# THE FASTEST MAN ON EARTH

*The inside story of Richard Noble's Land Speed Record*

*Best wishes,*

*Nov 19/92*

# THE FASTEST
# MAN ON EARTH

*The inside story of
Richard Noble's Land Speed Record*

## by DAVID TREMAYNE

633 CLUB
The Firs, 85 Kingshill Drive, Harrow
1986

Published in 1986 by
633 Club
The Firs
85 Kingshill Drive
Harrow
HA3 8QQ

ISBN 0 9512032 0 7

Typeset by Macrostar Ltd, Bookham, Surrey
Printed and bound by Tee & Whiten,
The Lincoln's Inn Press Ltd, London
All photographs by the author, Project Thrust
or Charles Noble (as indicated)

For Dick West and Leslie Weingartner,
Bev Osborn, Lena Courtney and the
people of Gerlach and Empire, Nevada

# Contents

# Acknowledgements

This book has been a long time coming, for all manner of reasons. And if it has exercised my patience I'm damn sure it has that of the countless people who helped to make it happen!

In particular, I gratefully acknowledge the Project Thrust team members whom I have so mercilessly interrogated over the past eight or nine years, and thank them for their (usually!) helpful responses. Richard Noble naturally deserves much credit, not only for having such a splendid dream in the first place, but also for putting up with the man with the microscope and notebook; while John Ackroyd merits some sort of sufferance medal for patiently explaining what, to him, were elementary technical points, to one whose grasp of physics and maths would have had Einstein rolling in the aisles.

Wesley Tee, Chairman and owner of the Teesdale Publishing Group which produces *Motoring News*, should also be singled out. Once persuaded a trip to Bonneville in 1981 was a good idea he sportingly insisted the paper should finish what it had started and cover all the record attempts in full. It's not as if I *needed* any persuasion, but it's fair comment that without his vital financial support in those early stages, this book would never have been possible.

Finally those members of the 633 Club who had the courage and faith to take the plunge, invest and support the project when it was decided to go it alone and publish, deserve special mention. Given the manner in which Richard had to fight every inch of the way, it is perhaps apposite that the book recounting his efforts should have had a far from easy birth. What is really gratifying, however, is that those who played such a vital part in breaking the land speed record, should also have such a crucial role in the telling of the inside story.

# *Introduction*

"Thank you *so* much for your contribution!"

The glare of Earls Court's arc lights highlighted the black hair of the speaker as he pumped energetically on the hand of a somewhat nonplussed onlooker.

The latter's name was Martin Preston. I had met him for the first time when we simultaneously began our journalistic careers with Marshall Cavendish forty-eight hours earlier. Sensing the opportunity to stick a pin into what he felt was a balloon of false bonhomie he replied, deadpan: "But I haven't given you anything", and withdrew his tortured arm.

The tall character rode the rebuff with commendable aplomb and moved smoothly on to another observer who evinced greater interest. With the practised air of a politician chasing votes on the eve of a vital election, he was making a point of thanking everyone who had shown interest – financial or otherwise – in his activities. Personally. About the only thing he didn't do was kiss babies, but that may simply have been because none was actually proffered.

It was October 5th 1977. The occasion was the first Motorfair and we were at the Project Thrust stand. The tall party's name was Richard James Anthony Noble and he was canvassing memberships for his Supporters' Club. His dream was to recapture the world land speed record for Britain. And no matter how many times he related the same story to members of the public that evening, the freshness of his enthusiasm never seemed to curdle.

To many who flocked round the stand, and there were literally thousands, he was certainly something unusual. From their expressions, some clearly thought he was just a well-groomed eccentric. The faces of others suggested they felt he was one of those dingalings you read about in the newspapers. Maybe they had a point, for behind him, cramped on to the small stand his smooth talking had won him from the show-organising *Daily Express*, a film of land speed record attempts played continually, attracting the punters like moths to a flame. A palisade of advertising hoardings shielded a giant Rolls-Royce aircraft turbojet engine. So large it had to be split into two sections, the latter was the stand's principal attraction. Bar a few smartly dressed personnel who looked as if they'd stopped off on their way home from the City, there was little else. The stand, like the project, was built mainly on dreams and determination. To many it seemed an odd way to launch such an exciting venture.

That occasion marked my first meeting with Richard Noble. As a land and water speed record fanatic, I'd become interested in him earlier in the year after reading of his exploits with his home-built jetcar Thrust 1, and I was there to watch him in action. I wanted to make an appraisal of his personality and level of seriousness before engaging him in conversation, if necessary to avoid the tedium of a lecture from an egotistical braggart. I couldn't detect any brashness, nor arrogant boasting of ambition, though. Instead, the project's skeleton staff simply radiated incredible enthusiasm for its aim: to erase Californian Gary Gabelich's right to claim the title of Fastest Man on Earth and to better his speed of 622.407mph set in October 1970 in the rocket-propelled Blue Flame. If Noble succeeded, he would be the first Briton since 1964 to hold the record.

Over the ensuing years I would get to know him pretty well, through my job with *Motoring News* and on a social level, but the memory of that first meeting remains fresh. During the following months I would watch those first seeds he planted blossom from dream to reality, and experience firsthand some of the numerous heartbreaks Fate threw at him. I would see that jet engine installed in a giant spaceframe chassis that was initially painted a stomach-churning shade of yellow, but which developed in stages as the project gathered financial momentum into a sleek streamliner christened Thrust 2. The fastest car in the world.

The vast machine's development was fascinating, but of even greater interest was the unravelling human story, that of a man, a dream and a record. Virtually six years to the day since that first meeting I would join with others to toast Noble's health in a tiny town one hundred and ten miles north of Reno, Nevada, as part of a British team celebrating a new 633.468mph land speed record.

Thrust 2 was a technical masterpiece, a product of the surrounding human element known collectively as Project Thrust.

This is that element's story.

*David Tremayne. London and Darlington 1986.*

# 1. Arrival on the salt

I could feel my eyelids losing the battle. My mouth was drier than Jack Benny's humour and my rental Chevette had an air-conditioning system that was sadly mismatched in its bout with searing ambient temperature. Every now and then I'd feel my hands clench involuntarily round the wheel rim as my mind threatened to shut down.

It was October 1981. Salt Lake City, with its seething crush of humanity and sky-clawing glasshouses, was fifty miles behind me to the east. Ahead stretched a seemingly endless ribbon of black tarmac. Interstate Eighty. The road to the Bonneville Salt Flats.

It was an ironic paradox. Since I was a kid one ambition had been to visit that forbidding expanse of nothingness that had dispassionately dealt out death or success to those bold enough to covet one of motorsport's glittering prizes, the land speed record. But weighing heavily against my mounting excitement in the battle of mind over matter were twenty-nine sleepless hours. My back still ached from a frustrating vigil at Salt Lake's airport, waiting vainly for the rental company's staff to come back on duty or answer their courtesy 'phone. My thoughts on an airline that had already put me way behind schedule through an unplanned stopover in Minneapolis were unprintable.

The radio set in the cramped car had become my only contact with the outside the world. The local station's country music fitted the unfamiliar surroundings well, but the news flashes were depressing.

"We are just receiving reports that Egypt's President Sadat has been gunned down by extremists. No firm news yet on the President's condition, but our sources suggest he received three bullet wounds when a gunman opened fire during a military parade. More details as we get them. . .''

Through the dusty screen heat haze danced mockingly on the road; behind, the occasional Mack or Peterbilt would loom large in my mirrors, pausing on my tail like the evil tanker in the Steven Spielberg film *Duel* before blasting its turbocharged way into the wide blue yonder.

Every so often I would surrender the crazy fight for alertness and pull over on to the hard shoulder but sleep, however brief, just wouldn't come. Every time I switched off the underpowered engine I'd wake up again. In a decent car the one hundred and twenty-two mile trip would have been a snap; in the Chevette it was purgatory. The spur was the knowledge that just outside Wendover, the stateline town between Tooele and Wells, Richard Noble and his Project Thrust team were attempting to carve their niche in history by attacking the American-held land speed record. They'd been on site now ten days and I experienced a moment's panic every time I found myself considering the possibility that I might arrive just too late to see it fall.

As events were to prove, that was a particularly naive worry. If I'd known then that I had near enough another two years to wait for that magic moment, I'd have pulled in and forced myself to sleep. . .

Mile tagged mile as the little grey and red saloon chugged through the barren scrubland, the monotony of the dry brush landscape relieved only occasionally by colourful but weather--ravaged advertising hoardings and very infrequent service stations. Then, directly ahead, the harsh Utahan sun began to wink invitingly on a white surface, like a guiding beacon. Presently Interstate Eighty carved its way through the white expanse. To the south was the old Wendover Bombing and Gunnery Range; to the north, the famed salt flats. Somewhere in the whiteness I fancied I could detect small figures, but I couldn't be sure. Then, abruptly almost, there was Wendover itself.

Like so many small American towns it is really only a main street, with a few back roads that dare tentacle away towards the surrounding mountains. There is the Wendover Museum, sometime home of the Summers Brothers' wheeldriven record--

holding car Goldenrod. There is Earl Heath's Best Western Motel. There is Motel Six, in which the Thrust team had established its headquarters. Halfway down Main Street, and so insignificant I missed it first time round, was the sole accommodation I'd been able to book, a scruffy little motel. The swimming pool the owners had boasted of in the guide book looked distinctly unfinished and contained as much water as the Sahara on a bad day. An aged Coca Cola machine, long vandalised, stood by the screen door to the office, like the empty shell of a long departed sentinel. I checked in, my arrival arousing a singular lack of interest until the proprietor remembered the deposit required.

I felt as welcome as a tax inspector.


The following day, refreshed after sixteen hours' sleep, I headed out of town on the two-lane blacktop that leads nowhere but the salt. As the scenery unfolded schoolboy memories of Bonneville pictures took on a fresh substance. Here was the first proper view of an area so cruel that in the mid 1840s the migrant Donner Party had been forced to resort to cannibalism while undertaking their hazardous crossing of the flats.

Either side of the narrow causeway stretched miles of harsh saline wasteland, suitable for little but potash extraction and the mad pursuit of absolute speed. As brine oozes up between cracks in the surface of the salt, it evaporates and the resultant hard deposits cause little ridges to form every few feet, so the whole area resembles an ill-fitting jigsaw puzzle. To the left, way in the distance, was the beginning of the Silver Island Mountains range, notorious as the backdrop for so many of those Bonneville photographs. To the right, vehicles on Interstate Eighty looked like children's toys, crawling along in slow motion as if pushed by invisible hands.

The causeway is probably only five miles long, but without reference marks it seemed to stretch for eternity. Yet somehow it was a comforting guide in that desolate region. As I progressed further I began to discern Floating Mountain, living up to its name as the heat haze directly ahead made it hover on the far horizon. Within a mile the road simply petered out, its termination marked by a tatty weather-beaten sign of welcome. It bore the legend:

'Bonneville Salt Flats International Speedway. A barrier of salt. The famed Bonneville Salt Flats, a remanent (sic) of ancient Lake Bonneville, historically has been a barrier to man, from the early trappers and explorers to today's supersonic rocket cars. It continues to provide a challenge to man and his activities'.

Beneath a sketch map of the area, the legend continued:

'Located approximately four miles beyond this sign, the Bonneville Salt Flats International Speedway is eighty feet wide and approximately nine miles long and is administered by the Bureau of Land Management'.

One or two visitors clearly felt some additional information to be of benefit. One offered the invaluable signed and dated news that 'Joe got high here' a short while earlier while another, in scratched grafitti, urged drivers not to drive on flats.

Beyond the sign lay nothing but white wilderness, the horizon sloping with the all too apparent curvature of the earth. With the Chevette's engine switched off it was so eerily quiet you could hear the blood pumping in your ears. Only a wobbly line of battered orange cones marked the route to Thrust's base camp, itself still invisible. Many of them had been knocked over where bored drivers had tried unsuccessfully to slalom through. A track had been dragged as a further guide, but hard salty crusts still crackled beneath the tyres. It was only another four or five miles to the camp, but it was like driving to the end of nowhere.

Then shimmering shapes of tents and vehicles haunted the skyline. A red and white panel truck emblazoned with Loctite logos. The distinctive red Jaguar XJ12 call-signed Fire Chase, which had been loaned by Jaguar Cars and converted by Chubb to act as a high-speed fire engine and interceptor. Several motor-homes. A yellow, brown and white monoplane.

On first impression the camp's atmosphere seemed tranquil. Nobody seemed in too much of a hurry and as I hailed familiar faces and was informed the day's wind was too high to permit runs I too was able to relax. In the cool shade of the huge white and yellow marquee used to house the jetcar and its plethora of back-up equipment, John Ackroyd looked up and grinned a greeting. He is a slim figure with barely an ounce of fat. In

October 1981 he was not far from his forty-fifth birthday but looking at him you'd have put his age much lower. Here was the man who had been selected from numerous applicants when Noble had sought a designer for his 650mph car. He'd been sitting on a beach working as a deck-chair attendant when he'd first learned of the vacancy, resting between jobs that had included spells with ERA, Britten-Norman, Dornier and Enfield Automotive. With the latter he'd designed the 8000 electric car and ultimately been responsible for supervising its construction. Ken Norris, who had designed Donald Campbell's Bluebird CN7 car and co-designed with his brother Lewis the K7 hydroplane, had agreed to vet applicants for Noble, and Ackroyd had had no trouble convincing him he was the only man for the job. He'd started work on Thrust 2 in his spare time while working for Porsche in Germany, and once Noble had been able to raise sufficient money to pay him fulltime he'd turned down a lucrative contract with Messerschmitt and gone to work in the kitchen of a derelict house Project Thrust rented on the Isle of Wight for the princely sum of five pounds a week.

Now, with his Swedish wife Birgit, he was in Bonneville facing the greatest technical challenge of an already distinguished career. So keen was his enthusiasm he'd actually ridden in the passenger seat of Thrust 2 during many of the runs made up to October 6th.

Strewn all round him were sheets of information from Thrust's onboard recording apparatus, awaiting analysis. He looked absolutely in his element. Behind him, panel specialist Brian Ball was hunched over one of the spare aluminium wheels. Typical of the calibre of skilled craftsmen attracted to Noble's project, he is a highly accomplished sheet metal wheeler with a love of his work and a fierce pride in Thrust 2. In later months he revealed in his broad tones: "When I was first invited down to the Island to discuss doing the sheet metal wheeling work on Thrust's double curvature nose I was pretty keen but I had plenty of things to get done before I could start. If anyone had told me I'd be starting work on the car virtually the next day I'd have laughed at them. Blow me, but if Richard didn't give me a lift back to the ferry and end up talking me into doing just that!"

On October 6th however, Brian was not a happy man.

"You a reporter?" he enquired aggressively before Ackroyd could speak again. " 'Cause if you are I hope you make a better job of reporting the facts than these idiots".

With that he pulled a copy of a London tabloid daily from his overalls and threw it at me. As I read the centrespread feature on Thrust his point became apparent. The copy was the usual jingoistic, naive stuff, and helped readers to a better understanding of Thrust 2's purpose and potential by comparing it with a milk float. . .

Thrust's tent looked a rather impressive affair, with white walls and a fancy yellow and white striped ceiling, all attached to a latticework of aluminium poles. It was only later that we discovered just how badly it had been erected. Crumpled groundsheets covered the salty floor and a large trestle table sagged under the weight of several parachutes. Mike Barrett and Bruce White were engrossed in the painstaking and critical task of folding and packing them before hammering them home into special bags with hide-faced mallets. Barrett was a fulltime team member, White was on loan fron GQ and had worked previously with Barry Bowles. The latter's rocket-powered dragster Blonde Bombshell had at one time seemed Noble's major rival in the race to produce the first pure thrust British land speed record car, before a televised accident at Pendine Sands in April 1978 scuppered its chances.

Initial problems had arisen deploying the parachutes at the end of the last run and they served to highlight the amount of ground the team had to make up on the Americans. Before Thrust Britain's sole jetcar experience had been gained with Campbell's Bluebird CN7, which used a gas turbine engine but relied on transmitting its power via shafts to the wheels rather than by employing pure exhaust gas pressure. In any case, Bluebird was built to comply with a set of rules since relaxed, and had a design speed of only 500mph. The Americans, by contrast, could draw on data from running some twelve land speed contenders powered by jet or rocket engines, starting as early as 1960 with the trail-blazing Flying Caduceus jet designed for Dr Nathan Ostich. Prior to that they had held the record only once in 32 years, through the efforts of Ray Keech and his White Triplex  at Daytona in 1928. Speed on land had long been the exclusive preserve of the British when the first jetcars appeared, but the explosion of speed made possible by the reaction-propelled projectiles changed all that overnight in the early sixties and literally blew the British away. The lost ground would not be won back easily.

Help however, was at hand and it came in the rotund shape of American Jim Deist. He is a short, barrel-waisted character rarely to be seen without an unlit cigar clamped between his teeth and in deference to the pioneer work he'd done using parachutes to slow high speed cars and hydroplanes he was dubbed the 'Daddy of the Drogue'. Ackroyd, ever one to seek and appreciate simpler solutions to engineering problems even if it meant admitting he'd been wrong, was candid about Deist's contribution at that critical early stage.

"Look. I spent literally ages on the Island designing our 'chute launching system", he said, pushing a small black object into my hand before standing back to observe my reaction, the way a small child might when sharing its favourite toy. "That's Jim's off-the-shelf 'chute launching mortar. Look how compact it is. We've switched over to them and saved ourselves so much trouble".

He put the device back in its tray and turned with a shrug. "That's what is so important about getting out here to Bonneville and actually running under in-the-field conditions. Every time we run that damn car we learn something new and close the gap the Americans opened".


Outside, once again basted by a sun so merciless you could suffer from its reflection on the salt by getting burned up the legs of shorts or inside your nose, I bumped into Geoff Smee. He is normally employed as a pilot by British Caledonian and is a wiry character with thinning hair who'd been responsible for wiring Thrust 2's electrical systems. That morning he was preoccupied as he strode towards the marquee and his response to the inevitable question was terse.

"Things aren't going to plan. So far we've only got the thing up to 395mph". He kept on striding.

Not her. Not Thrust 2. Not even it. The thing, he'd called the car on which he expended so many hours of loving attention. His choice of words spoke volumes. By that day the team had been on site since late September, and some of the boyish enthusiasm and confidence with which many had set out on the Great American Adventure had already become a casualty of the intervening problems.

Thrust 2 was still somewhere down the course after the day's aborted start, near the southern end, but just then Noble arrived back at base camp, dressed in his pale blue pin-striped overalls. On many occasions I was to experience his peculiar knack of entering a room and immediately stamping his personality on its occupants. Sir Malcolm and Donald Campbell were both said to have possessed a similar ability. Though he now approached across an open expanse of salt, Noble's trick once again had its effect. It was as if everyone geared themselves up another notch, and suddenly the place crackled with an electric atmosphere. He crossed from his car in a purposeful stride, arms swinging loosely at his sides. The slight breeze tugged at his long hair and caused it to flop over his eyes. He looked fresh and relaxed and smiled a greeting.

"Good to see you, man! You've arrived just in time. We've been having a few problems, but now we're *really* beginning to get somewhere at last".

He pumped vigorously on my hand before sweeping his hair back with the almost impatient gesture that had become so familiar.

"Hey, you know", he continued, rocking from one foot to another, "this really is a *fabulous* place. And we're learning so much about old John's car".

It was all still there. The almost caricature gestures and expressions. The boyish sense of excitement in his own special role. Like Ackroyd he was in his element. And he seemed particularly cheerful as he outlined the great car's performance at the speeds he'd achieved in the past days.

"You know, driving Thrust 2 on these metal wheels and on salt is one *hell* of a lot different to running it back home on rubber tyres and tarmac runways. Out here it's a bit like driving a bloody great American jalopy with vague power steering and bald tyres on packed snow. I thought it might be like drag racing, but it's got nothing to do with it! Instead you need to be a combination of rally driver and fighter pilot!".

When excited he has a tendency to exaggerate for effect as his keenness and imagination get the better of him. Even his normal speech is heavily italicised. His enthusiasm now well fired, he moved into top gear.

"What we've managed to do so far is sort out the low speed handling by altering the front suspension toe-in settings, and we've got the 'chute deployment working properly. We're just beginning to get to grips with this track. You haven't really missed anything so far, but from now on things are really going to start happening.

"The biggest problem we're finding is that for once the damned surface here is almost ideal for a rubber-tyred car such as Gabelich's Blue Flame, but our metal wheels are digging slight ruts every time we make a run. And believe me, when you hit them at any sort of speed it's like hitting Clapham Junction at 250mph! I've been getting into some *hellish* four-wheel drifts!"

If he was daunted by the troubles, it didn't show. Shading his eyes from the sun, he continued: "The real thing is, of course, that you are inevitably going to run into problems when you try developing this kind of vehicle. We've just got to overcome them as quickly as we can".

For all the dramas he seemed buoyed by the experience, almost as if he was glad of the opportunity to prove that even in adversity he could cope with the driving aspect of the role he'd spent the last seven years fighting to be cast in.

Later that day I had a desultory conversation with the few American pressmen who'd ventured out to see what all the fuss was about. They'd been on site longer and it was intriguing to hear their reaction to Noble's progress.

"He's lost his nerve, hasn't he?" asked one red-bearded character who looked like a refugee from the ZZ Top band.

"He just wants to keep that pedal to the metal and go for it".

"I sure wish he'd get on with it and get it over so we can get the hell out of this goddam place".

"It wasn't like this with Breedlove or Arfons. Those guys really knew how to turn it on!".

It shouldn't have been surprising. Most record breakers go through patches where their nerve is called into question. It's an occupational hazard. Donald Campbell had to live with such accusations throughout his prolonged land speed venture, and went through it all again with the boat in the weeks leading up to his death at Coniston in 1967. What was surprising was that the accusations were coming so early in Noble's campaign. What was it he had said so often?

"Record breaking is all about having the patience to minimise the risk, whether by allowing that little bit extra time for design research or by building up speed in gradual, planned stages".

Whatever anyone might be saying behind his back, it was clear he wasn't going to rise to the bait and try progressing too fast, too soon. Campbell had done that at Bonneville during the great confrontation of 1960, had flipped Bluebird at 360mph, and been lucky to survive a spell in hospital with nothing worse than a fractured skull.

In any case, there was no way the timing officials were going to allow a rookie who'd never exceeded 200mph before stepping into Thrust 2 to go flat out, straight away, even if he did hold the British land speed record. Under the leadership of Dave Petrali the United States Auto Club officials were responsible to the sport's governing body, the Federation Internationale du Sport Automobile, for ensuring the rules and regulations laid down to cover record attempts were strictly observed.

Petrali is a professional photographer who had taken over the mantle of USAC Chief Steward from his father Joe, who had himself succeeded the legendary Art Pillsbury. Between the three of them they had covered just about every major record attempt made at the flats. Petrali made USAC's position clear right from the start.

"The days when some hothead could come out here one day and run for the record the next are long gone. Part of our job is to determine whether a given car and driver combination is in good enough shape. We do that by making sure they increase initial speeds in relatively small – say 50mph – increments until we're satisfied. After they've done that safely they can get cleared for larger increments. But nobody gets away with going for broke these days".

He was alluding to attempts such as Athol Graham's in 1960, or Glenn Leasher's in 1962. Both had ended in tragedy.

By the 6th Petrali and his crew knew Thrust 2 was no ordinary record contender. Twenty-seven feet long by eight feet wide, and weighing close to four tons, it is a lot of car. That it had endured and survived several yaws as great as twenty degrees said a lot for its design integrity. John Ackroyd's concept of weathercock stability, with the car's centre of gravity near the front and the centre of aerodynamic pressure – the real air resistance – much further back, gave it the qualities of a dart or arrow and obviously worked as intended. Most previous land speed contenders would have tripped over their own wall of air and rolled end over end at smaller yaw angles.

Petrali had seen American Slick Gardner's efforts at Bonneville in the ex-Arfons Green Monster – a triple record holder in the mid sixties – and knew from the frights he'd received with it on new solid metal wheels that technological advances need time to be assessed fully. Thrust 2 would run straighter still once it hit speeds at which the aerodynamics really began to bite – Ackroyd estimated 375mph and over – and he felt the team was now ready to try for them.


By midday hopes that a run might be made had faded. While the wind had dropped considerably, the sun's heat was drawing the moisture to the surface of the salt, making it mushy underfoot and too soft to bear Thrust 2's weight. In some places a good kick with the heel of a shoe was enough to bring water flooding into the depression.

While Thrust might not be able to run, however, it could still attract attention. That afternoon it was trailered back to base camp and time was devoted to the cameramen present. The dominant figure to emerge was Bob Pakes, an aggressive Cockney from the Isle of Wight. He'd gambled a lot to travel to America as team photographer, and he was determined to come out ahead.

It was a curiously laid-back couple of hours, as Pakes moved team members here, there and everywhere before recording them on celluloid. The sun continued to burn its victims but nobody seemed all that anxious to avoid its rays. Given a drop of water and a yellow tinge to the salt, that afternoon at Bonneville might have doubled for a day-trip to the seaside.

"Smile like you had it last night", Pakes ordered as he lined up a team and car shot, and everyone cracked up. The spirit seemed high and morale strong, even though there were inevitably one or two disappointed individuals who found it difficult to comprehend why  their wonder car hadn't already done its stuff. Pakes finished his shot and began lining up another when somebody wobbled a strange-looking creature into the frame, on the end of a length of cord. Its papier mache body looked of interest to Colonel Sanders' recipe chiefs, but as soon as Ackroyd saw it he was quick to identify it.

"It's a salt rabbit!".

As the horseplay continued somebody noticed something formidable protruding from transporter driver Terry 'Orrible' Hopkins' overalls – a snakelike length of parachute rope which was quickly christened Hissing Sid. At risk to his personal wellbeing Orrible was deprived of his pet, which was to assume the status of team mascot.

Project Thrust had now been in Bonneville for just over ten days and had a best speed of just under 400mph to its credit. Over dinner at the noisy Stateline Casino that evening, amid the monotonous calls of the Keno players and the chimes of one-- armed bandits operated endlessly by grandmothers with blue-- rinsed hair and those awful stretch nylon slacks, the general mood was optimistic. After all, problems were to be expected. Nobody in the record game escapes without some setbacks. The indications were that the gremlins had been identified and eradicated.

The following day, Wednesday, would see a concerted attack on 450mph, with 500 by Thursday. By the weekend the record should be in sight. . .


The 7th dawned cool but again it was dry, and sleep-numbed hands reached clumsily for steering wheels, gear selectors and headlight switches as Thrust's disciples made their way to the

Western Café for an early breakfast of hash browns, scrambled eggs and ham, washed down by the bitterest coffee this side of a Mellow Birds' television commercial.

Involuntarily I'd overslept and by the time I trailed into the Western everyone bar a grey-haired man in a vivid blue anorak had long departed for the salt. Across the back of his jacket was emblazoned 'Rocketman Productions'. This was Mehl Gabelich, the current record holder's father. The Americans were taking the British effort seriously and the advance scouting party had already reached town to monitor events.

Over a shared breakfast, Gabelich Snr came across as a generous-minded and likeable man with no trace of rivalry, and it soon became apparent that the Americans were as anxious as the British to see the record fall.

"You see son, the problem with holding something as patriotically linked as the land speed record is that the country already has its hands on it, so it's real tricky getting people to back you to break it. It's even worse if you're shooting for your own record. Now if you guys were to break Gary's mark things'd be a lot different. National pride would be stung and just maybe there'd be some backers prepared to spend big to redress the situation. Gary already has the car on paper".

By nine thirty we'd driven out to the causeway, only to find it blocked by a red saloon drawn across the road. A tall man leant nonchalantly enough against the driver's door, but behind his sunglasses his eyes were watchful as we drew alongside.

"Sorry, can't let you through for a bit. There's going to be a run any minute".

His manner was apologetic but firm and we fell into conversation. His name was Mike Hearn and he was managing director of MWG Impex back home in Weybridge. A longtime Thrust supporter he'd made the trip with his wife Ninetta and their two daughters and had been adopted as a team member. A charming individual with a penchant for the most excrutiatingly corny jokes, he would offer the solution to the fuel surge problem that dogged Thrust 2 in its final runs leading up to the successful record attempt in 1983.

"Conditions are near as dammit perfect. Better'n when Gary was here in 1970", offered Mehl as we waited, giving the salt the odd kicks the way a half interested buyer might kick tyres when assessing a secondhand car. Within minutes, however, we all felt the breeze begin to ruffle our hair and it wasn't long before a message came through on Mike's hand-held radio to say the run was off. Further down the track the wind was already gaining strength by the moment, gusting to double USAC's 5mph safety limit. If Noble tried to drive Thrust 2 in the conditions there was every chance it would be blown badly off course, even though the toe-in changes had gone some way to improving its directional stability. Hearn was told he could open the access road for the time being and as we drove to base camp the wind became noticeably stronger as it pushed the Chevette off line. One of record breaking's many frustrations was already outstaying its welcome.

I meandered around camp until Jack Nichol of Loctite collared me to join in a new pasttime developed to alleviate the boredom of waiting. It comprised estimating the distance from the cream and brown Loctite motorhome to the edge of the Silver Island Mountains. Jack opened with five miles and Tony Jeeves, the GKN man handling Thrust's public relations that year, offered four. I chipped in with two. It simply proved our collective unsuitability for such tasks. By the time we'd driven the motorhome to the point where it was threatening to sink into soft salt we'd clocked seven point five miles on the odometer, with what seemed a similar distance to go.

On the way back we came across one of the region's most remarkable inhabitants, a tarantula which had apparently wandered on to the salt from the mountains. On the drive out we'd spotted a small black blotch that stood out against the salty white background and we were all intrigued to see it moving steadily in the direction of base camp. It was a good couple of inches in diameter, with long hairy legs and a markedly unpleasant mien. We called it Loctite on account of our hosts and scooped him into a KP peanut tin. Back at camp he helped counteract the tedium that was fast setting in amongst those who had no specific jobs to do. Very few managed to maintain their cool when they were offered a peanut only to notice the furry form on the base of the tin just as their fingers were about to make contact with the rim!

These insects actually live on the salt, where they are one of the few species able to sustain life in such an inhospitable environment. Small wonder they can be so lacking in the social graces.

Not long after that episode Pakes caught a baby rattler during a trip to the mountains. This, like Loctite, was later released as most objected to its house manners, but nobody knew quite where it was freed. Many were thus wary when using the tatty portable toilet situated a discreet distance from the camp. And rumour had it those whose duty it was to act as night guards made very careful checks of their tents and bedrolls before turning in.

With the enforced lull in activities I was glad when Noble suggested the diversion of another look at Thrust 2, still parked at the southern end of the eleven mile course after its morning abort. I drove up the access road and then walked the mile or so across the uneven salt until I came to the specially smoothed section of the prepared track. I'd seen the finished version of the car in Birmingham when it was launched to the press shortly before shipment to America, and of course it had been on display the previous afternoon. But somehow seeing it now on the salt, away from anything else, in its intended element, it looked very different. Aesthetically I'd never found the chunky shape very pleasing, but now I saw it in a different light, as a machine with beauty in its functionality. The whiteness of the salt complemented the car's gold paintwork perfectly and it became apparent just how well the colour had been chosen. As I stood close to the jet-powered brute I felt an awesome regard for its capability, and a new respect for the man who was prepared to drive it to its maximum, whatever that might prove to be.

It was a rare moment, for there were only a handful of people around the car and for once it did not command everyone's attention. Already I'd lost count of the number of times efforts to photograph it on its own had been frustrated as someone wandered into the shot or popped up unexpectedly after kneeling round its other side.

Perhaps Thrust 2's squared off shape was too reminiscent of Art Arfons' Green Monster to be regarded as fresh, and therefore modern. Perhaps it was because the Blue Flame's pencil-slim shape came closer to every schoolboy's idea of what the fastest car on earth should look like. Whatever, many of the people I'd discussed it with had reservations about its ultimate potential. Even Ackroyd and Noble had once related a story about the original transonic wind tunnel tests of the scale model and how sceptical experts had been until they got the results. Within Thrust's aluminium-clad frame the Rolls-Royce Avon 210 from Motorfair had been replaced with a more powerful 302 version and this occupied the entire length of the centre section, its huge maw protected before and after runs by small wooden panels, its vast jetpipe smelling intoxicatingly of burned kerosene even days after its last outing. Noble had obtained the new engine after setting six British land speed records and at twenty-seven feet in length it was rated at 17,000lbs of thrust at sea level. That amounted to some 34,000hp, or about the same as 40 race-ready '86 turbocharged Grand Prix cars. . .

Above all, Thrust 2 was beautifully built, right down to the last flush rivet. By his own admission Ackroyd had placed the greatest emphasis on primary and secondary safety, the former concerned with preventing an accident, the latter with protecting the driver in the event of one. Sturdy suspension components transmitted surface shocks to rubber springs specially developed in conjunction with the Malaysian Rubber Producers' Research Association, while the solid metal wheels aroused considerable interest and comment. Ackroyd had once explained how he had designed them by rule of thumb and run stress tests on them, finding them to be totally satisfactory.

"Then I decided to design them by the book rather than by eye and I wasted a load of time trying all the fancy methods. In the end I came back to the first design, which was far superior and took far less time to produce!"

Each wheel measured thirty inches in diameter, to provide the right ground clearance, to fit neatly under the front cowlings which would be within the driver's line of sight and to stay within the limits of aluminium alloy at the envisaged rotational speed of 8,000rpm, or around 705mph. They weighed in at around a hundred pounds apiece, and each rim was bead blasted to provide some extra grip. Although the front and rear wheels were an identical four inches wide, the former had radial and lateral grooves to create a degree of understeer while the latter had raised keels in the centre of the tread to enhance directional stability.

Once Noble wound Thrust 2 over 250mph it would literally rise on to those central keels, planing like a very fast unlimited hydroplane. Partly as a result of this drag from the surface was reduced, to the benefit of top speed, and a huge roostertail of salt spray would chase the car down the flats whenever it ran. For the first time in a land speed contender rack and pinion steering was employed, Ackroyd finding a modified heavy-duty design normally provided by Adwest for Leyland buses to be perfectly suitable.

Presently Noble offered me a lift back to my car and seemed surprised when I said I'd walk. I wanted to be on my own to think about the past of Bonneville, to soak up the atmosphere and remember men such as Abner Jenkins, Sir Malcolm Campbell, George Eyston and John Cobb who'd all done their bit to establish the venue as the capital of speed. And as I trudged across that crunchy jigsaw I also remembered Mormon preacher Graham who had seen himself breaking the record in a dream he came to regard as divine inspiration. When he had crashed his home-built City of Salt Lake it transpired he'd been so blasé he hadn't even bothered to fasten his safety straps. Then there was Otto Anzjon, a leukemia victim who had painstakingly rebuilt the car and survived an accident of his own in it before succumbing to his illness. Or twenty-six year-old San Franciscan Leasher who had promised Joe Petrali he would work up to fast speeds in gradual steps, only to turn to his crew as soon as the older man had moved out of earshot to declare: "This time I'm gonna go for broke". The accident in which he died convinced jetcar drivers a tail fin was essential for stability. Leasher's Infinity had not been equipped with one and he had paid dearly for his youthful impatience. For years the wreckage of his car lay abandoned and forgotten at the entrance to the flats, the remaining tattered shards of his broken dream.

Now Richard Noble had applied to join the elite. This was the place to which he had brought his giant streamliner in search of the ultimate. Bonneville Speedway, steeped in history and watched over by the ghosts of speed, looked every bit the desolate place in which *his* dream would be realised – or destroyed.

# 2. Storms

The young girl on the video screen was twisting into some strange contortions but her performance didn't seem to be having an adverse effect on her male companion. The smile on his face indicated he was more than satisfied. He was Mr Greenfield, she was Debbie. The film was dedicated to her exploits in Dallas.

Six faces turned in surprise as the mounting wind threatened to wrench the door from my grasp as I entered the team motorhome. Each registered a momentary expression of guilt like schoolboys caught having an illicit cigarette. As I slammed the door the fleeting guilt turned again to amusement as Mr Greenfield began a fearful moaning. From the brief nods that were exchanged it was obvious conversation was temporarily discouraged.

We were quite an assortment. There were Brian Ball and Geoff Smee, sandwiching burly, bearded John Griffiths of the *Financial Times*. There was Salt Lake City fireman and keen radio ham Richard T.Briggs, who had the most laid-back accent since Jack Nicholson. There was bespectacled USAF engineering student Tom Palm. An undergraduate with aspirations to break the record with his own jetcar called Minnesota, he'd simply strapped his ten-speed racer to the luggage rack of his primer grey Ford and driven west to watch Project Thrust's activities as soon as he'd heard it had arrived. Before long he'd been roped in as a team member, acting as night guard and sleeping in the small tent that was his sole accommodation. I'd really driven out to the flats that night to discuss his project but right then even he had other things on his mind.

Then there was Richard Noble's younger brother Charles, a Winker Watsonesque character on leave from his job at

Buckingham Palace, where he is responsible for the Queen's paintings. A keen photographer, he would become the official team lensman for both attempts at Black Rock in 1982 and '83. At that moment, however, he had a different kind of exposure on his mind and was letting his hair down. It was doubtful he could have focussed even an automatic camera, as he was laughing so heartily tears streamed down his cheeks.

Mr Greenfield looked and sounded near the end of his tether when it gradually began to dawn on us that the wind velocity was building to equally climactic proportions as the motorhome began to rock. Above its scream was just discernible the sound of things rattling around outside. Reluctantly someone suggested we should take a look. Since he was still wearing his coat and was seated nearest the door, Griff was volunteered. As the first indication of what lay in store, the door was torn from his hand as he left, slamming back against the side panel. Mother Nature's ire had been aroused. Feeling rather as if John had become our Titus Oates we sat silently exchanging uneasy glances – in retrospect, a case of no *FT*, no comment – until he came rushing back to announce breathlessly that the marquee was in serious trouble.

As we tumbled into warm clothing and raced outside, the yellow and white edifice was gripped in a struggle for survival that it showed every sign of losing. The bitter cold wind screeched round the camp and the tent's plastic sides were billowing frantically in and out like the lungs of an obese man desperately trying to regain his breath after a sudden sprint. Thrust 2 was parked inside the marquee and nobody needed reminding that the giant car had to be protected at all costs. No car, no record.

Inside things looked even worse, although mercifully we had some degree of protection from gusts strong enough to tug at our legs with the force of an All Blacks' tackle. Smee and Griff raced to Wendover in the Jaguar in search of help, the rest of us left to do the best we could. Whoever had erected the marquee, to use Briggs' vernacular, was a turkey. The design itself was efficient enough, an intricate confection of interlocking aluminium poles, but the contractor hadn't bothered to insert any locking pins. As the plastic covering expanded with every wind gust the poles simply began to pull apart. If they came down on those precious tail fins — Richard Chisnell's Initial Services fins — or crushed Brian Ball's nose panels, there was no telling how much damage might result.

Outside, above even the scream of the gale, came a fearful crashing sound as Briggs' expensive radio mast was dashed to the ground, but at that moment all anyone cared about was grabbing a pole each and hanging on to it as if our lives depended on it. Try to break the land speed record? There wasn't time to give it a thought. All anyone dared think of was keeping that damned marquee together until help arrived.

As the weightier Brian and Charles clung like limpets to corner poles, Tom and I shinned up them to pass ropes around the upper poles, until eventually we were all left hanging on to a rope at each corner, pitting our puny weights against the angry elements in an effort to keep those poles interlocking. The ordeal probably lasted half an hour as they jerked with a frenzy that made the ropes bite deep enough into wrists to draw blood, but at least the cold numbed feelings. All the while the wind still threatened to win.

Then, way in the distance, was just discernible the flashing blue light of the Jaguar leading the rescue convoy, the wail of its siren ripped away in the angry night. We swore at the length of time it took on the run down to base camp. We swore at the marquee contractor. We swore at just about anything. Lenny Bruce would have been proud of us. Ten minutes later the Jaguar skidded to a halt, but it could have been ten years. Then suddenly the place seemed alive with people. Leading them, as expected, was Noble, and you had to take your hat off to him. Within seconds he'd grasped the situation and began rattling off crisp orders, deploying a small army here, an individual there. A stepladder was dragged in and Noble himself got a line round the ring at the top of the marquee, into which the six roof support poles slotted. One had finally slipped from its socket but the crisis was averted and some semblance of control was restored. The line was lashed to one of the heavy Palouste gas turbine starter engines, others to Thrust 2 itself. Everything else that could move was lashed to something heavy enough to resist the manic gale.

Meanwhile Briggs, rushing to his motorhome for extra rope,

was hit by the door as it rebounded off a tyre hidden in the darkness and swung directly into his temple. He fell as if poleaxed.

It took four long hours to win that battle against nature, and nobody cared to contemplate how close Project Thrust had come to disaster. It had been a very fine-run thing as the wind ran amok, but it could carry on, and that was all that mattered. As tired men climbed into their cars the Jaguar lead the convoy back to the causeway. Nobody tried going back alone. The 50mph wind was too awe-inspiring, as if Mother Nature was firing a warning shot at those who dared reach beyond the achievements of other mortals. Certainly nobody ventured away from base camp on foot, even to go as far as the portable toilet. In the frightening maelstrom the chances were that anyone foolish enough to stray too far would be courting disaster of another kind.


Not surprisingly the following day was a washout, the course dampened by light rain that followed the gales in the early hours. As an indication of the dedication of those involved with the project however, men who had turned in at one o'clock that morning reported for duty at seven to tidy the battered workshop and effect more lasting repairs. The wind still ran high, but was no longer strong enough to pose a real threat. The one benefit from its continued presence lay in its drying power, for locals advised that the track would be usable the following day if further rain was avoided.

While the finishing touches were put to the parachutes intended for the next runs, Ackroyd supervised suspension modifications. He'd decided to take an inch out of the rear suspension struts to change the rake of the car, explaining: "At the moment we have so much downforce generated by the venturi beneath the car that we've decided to reduce it by altering the angle of incidence, the angle at which she runs to the ground. We think we're tending to dig ruts in the track each time we run because of the excess downforce, so if we reduce it there should be a beneficial trade-off in terms of reduced surface damage. At the same time we'll also reduce our rolling drag, so we should go faster for the same amount of run-up".

The struts were simply removed and clamped in a vice, and the required inch cut out laboriously with a hand-held hacksaw. The two sections were then welded neatly back together.

Noble, looking tired and for the first time slightly edgy, watched the work with visibly mounting uneasiness. Finally he could contain himself no longer.

"Christ, John", he enquired of Ackroyd, who'd been watching his apprehensive expression with a wry smile, "is it going to be safe welding them back together again?".

Ackroyd's face broke into a grin and he waved an arm at the car. "Of course it is, Richard. How else do you think the rest of this thing is held together?".

That night there was one of the more unusual sights of Wendover to sample, not that there were many. I happened into the Stateline Casino in time to tag on to a posse of cars headed for an apparently deserted backstreet hangar in which local eccentric Robert K. Golka conducted scientific research. Cynthia Page was heading a BBC television crew on site to film Thrust's efforts for the Q.E.D. series and her suggestion that Golka might make an interesting topic for a *Tomorrow's World* feature was seized upon by Thrust members anxious for something to do. As the heavy door was eased open, complete with mandatory Hollywood-style creak, several sets of eyes peered into the gloom. Piles of junk littered the place, each bearing a sign proclaiming: 'Everything in here for sale'.

Towards the centre of the hangar something resembling a child's crude playpen reached up to the ceiling, with what looked like a ten year-old's idea of a space rocket standing to its right. Resplendent in a spotless white three-piece suit that added an even more incongruous note to the proceedings was the flamboyant Robert K. He fired a powerful generator and suddenly electricity began to flow round the top of the playpen before passing via a high-tension cable to the space rocket. At that point the latter took on a life of its own, stabbing purple fingers of electrical charge into the air. Every so often more powerful fingers speared the concrete floor, accompanied by an acrid stench. The rocket now looked like an angry tyrant flaying its subjects and was somehow sinister in the dingy building.

Golka is known locally as 'the Twenty Million Volts Man' and has been working for years to harness the plasma in ball lightning. The latter is a natural phenomenon that occurs infrequently, which must make research less than easy, so in the circumstances he had put his giant Windlass machine to good use to provide some footage for the television cameras. As a spectacle it was quite breathtaking while it lasted, and it killed half an hour of ennui, but what it proved or disproved was way beyond my understanding of physics.

As we left Cynthia to it, Golka was preparing to don his 'Faraday' suit so he could walk directly into the field of electricity his toy rocket produced. As the subsequent programme revealed, he survived. . .


The ham was tough and the eggs anaemic, but it's doubtful if anyone noticed as breakfast was bolted down the next morning. It was six thirty and there was an exciting air of expectation mingling with the cigarette smoke in the Western. In stark contrast to the previous morning Friday had dawned cool and crisp. The wind had died to a mere breeze. Today, Thrust 2 would run. Today, Noble would be aiming at 450mph. The promise of action had everyone talking animatedly, anxious to be getting on with the job.

By seven thirty the complete team was on the salt, blue-clad figures scuttling busily beneath a pallid red sky. The puffiness of the few clouds was like that around a hard drinker's eyes, as if Mother Nature had a hangover after her recent excesses. If that was the case, Project Thrust was determined to make as much noise as possible with its jetcar.

Hopkins had driven the Leyland T45 down across the access road and across on to the rough salt, to begin the ritual of unloading Thrust 2. First the cab's swan-neck was tilted backwards until its locking eyes on the Crane Fruehauf trailer could be disengaged, then the truck was moved away. A small army of men then unloaded aluminium runners and assembled them at the front of the trailer before placing strips of rubber on top of them to prevent damage to Thrust's metal wheels. Then, very slowly and carefully, the gold monster was winched down the ramps, the final operation being completed as a tow-line was attached to an eye beneath the jet's air intake. Gently, Thrust 2 was then towed by Range Rover to its intended starting point on the prepared section of track.

Personnel swarmed around, lovingly checking and rechecking every system and leaving nothing to chance as Ackroyd's detailed lists were followed to the letter. By ten the streamliner was nearly ready for action. Smee unbolted the orange towbar bracket fitted beneath the jetpipe, and engine specialists John Watkins and Tony Meston hauled one of the Paloustes into position. The sense of excitement was intoxicating. Noble, as he always did, took infinite pains to ensure his windscreen was spotlessly clean. His obsession with cleanliness gave rise to numerous jibes about Howard Hughes, but it wasn't quite so funny when you remembered his life depended on that sort of attention to minor details.

That task completed, he was joined by his wife Sally, a statuesque blonde with a quiet dignity that brought a breath of fresh air to Bonneville. She is a remarkable woman. She seemed reserved most times I talked to her, leading to the assumption that she disliked the press, particularly those dreadful people who continually besieged her home to talk endlessly with her husband about his ambition. But you didn't have to think about it long to appreciate the potential of the strain she had to face.

In England she'd had to watch her husband roll Thrust 1 at 140mph in March 1977, and since that harrowing moment Project Thrust had virtually invaded her life as it developed from a part-time occupation to a fulltime obsession. She was a director of Thrust Cars Ltd and had always played a role in the vitally important Supporters' Club, at the same time bringing up daughter Miranda (Mimi) and preparing for the birth of Genevieve (Genny) in early 1981. Now, in Utah, she was having to adjust to existence in a backwoods town while worrying about her daughters back home. And throughout the stay she was surrounded by fleeting reminders of the accident sequences she had seen so many times on the land speed record film. Accidents which had killed men like Graham and Leasher at the same venue.

The parachute problems were another unpleasant reminder, for in 1964 Craig Breedlove had crashed into a brine lake at the end of the Bonneville course after *his* had failed over 500mph. All along she also had to watch her husband fighting similarly dangerous odds as he struggled with Thrust 2's low-speed handling problems and stopping difficulties.

Worse, she was astute enough to realise a worrying wife was the last thing he needed at the very moment he had to summon every ounce of confidence and concentration for the job in hand. Tonia Campbell had had her singing career to fall back on during her husband's record attempts, but Sally had nothing like that to distract her. Bringing up the girls was her career, with all that that implied should there be an accident. And right then Mimi and Genny were six thousand miles away.

Sally Noble, however, is made of stern stuff. She'd met Richard in the first place because her adventurous spirit had led her to reply to an advertisement he'd placed seeking companions for an overland expedition to Cape Town in 1972. This, however, was something very different. Land speed record breaking isn't a thrill you can share, like facing an alligator or braving a crossing of a parched desert. Only Noble could take the ultimate risk with Thrust 2, and that meant those who cared about him could do nothing but watch and wait. Sally was trapped in an awful situation. If she was the type it could have been very deadly and very frightening. Two years later on the Black Rock Desert she told my wife: "I never really thought Richard was serious. Not even after he crashed Thrust 1 at Fairford. When that happened I thought 'Thank God he's alright'. Then I thought 'Good, that means it's all over'. But it wasn't. It was only when we got to Bonneville that I finally realised he would never give up until he got the record or something dreadful happened".

To many, she was the bravest person present.

That day, as she went through her routine with Noble's kit, her feelings were well masked. Like her husband she too had perfected the poker face. He sat atop the car as she handed him his black driving shoes, red flameproof gloves, white flameproof balaclava and black Cromwell helmet, of the type worn by Harrier jump-jet pilots. It was a scene not dissimilar to a lady bidding farewell to her crusading knight. Twisting the hessian carrying bag unconsciously between her fingers she walked slowly back to her hire car and awaited the next stage in the ordeal. The start up.

By ten past ten Operations Manager Eddie Elsom announced a start in five minutes, but it was actually another ten before the Palouste was connected to its small socket by the offside front wheel. Due to the size of the Rolls-Royce Avon engine and the weight and initial inertia of its turbine shaft, plenty of energy is required before it will spin over fast enough to sustain ignition. An electric starter system would have required far too many heavy batteries, while onboard compressed air bottles would have required continual replenishment. Instead, Noble had managed to acquire two Paloustes, one for each start during a pair of runs. The Palouste is a small gas turbine, in this case mounted on a wheeled pod, and the compressed air each unit generated was fed to the Avon via flexible trunking.

As American pilot Bill Woffinden swooped aloft in the small monoplane Speedy Two, to act as aerial emergency spotter, the Palouste whined into life as Watkins cranked it over. Flames darted from its exhaust and suddenly the flaccid trunking became rigid as compressed air whistled down it. Noble, Speedy One for radio communications purposes, was safely strapped in monitoring his instruments, pressing the Avon's starter button as it began to rotate at its correct percentage of overall revs. Beneath the scream of the smaller engine became detectable the deeper rumble of the ex-Lightning fighter power unit and as a shimmer of heat haze issued from Thrust's jetpipe we knew the larger engine had fired. All extraneous personnel were cleared from the immediate start area and as the Palouste was switched off its trunking was disconnected and Brian Ball's deft fingers rapidly replaced the socket panel.

There was something eerily final about the closing of the cockpit hatch, always the last external section of the start-up, and for Noble there was now no escape until he had completed his task. The rumble of the Avon had now been superseded by a fearsome bellow as he built up power against the Lucas-Girling disc brakes, which had been specially designed for their demanding role. Then, just as it seemed something had to give way as the noise reached a crescendo, Noble took his foot off the brake pedal and Thrust 2 rolled forward. At first it seemed deceptively slow, but within a second it spurted ahead, its jet efflux flicking up salt particles in an ever growing cloud of white dust. In an exhibition of pure, raw power the monster car blasted down the course, assaulting the ears and making the very ground beneath our feet tremble with its passage.

A stench of kerosene hung in the air and everyone eagerly watched Thrust 2 slam its way into the distance until all that could be seen was a cloud of salt spray as the roostertail obscured further progress. Even after the cloud had disappeared over the horizon the now muted thunder and Buck Wetton's voice crackling over the radio could still be heard.

"That looked like a good one. That looked like a good one".

And indeed it had. We weren't at the stage yet where post-run talk centred on how well observers felt the reheat had lit. So far Noble had not employed that device which injected fuel into the stream of burnt exhaust gases to ignite unburnt oxygen and augment thrust by boosting the gas velocity from around a thousand feet per second to something closer to two and a half thousand. Nevertheless, it had been a moment of sheer excitement, unlike anything I'd experienced before, and every-body was absolutely delighted just to see the giant car finally doing what it was intended to: travel very, very quickly.

With the tenth mile of track still wet Noble had pulled up by the eight and a half mile mark and as the timekeepers declared the course clear everyone began a mad rush for transport for the dash to the north end. While we were permitted to watch starts nobody was allowed by USAC to await Thrust at the end of a run just in case it ran out of control. Minutes later, the rough salt scarred as cars slewed to a stop, the official speed was announced: 398.6mph through the measured mile. It was Noble's best to date. It also seemed the changes to the front suspension geometry had enhanced directional stability and stopped the car lurching badly off course. The aerodynamics were now also contributing more to its ability to maintain a steady course. Things were looking up.

FISA stipulates that records must be the result of two consecutive passes through the measured distance. One hour is allowed between the time a vehicle breaks the timing beams entering the distance – which may be a mile or kilometre according to preference – on its first run and breaks them clearing it on the second. If Noble could make a return run at 411mph or better he would have travelled faster on land than any Briton in history. There would also be the added psychological boost of going faster than his boyhood idol John Cobb, who achieved a one-way best of 403mph while setting his final 394mph record in 1947.

By eleven seventeen just over eight minutes of the allotted hour remained. In the intervening period Thrust 2 had been towed round to face back along the track, checked thoroughly, and refuelled from an ageing white tanker. Barrett and White had repacked the parachutes and re-armed the launch mortars. The wheels had been laboriously scraped clean of every speck of salt that had adhered to the rims during the first run, so that there was no risk of a build-up leading to high-speed imbalance. Unlike Bluebird there was no need to swap wheels and tyres between every run, but part of the time saving was eaten away by this need to scrape away any salt deposits. Nevertheless it was an important discipline. In any case, Ackroyd always insisted on having the front wheel covers removed so that full front suspension checks could be made. Throughout the car's history nothing was ever found amiss during this procedure, but even when it was suggested during the 1983 attempt that the check be deleted he was adamant it should be carried out just in case. That illustrated his commitment to safety and his abhorrence of allowing any element of unnecessary risk to creep in.

Throughout the 'controlled panic' Noble stood impassively, arms folded across his chest, chin dropped. His expression was relaxed, if anything thoughtful. If he felt any strain he gave no sign of it.

By eleven twenty-four he had again donned mask, shoes, gloves and helmet and fired the engine. But even before he had slowed at the southern end hopes for a new British car and driver mark had been dashed. Around 385mph he had felt Thrust 2 slip into its previous ruts and rather than attempt to wrestle it back under control he had deliberately throttled back and let it run where it chose. He veered  eighty feet into the rough salt before deploying the parachutes and rolling to a stop. It was a setback, but he remained calm and looked even more thoughtful. Yes, there was a problem, his manner suggested, but there had been many on the road to Bonneville. The team would simply have to find a solution.

"When she begins to run out of control like that", he explained quietly, "there really is no point in trying to bring her back. You just don't drive Thrust with white knuckles and wrestle with it. What you have to do is maintain a very delicate hold on the wheel. Once she gets out of shape it's best simply to let her run where she wants to go and slow down as gently as you can. There's plenty of space to manouevre out there, so it's not a dangerous situation".

Once again the jetcar was left on the track, and team principals returned to base camp for a high-powered rethink. Jim Deist suggested the independent rear suspension might be the culprit for Thrust's lack of low-speed stability, and went on to suggest the two lower Y-arms should be linked to form a simple beam axle. If Ackroyd was sceptical he had the politeness to disguise it, and with open-mindedness agreed to explore the avenue even though it might show he'd taken an incorrect design route. Straight away the modification was effected and later that afternoon Noble blasted down the remainder of the course to the southern end. He probably ran little more than a couple of miles, but it was enough to provide an answer. The modification made Thrust even less stable and it was returned to base and converted back to its original specification.

In several quarters the situation had now developed a fair degree of tension. What all the morning's dramas had done was compound an underlying sense of impatience felt by some of the crew, many of whom simply couldn't appreciate that their beloved car might be at fault. Already more than one individual had pondered aloud why Noble hadn't yet used the afterburner. He had responded that to do so would probably compound the handling problems, especially when Thrust hit its own ruts. Better to walk than try running too soon. He was distinctly unamused when the irreverent Watkins posted a notice on the motorhome's information board which read 'Reheat is a myth'. It began to look as if team, car and driver were in danger of reaching a performance plateau, even though beneath the surface Ackroyd still had plenty of fresh ideas.

The most serious cause for concern now though was the state of the track itself. Even with the reduced downforce Thrust was still cutting deep ruts that were destroying the prepared salt surface. Part of the depth was a result of the jet efflux blowing away salt loosened by the metal wheels and there was no denying that the faster the car went the greater would be the downforce it developed and hence the damage inflicted. Noble knew all about the dangers such ruts presented, from his own recent experience and from reading of Campbell's similar problems on Lake Eyre.

One obvious but expensive solution remained. Each time Thrust ran it would have to use a fresh section of track, and that meant spending even more precious financial and time resources on preparation. In the history of the record such a drastic move had never been necessary, but the technology of the metal wheels brought with it fresh demands and new problems, as the American SMI Motivator team already knew. Initially, three two hundred foot wide tracks eleven miles long had been prepared, with a fourth readied for the record attempt. The work had been carried out under the auspices of GKN Automotive, one of Noble's sponsors. GKN's American branch under Earl Sperry had invested some four hundred man-hours and countless dollars. Now, with all three tracks ruined despite the greater width designed into them to avoid the rut problem, urgent further action was needed.

Part of the root cause lay with local industry. Over the past twenty years local pumping stations had extracted some 350,000 tons of salt annually, for its potash content. The salt itself was eventually replaced but its lack of potash had a detrimental effect on its ability to heal itself whenever damaged. Now, even though Bonneville was said by experts to be in its best condition for fifteen years, it was still too soft for a high-downforce-generating four-ton car running not with rubber tyres but on metal rims.

For the rest of the day the ruts from the last runs were carefully filled with fresh salt in the hope that they might heal sufficiently to permit test runs within a couple of days. Under the supervision of a tomato-red-faced Briton from GKN called David Hannay, work was also started dragging a new course with enough tracks to allow two runs in each 'lane'. Poor David had a rather unfortunate manner of dealing with people, as if he was ordering about charwallahs in India, and his well-meaning aims soon earned him the nickname Colonel Salty.

The rough salt was dragged first with heavy metal scrapers before a belly-loader truck was employed to sprinkle fresh salt into any perceptible depressions. Then local contractor Dave Shelton moved in to tow a huge, ladder-shaped drag up and down the course at a monotonous eight miles every hour to pack the surface tight.

It was hard, time consuming work, compounded by the need to reposition the existing course marker flags. But at least it was action of sorts and it gave everyone plenty to do to keep their minds occupied and ward off the boredom and frustration that seemed to lie in wait for every setback.

While the work was progressing Ackroyd supervised further suspension changes. He had decided to take another half inch from the rear struts to reduce rake further but this time the locating eyes had sufficient adjustment thread to cope with the alteration and they were simply screwed home without the need for cutting and welding. As we turned in that night the reluctant decision was taken to hold the following day's runs on the track hitherto reserved for the record run. It was a sign the chips were really down.


In retrospect, Saturday October 10th was the project's most crucial day as far as the 1981 campaign was concerned. The sky wore a slightly less hungover expression but otherwise little was different to Friday. What had changed, however, was the atmosphere in the Western Café. After all those runs at the high end of the 300mph bracket a breakthrough in speed was absolutely essential, to give the project the fresh impetus it needed so desperately and to bolster morale which had begun to show definite signs of flagging. The one essential ingredient for safety in record breaking is patience, and Wendover's deadly ennui had already done its best to create an environment in which that fact could easily be overlooked by some crew members. Everyone, Noble included, was quiet over breakfast that morning, and more than a little edgy.

Just after nine o'clock Noble was ready to go and as the quarter hour came Thrust 2 again barrelled towards Floating Island. From the sidelines the run looked quicker than the previous day's, and he had seemed to hold even more power against the brakes. It is virtually impossible to judge such speeds by eye though, and when an official speed announcement came through it was to the accompaniment of disappointed groans. 392.720mph. Slower than Friday.

This time the turnaround seemed to progress well, a sign that the crew's prowess was improving, but then came a delay when the fuel tanker broke its prop-shaft, forcing the team to fall back on time-consuming manual refuelling. Noble appeared oblivious to the disappointment over the speed, and could be heard over the radio calmly informing Ackroyd that the Revtel speedometer wasn't working and that there was an unpleasant electrical burning smell in the cockpit. The mess-up with the fuel bowser had infuriated him however, and he determined to try a new ploy on the return run.

Six minutes later Elsom's voice broke the airwaves. "She's rolling. She's rolling. There she goes".

This time it was different. Very different. This time when Noble released the brakes and Thrust 2 began to surge forward there was only a brief moment when the salt cloud behind it was pure white. Then a great belching finger of orange flame stabbed from the jetpipe and suddenly Watkins grabbed Sally Noble in a crazy bearhug and began to scream at the top of his voice. "Reheat is no longer a myth!"

A grin of unalloyed satisfaction lit his face. 'One-Take', so called because of his unfailing ability to perform faultlessly for the film crew first time, every time, had at last seen his baby producing its real power, as he had always known it should. For the first time at Bonneville Noble had used the afterburner.

As we all stood grinning foolishly at the rapidly departing cloud, open mouths were choked with gritty flying particles of salt, but nobody cared. The euphoria of the moment had swept over everyone and put such trifling matters as personal comfort well beyond consideration. For the first time at Bonneville Thrust 2 was running in full reheat and the spectacular sight brought about a surge in spirits. Significant progress had at last been made.

"He's approaching the six. He's through the six mile. He's through the kilo. He's through the five mile. It's a good one".

With practised monotone, USAC's Buck Wetton charted Noble's lonely progress from his vantage point in the timekeepers' hut in the measured distance, and by the time the gold machine had completed its day's work those of us far down the track had barely had time to proffer congratulatory cigarettes, let alone light them.

It was staggering how speed and that spurting orange flame had killed off the apathy and bad feeling. Everyone had been anxious for action and Noble had provided it. Once again he was everyone's friend.

Two American photographers had hitched a lift down the course. To them the assignment to cover Thrust had been just another job in a not particularly enthralling location. They had been sceptical and couldn't wait to leave. Now their conversation had changed. The reheat had really turned them on and they no longer spoke in pessimistic terms of if. Instead they measured progress in terms of *when* the record would fall. And secretly everyone felt that had to be within the next few days.

At the southern end Thrust 2 sat quietly, hazy sunshine glinting on its polished paintwork. Like some huge circus animal it seemed to be awaiting praise for a job well done. Noble stood alongside, a huge grin across his face. He repeated himself many times, his italicised bellow again stretching his adjectives.

"Wow! Wow! That was absolutely fantastic. She felt ab-so-- lutely tremendous! She is so bloody stable with reheat on. Do you know Ackers, I think we've just found the answer to our stability problem!"

Shoulders hunched, hair flowing, he danced from foot to foot, no sooner finishing shaking hands with one well-wisher than another would grab him with congratulations. The cameramen had a field day.

"Stand by the car and look back down the track, Richard".

"Let's have one of you shaking hands with Ackers".

"Where's Sally? Let's get her in on this".

Hysterical laughter rent the air, and Noble kept yelling "Hurrah!" at the top of his voice. Practically every man and woman present applauded him on a superb performance. Many didn't know the exact speed figures, but everyone was certain the British car and driver mark, though not really an official record, had fallen. Little Butch, Jim Deist's nephew, had seen Breedlove, Arfons and Gabelich on the salt in their heydays. Now he waited patiently for Noble to be left alone, a forgotten, sad little figure, before grabbing his hand and shaking it longer than anyone else. It was the only time I ever saw Richard have his hand outshaken.

Still the camera shutters clicked away and as Sally almost shyly joined her husband they were posed and re-posed remorselessly. Noble continued to laugh, admitting: "God, this sort of thing embarrasses me".

The final speeds were revealing. Noble covered the mile at 440.906mph on that second run, the kilo at 447.029. A solid increment. For some reason USAC hadn't caught a mile speed on the first run, but the kilometre average of 418.118mph was enough to make him the fastest Briton in history and Thrust 2 the fastest British car. It was a long way from Gabelich's 622mph record, but it was a significant improvement nonetheless and everyone was delighted.

Even more telling though, was the subsequent analysis of the reheat run. At first, in the ensuing euphoria, there had been talk of rapidly turning the car for a third run, which would act as a back-up to the second and might thus boost the new averages, but Smee was worried about the electrical burning smell and was adamant the car should be checked before it ran again in anger. As it turned out he was right, for inspection revealed a faulty battery connection which partly accounted for the Revtel's antics and, even more important, a massive fluctuation on the recorder print-outs. The latter revealed that Thrust 2 had approached the measured mile well over 480mph – almost 50mph better than its previous peak – only to stutter as the loose lead cut out the fuel pump and created the hiccough. The Revtel problem, it transpired, had also been caused by a fault in the black box recorder's voltage regulator. But for the electrical problems, Thrust 2 would undoubtedly have peaked over 500mph. The British were beginning to make up the lost ground.

As preparation work on the new tracks continued that afternoon, the base camp area was strangely quiet, the only sounds to disturb the tranquility the rhythmic hum of a generator and the repetitive patter-pat of a child playing with a bat and ball. As Charles and I continued moving marker flags though, the first signs of fresh trouble reared their head. While we were engaged in the work we were forced to take temporary shelter from large rain spots as the sky developed a blackening hue, but the storm which had been threatening since lunchtime suddenly veered off the flats. Later, as we dined in an atmosphere of justified optimism at the Stateline that evening, it returned with a vengeance. Huge spots splattered on the roof and by the end of the meal Wendover's streets were awash and the whole of Utah's skies seemed filled with rain clouds.

Sunday's target of a 500mph average had just been drowned.

Standing on the causeway on the 11th, the transformation was simply breathtaking and almost unbelievable. Mournful team members stared aghast at what had been the salt flats. Now the scene resembled something from the Arctic. The Silver Island Mountains were faithfully reproduced as reflections in four inches of standing water, the odd salt mound that broke the surface here and there looking for all the world like floating pack ice. The previous night Hopkins had trailered the jetcar to the sanctuary of the deserted Northern Nevada Aviation Inc hangar at Wendover's disused airbase. Now the rush was on to break camp, to salvage the precious equipment before further bad rain that was forecast made things even worse. Some local weather sages spoke of the course drying out at surprising speed if the rain held off, but with water as far as the eye could see it was difficult to take them seriously. Worse, weather reports mentioned snow at four thousand feet, only five hundred above Bonneville's elevation from sea level. Winter, it seemed, had hit Utah early and literally washed away Richard Noble's hopes.

By Monday 12th, Columbus Day, the situation had indeed worsened. The previous night there had been more rain and now even the salt mounds were invisible. We spent the afternoon getting the remainder of the equipment to dry land, a GMC pick-up laden with a Palouste having to tow the team's stricken Pace Arrow motorhome from the sodden flats. Both were up to their wheels and somehow seemed to summarise the frustrating unhappiness of it all.

"When the airbase was operational guys used to call Wendover Dead End Road, the armpit of the world", said one of the locals in an attempt to lighten the brooding mood that descended on those who paused on the causeway for one last, malevolent glare.

"Well I reckon this place is more like a lower part of the human anatomy", someone else remarked. International photographer Leo Mason, on assignment for the past few days, added quietly: "If that's the case maybe we should remember we're all passing through it, so what does that make us?". It was a clever remark, but nobody felt inclined to reward it with the laughter it merited.

When he had stood in the same spot the day before, Noble had been impressive. He was the one, after all, who stood to lose most, and he knew only too well that his dream, as far as 1981 was concerned, had been frustrated. As Neil Parker's subsequent documentary summarised, it had been destroyed by an act of God. The manner in which he conducted himself, publicly at least, was exemplary. There were no tears of bitterness, no curses; there was no sign he felt hard done by. Equally, there was no sign whatsoever that he felt ready to quit. His face a hard mask wetted by occasional rain spots, he responded quietly to an observer's comment.

"Yes, it looks like a wrap. For this year at least. . ."

Back in Britain his many sponsors, who had been kept informed of developments throughout the attempt, had held a meeting and agreed tentatively to carry on into 1982. At a summit meeting at the Wendover airbase team members were paid off and the attempt was officially abandoned for the season.

It was probably Ackroyd who took the defeat and the decision most philosophically, as he reflected on what the team had achieved.

"You know, in a way I think the postponement is probably the best thing that could have happened. You mustn't forget that we came out here with absolutely no experience of running Thrust 2 on salt, nor on its metal wheels. We were raw beginners. Since we've been here though, we've amassed an incredible amount of knowledge that we never could have acquired six thousand miles away back home. We've sorted out the front suspension geometry and we now know the car is much more stable when we use the reheat.

"It's funny, but we virtually feel about the salt like sailors feel about the sea; you never know what it's got up its sleeve. But now we've got the time to incorporate a few more ideas into the car in the light of our experience, and we can polish up our act. To be frank, we've been very near the bone at times, as far as our organisation is concerned, but we'll get it better and we'll come back next year a far stronger team".

# 3. Building the cathedral

The six-year-old boy stares wide-eyed as the mysterious waters of Loch Ness slip by the windows of the beige Hillman Minx. At its wheel a burly man of military bearing, the child's father, smiles contentedly as he and his wife savour the pleasures of a bright, still day's holiday in one of the most picturesque yet brooding parts of Scotland. On the back seat the dark-haired youngster watches hopefully across the loch, heart pounding at the possibility of some prehistoric monster rearing suddenly from the inky depths, to defy all the grown-up disbelievers. He is lost in a world of his own, half-fearful, half-expectant.

Mile after mile of road speeds beneath the Hillman's wheels without sign of the fabled beast, but the fear of missing even a fleeting glimpse keeps his eyes rivetted on the water. Then the man at the wheel changes down a gear and slackens the car's pace, and rain-greened hedges cut off the boy's view and interrupt his reverie. As they turn into an opening to the right of the road and brake smoothly to a standstill, he is brought back down to earth. The man and woman in the front seat turn to him, their faces smiling.

"Let's see what all this is about, shall we?"

The boy is already beginning to form the suspicion that Something Is Going On. There is Something In The Air. By the waterside is a giant black crane with the name Coles painted in large letters on its side. Nearby is a wooden shed with weatherbeaten doors, over which hangs a green, white and red Castrol sign. There are groups of people standing around, looking at the jetty. And there, proud and massive, is the focus of their attention. Something huge and sleek and silver and goldfish red that seems to dwarf everything else.

*And deep within himself the child feels something primitive stirring, as though answering a distant call. It is beyond his ability to put the feeling into conscious thought, yet he is captivated immediately by the thing, the most awesome boat he has ever seen.*

*"That's John Cobb's Crusader", his father tells him.*

*The names become etched forever in his mind. John Cobb's Crusader! The importance of the loch's legendary monster might never have gripped his imagination.*

*He listens with mounting excitement as his father tells him more. John Cobb – holder of the Land Speed Record! The Fastest Man On Earth! – is to drive Crusader. He stares at the huge craft, taking in its space-age shape. With a surge of exhilaration he imagines the sleek projectile skimming across the loch's black waters faster than any other boat has ever travelled. Capturing the Water Speed Record for Britain! What a fantastic machine! What a tremendous thing to do!*

The seeds of his dream have been sown. As a result, the dark-- haired schoolboy will now spend all his time dreaming of that silver boat. He will collect everything he can relating to speed and speed records. Men such as John Cobb will become his heroes. He will even go so far as to spend hours crawling all over a scrapyard on one occasion seeking just the right shape spark plug to double as the centrifugal compressor when he builds a model of a jet engine. By his tenth birthday he will have read Eric Burgess' book *Rocket Propulsion* from cover to cover.

That day in September 1952, only weeks before the burly Cobb lost his life when Crusader nosedived and disintegrated at 240mph, a die was cast. The Great Bonneville Dream had begun. When Richard Noble related it one day in 1977, its effect was contagious.

"It wasn't the boat itself that was my inspiration", he said the day he outlined it and explained why it was the land and not the water speed record that had captivated him. "It was the speed element, really. It was just so outrageous, and it was that concept which appealed. At that time people were playing about with fifteen to twenty horsepower boats, and here was one with a 3,500lb thrust de Havilland Ghost jet engine from an aeroplane!

"Now the water speed record, as Cobb proved, is just very, very dangerous. At least when you're dealing with a car you can control your variables; with water you can't. That's why my dream always centred on the land speed record".


Every record breaker begins with a dream, and usually it is the same one. What differs is the way in which each man turns his dream into reality. Glenn Leasher became one of the record's victims, not just because he died attempting to push his Infinity to 400mph, but because his courage and efforts are remembered only by a few. Ever since he quit school he had dreamed of the record, while contemporary Craig Breedlove, second only to Sir Malcolm Campbell in the roll of success, dreamed of it when he was ten and worked through at least one marriage to break it.

Mormon preacher Athol Graham, another casualty of the great challenge of ultimate speed who died in City of Salt Lake at Bonneville, literally *did* have that dream about the record. It happened in 1947 and thereafter he regarded it as divine guidance for his secular mission.

But dreams come cheap. As the old Indian adage has it: 'Talk cheap, white man. Takes money to buy whisky'. Anyone can be bold enough to covet the land speed record, and there have been some great talkers over the years, but only success can elevate contenders into that elite that has achieved something no other mortal has. Turning dreams into reality is what really makes the Breedloves, Campbells and Nobles different from their fellows.

When Noble began putting wheels in motion for his first record breaking steps in 1974, there were plenty of observers ready to begin firing the age-old questions at him. What qualifications did he have that made him a suitable candidate to drive a car faster than any other man in history? Where was his background in drag racing? Where was his astronaut training? Why, he didn't even have a family background steeped in record breaking, like Britain's last speedking Donald Campbell! The next question would be inevitable: 'What's the fastest you have ever been in a car, Mr Noble?' And Noble would look his interrogator straight in the eye, like a forty-five year-old society hostess rudely asked her age, and say: "I've done around 120mph in my Triumph TR6".

The questioner would look askance as if he was some kind of Don Quixote in racing overalls tilting at the windmill of ultimate speed, and would paint a patronising smile across their face and nod sagely. In doing so they would overlook one of his most precious assets: a clear-headed, almost cold-blooded assessment of exactly what he would need to do to get a jetcar to the Bonneville salt, or Australia's Lake Eyre, or wherever else Fate might take him. No, he didn't have Breedlove's drag racing experience, nor had he been a part of such intensive physical and mental training as had current record holder Gary Gabelich when he was involved with NASA's space programme. All he had was some Army Outward Bound School experience and an addiction to speed, which he admitted was a tremendous influence on his life. He hadn't even driven a racing car, although at one stage subsequently he would consider a season of Sports 2000 in Britain to hone his reflexes. But in the seventies the requirements for record breaking had changed somewhat since the happy-go-lucky days of the sixties, when the first jetcars appeared. Now, the days of the backyard jeans and tee-shirt land speed record project were over, and the sport had moved into the realm of the corporate budget. What Richard Noble *really* had going for him when he decided he wanted the record was the ability to raise the money.

Ken Norris, who with brother Lewis was responsible for the design and development of Donald Campbell's Bluebird K7 jet hydroplane and CN7 gas turbine car, has long summarised the requirements for record breaking as the Four Ms: Man, Machine, Medium and Money. With the high technology equipment he was going to need, Noble was fully aware from the outset that the single most important would be the money. No money, no project. The driving skills could be mastered along the way, likewise the design of the car and the choice of the medium. The money had to come first and he knew how to get it.

Another arrow in his quiver, of course, was an adventurous spirit, for without it he would never even have dreamed of the record. He was as full of stories of his overland expeditions at that stage as he later would be of his record attempt adventures, albeit only when talking with friends. Behind him lay the sojourn to Cape Town in 1972, with a six-strong band of fellow adventurers who travelled in a thirteen year-old Land-Rover he had prepared and rebuilt himself. That was where he met Sally Bruford, who joined his team after responding to an advertisement he'd placed in *The Times*. Before long she was to become an indispensible part of his life, and they were married on July 30 1976.

By extraordinary coincidence, it transpired Sally's uncle had visited the Bonneville Salt Flats in 1947, the year in which Cobb made his last automobile record attempt, to see the English fur broker achieve 394mph.

Four years prior to his marriage, Noble's wanderlust had taken him from South Africa to Afghanistan via India. When, in 1984, he became another unwitting victim of Eamonn Andrews' *This Is Your Life* programme, he was genuinely embarrassed as his companions were called on to relate tales of his bravery.

It was while working as a twenty-eight year-old consultant writing training courses in pure management that he finally decided to do something about his dream, and typically it didn't take him long to make his resolution.

"Whenever you get into something like the land speed record", he related during our first interview, "there is inevitably a time when you have to ask yourself one two-part question. 'Am I going to do anything about it, or shall I let it go?' And I simply decided I *wasn't* going to let it go".

The decision taken, he began designing the vehicle he would christen Thrust 1. It was an apposite title, since nobody in Britain had ever built a car that relied purely on the thrust of its exhaust gases. He knew precious little about engineering, but what did that matter? Thrust 1 was never intended as the record attempt vehicle, but simply as a starter machine that would give him experience, publicity and, above all, credibility.

Something else he did know, however, was how to be disarmingly persuasive or just plain cunning, and the early days of Thrust 1 were littered with examples of both. He tracked down one of the last serviceable Rolls-Royce Derwent 8 jet engines in the country at an independent engine dismantlers and paid £200 for it. The French Air Force had also been interested in the unit, but Noble beat his foreign opposition to it, sneaking the engine out of the yard just before the French government inspector arrived to make his purchases.

The Derwent was an old-fashioned type of jet even then, and its centrifugal compressor design endowed it with prodigious girth. But on the credit side it was cheap, reliable and gave three and a half thousand pounds of thrust. That wasn't anything like enough to get the record, even if Noble subsequently chose to instal it in a more sophisticated car, but it was ideal to get things going.

As he set about his new project with his usual unstoppable enthusiasm, his public school brand of self-confidence helped him to shrug off setback after setback, denial after denial. And his ability to sell himself and his project slowly began opening doors closed after industry's disappointment with Campbell's prolonged Bluebird CN7 struggle. The final asset on his decidedly lop-sided balance sheet was his ability to enthuse others, to get things and people rolling. And the opportunism continued unabated.

For many record breakers, getting an engine is the easy part. You contact the Ministry of Defence, get on its mailing list which is circulated every time various types of engine come up for disposal, then tender a bid once you have inspected the units. Putting a chassis beneath an engine bought in such a manner has often proved the stumbling block, on grounds of design and construction expense. It was not so for Noble. While employed by GKN he went prowling round the GKN Sankey works at Telford with the Works Manager, but found nothing suitable. They returned via the research and development section and there he came across a ladder-type chassis lying on the floor covered in dust. Instantly he tackled his guide.

"That would be absolutely ideal for the project".

"But we couldn't possibly let you have it; it was part of an experimental project, a one-off. It cost a fortune to make".

Noble looked reflective and shook his head as if he hadn't heard a word. "Mind you, it's about eighteen inches too long. . ."

At that the manager's expression brightened and he signalled to one of his men who was wielding an oxy-acetylene torch nearby. The latter promptly burned off the offending eighteen inches. Turning to Noble the manager smiled. "It's damaged now. Not much point in holding on to it, is there?"

Noble would tell a similarly satisfying tale about the wind tunnel tests conducted on Thrust 1's proposed design.

"There was a lovely time when we went to British Aerospace in Filton to ask if they would be prepared to do some tunnel tests as I was a little bit concerned the proposed front section might develop some positive lift. They said it probably wouldn't once they'd examined the drawings, but that you couldn't always tell. They offerred to do the tests for £400. Of course, that was quite reasonable but I had to say 'Sorry, that's forty per cent of our budget. There's no way I can spend that sort of money. I'll just have to suck it and see'. Eventually they said they might be able to do something for £100 but I still had to say 'Sorry, but we are building Thrust 1 on an absolute shoestring budget and I don't think I can afford even that'.

"But they were interested. Three or four days later they rang up to say a rare opportunity had arisen and that I had nine days to get a wind tunnel model together. They said if I could do that they'd run some tests for nothing. I can tell you, getting a wind tunnel model built in that time is quite a hassle!".

Through 1974 and 1975 Noble spent every spare moment he could steal working on his jet machine, first in his home near Chiswick, later in a garage in Thames Ditton. Finally, with the assistance of a band of enthusiastic friends it was finished. What emerged from that garage was desperately crude and without the finance for a trailer he once had to tow it across London roped to the GKN Ford Cortina company car. On the way the unique entourage was stopped by an appalled police officer who took a few steps back as he regarded the huge jet engine perched atop a set of Wolfrace wheels with a mixture of awe and horror. After going through the usual procedure he finally allowed the future land speed record holder to carry on.

"But three things. First of all you never saw me. Second, get there as quickly as you can. And third, for God's sake don't start it up on the way. . .!"

Noble was all too aware of Thrust 1's design shortcomings and was the first to dub it a 'cathedral on wheels'. He had based his concept on Grand Prix car principles, overlooking the fact that they are designed to corner as fast as possible, where jetcars should be designed in a very different manner so they run as straight and stable as possible. It didn't take him long to appreciate that he'd taken the wrong route as Thrust's inherent faults became apparent after its maiden run at RAF St. Athan in 1975. It was fast enough and spectacular enough, however, to attract a great deal of attention and publicity was something whose value he already appreciated, even at this formative stage. What was more, Thrust 1 had been very cheap to build. He had sold his beloved Triumph TR6 to raise its £1,000 budget.

The run at St. Athan was more than enough to convince him he had done the right thing in pursuing his dream. "I sat in the cockpit and saw the revs rising. Then I eased the HP cock open and suddenly there was a bloody great whoomph as she lit up and then we were away. We were on forty per cent idle and cruised at 50mph to get the feel of things, but from that moment I was absolutely and totally hooked".

Subsequent runs were made at significantly greater power and speed, especially after the suspension had been lowered, and before long Richard Noble and Thrust 1 had appeared on several television programmes, including *Tomorrow's World*. On one occasion he actually drove the jet monster round the short Indy circuit at Brands Hatch. He nearly blew over a camera crew's pursuing Range Rover when he used a bit too much power climbing the hill up to Druids bend and the Derwent's jet blast got a mite too potent.

The Thrust 1 story came to a sticky conclusion on March 5th 1977 when he was making a series of test runs at RAF Fairford in Gloucestershire. The perils of his chosen new profession were brought home forcibly when, following a successful 150mph warm-up run on part throttle, he embarked on one intended to edge closer to 200mph. A wheel bearing seized at 140mph and pitched the crude monster into a horrifying series of airborne rolls. Thrust 1 lurched over once. Twice. A third time. By the time it had expended its energy and ceased its destructive threshing, and a shaken but otherwise unharmed Noble had been released from his safety belts, it had passed into history. During one bounce the Wolfrace rims had touched the runway for a millisecond, leaving two perfect aluminium circles in the tarmac.

The incident could have dealt a crushing blow to the fledgling project, but Richard refused to see it in anything but positive terms. Years later he still drew satisfaction from his own reactions during the crisis, as if the memory remained of a moment in which he'd really proved something to himself. Perhaps it was one of those record breaker's moments of truth.

"You know, I can distinctly remember switching off the fuel supply while we were upside down in mid-air at 140mph", he recalled, and lurking in his eyes as he spoke was a gleam of satisfaction at his own self-possession. It spoke volumes.

Over some consoling drinks immediately after the disaster he addressed himself and the team to the problem the day's events had introduced. There were a number of alternatives. The most obvious was to call it a day, be thankful for the chance to have done something unusual and exciting and be heartily grateful to have survived without injury. That didn't take much time to consider.

The second was to build a second version of Thrust 1, with some design rectifications, and continue the programme. That took a while longer to assess.

The third was to move on to a wholly new car. When Noble had set up Thrust Cars Ltd, Project Thrust's background company, he had always envisioned a series of cars, and it was more than obvious the team had learned as much about Thrust 1 as it was ever likely to.

In a short space of time the third alternative was chosen. In many ways Noble had reached the crossroads Donald Campbell had faced in 1951. He had inherited his father's K4 hydroplane, had had it converted back to Rolls-Royce piston power after Sir Malcolm had experimented with jets after the war, and had vowed to defend his father's record from American attack. The Americans had succeeded and on a run in 1951 Bluebird had been disembowelled at above record speed when it hit a sunken railway sleeper. With the boat wrecked Campbell had eventually made his decision to carry on with an all-new jet-powered craft. Now Noble made a similar decision. This time, however, things would be done properly. The backing would have to be raised from commercial sources, as none of the team was wealthy and Noble had no desire to see anyone mortgaging their houses or risking bankruptcy, a fate which nearly befell one of his contemporary rivals. There would be a professional designer, the car would be built by skilled engineers and immaculately turned out, and would act as a high-speed showcase for the team's talents in the interests of raising further backing for Thrust 3. That would be the land speed record attempt vehicle.

On the way back to Project Thrust's Twickenham base that night the shattered remains of Britain's first pure-jet car were simply dragged off and sold to an Irish scrap dealer on the Great West Road. As he viewed them, running a dirty palm across his stubbled jaw, a faraway look came into his eyes.

"It's no problem. With a bit of welding we should be able to get her going again", he calculated as he doled out £175 for his new possession. At that, the horrified recipients surreptitiously removed enough parts from the Derwent to frustrate any aspirations he might harbour. . .

# 4. The birth of Thrust 2

If the decision to step Project Thrust up another gear was bold, Noble's manner when he started planning Thrust 2 was convincing. In one of our numerous interviews in the early phases of the undertaking, he outlined his criteria. "Basically, to do something of this nature you need dedication, determination and money. In that order". It was a credo that was to hold good throughout the project's life.

At that point, however, Project Thrust had only the £175 proceeds from the sale of Thrust 1 in the bank, even if Noble did have dedication and determination oozing from every pore. Just how do you go about initiating a project that will eventually swallow the better part of one and three quarter million pounds in such circumstances?

"There are three ways", he would list, underlining his grasp of record breaking's realities. "You can build your project on the back of something that is already successful. If you really strike lucky you might snare a multi-millionaire who is willing to let you go ahead in strict secrecy until you are absolutely ready to go public. Or you can do it the way we've had to, building as much publicity as possible and chasing people endlessly for support. And to get away with that you'd better make damn sure you have a logical programme of development and that you never let the momentum slip".

Very shortly after the Thrust 1 accident Paddy Hine of the Ministry of Defence, now Air Marshal Sir Patrick Hine, invited Noble to give a lecture on Project Thrust to a host of very senior RAF directors in a little cinema in Adastral House. They were very keen to help but when they asked how they could, his response came as a dramatic shock.

"We want a Lightning fighter!".

Predictably, this rash request met with gasps of surprise and protestations of impossibility, but as was his custom Noble had done his homework well.

"Come on gentlemen. I know you're breaking several Lightnings at RAF Gutersloh, and we're only interested in certain bits. . ."

On that occasion even his persuasive technique wasn't quite enough. He didn't get his Lightning, but as a direct result of his lecture and his extraordinary request a Rolls-Royce Avon 210 turbojet from one of the airframes was made available for a paltry £500. This was the mighty power unit seen by thousands at Motorfair in October 1977. Thanks to its coaxial compressor system it was relatively slim but with its reheat pipe it measured more than twenty-five feet in length and weighed 2,938lbs. With 15,000lbs of thrust it was at the time thought powerful enough to break the record and it had the added advantage of being a sensational publicity tool. Few residents of Twickenham at that time could boast ownership of an ex-Lightning F2 fighter engine! Noble's £500 outlay bought him some very economical power at 30lbs thrust per pound sterling, and he couldn't resist pointing out that when he transported his new toy back to the garage behind his semi-detached house he had to borrow a truck and crane. The idea of paying to hire one never even crossed his mind.

With the new engine came a fresh round of television interviews on the programmes that had shown interest in Thrust 1. The latter's flip had been well covered in the daily papers, thanks to some astute public relations work by George Myers, so the prospect of a driver who had survived that sort of incident being prepared to have another go in a vehicle three times more powerful attracted a lot of comment. The really big break, however, came in October. Noble's smooth talking again won the big prize: one thousand square feet of display space at Motorfair from the show-organising *Daily Express*. But even that meant a major gamble. With precious little time in which to do it, he sold advertising space on the stand to pay the stand construction bills, and just made it in time. Having drawn countless blanks, he simply sat down and called the chairmen of all the companies he'd approached and chivvied away until they finally succumbed.

On paper that Motorfair stand boasted little, yet it was by far the most popular and, exactly as Noble had hoped, the most televised. During the course of the show the project received valuable airtime and was visited by thousands. Noble estimated the figure at 35,000 in the 13 days. There were several useful spin-offs. The first was the boost to the Project Thrust Supporters' Club. This was a hangover from the Thrust 1 days, when it had been known as the Supporters' Association, and was little short of a stroke of genius as it gave the public the chance of involvement in the project for a mere pound a year. Better still, it gave sponsors a chance to advertise to already sympathetic consumers via the club's regular newsletter. Loctite, one of the first backers far-sighted enough to put money into the project, picked up the tab for the printing costs and the newsletter graduated over the years from a two-sided newsprint sheet to a wholly professional glossy four-pager. At its peak the Supporters' Club had over 2,500 members, and while it didn't raise a fortune it was further proof that Project Thrust was prepared to explore every avenue of self-help and wasn't just another outfit looking for handouts. Sally started the club, then Sue Brinn, wife of Thrust Cars' Company Secretary David, handled the post of Club Secretary before Sally took over again in September 1980. Even the postage costs were sponsored, Mike Hearn's MWG Impex concern looking after that side to help the project maximise its income. As a nice historical touch and a respectful gesture, the Campbells' right-hand man Leo Villa was made the Club's first official life member.

The most significant breakthrough of Motorfair actually threatened to bankrupt the project, yet its effects were to prove far-reaching. On one of the days the Publicity Director and public relations agents of Tube Investments travelled to the show to assess the worth of Project Thrust in response to a proposal Noble had put before the management. He had expected a couple of people but was inwardly horrified when six turned up. When it was obvious they weren't ready to leave by noon, he invited them to lunch. The meal lasted two hours and the bill came to £65, exactly what Project Thrust had left in the kitty! Noble, however, had achieved his goal. Soon after Tube Investments agreed to build the £25,000 spaceframe chassis for Thrust 2, using its world famous Reynolds 531 round and square-section tubing. The company wasn't able to offer any financial assistance, but charged Noble nothing and told him he could use its name in any way he liked that might help the project and encourage other companies to become involved.

John Ackroyd had agreed to join the project by September 1977, but had been unable to attend Motorfair as he was still on contract work for Porsche in West Germany while Noble sought the backing to employ him fulltime. The manner in which the latter had advertised the post of designer was typical of his resourcefulness and shrewdness, while the way in which Ackroyd went about securing it was typical of his enthusiasm and determination.

Placing an ad for a 650mph car designer would have cost far too much, so Noble simply circulated a press release to the specialist motoring magazines. Predictably, the result was considerably more coverage than any advertisement would have attracted, at negligible cost. Ackroyd read it in *Cars and Car Conversions* while 'resting' between contract design jobs and working as a deckchair attendant. Here was an ultimate challenge. After a delay he was interviewed by Noble, having already telephoned to ask why he hadn't heard from him, and though he was shown the Avon engine and not much else he was still keen to get started. He assessed the resources for himself: "We had one Rolls-Royce Avon 210 engine with reheat. But we had nowhere to build the car, no materials or components, no tools, no team, no experience and no money. At least that meant we could start with a clean sheet of paper".

Noble, however, ever keen to have everything double-checked, wanted Ken Norris to vet all applicants and called him the following day to tell him about John Ackroyd and to arrange an interview.

"He's been here since nine o'clock", came Ken's reply. . .


Slowly the threads were drawn together. Initially there weren't the funds to employ Ackroyd fulltime, so he took the contract design job with Porsche and made the fullest use of the German company's library facilities during his spare-time work on Thrust 2. Noble's contribution to the vehicle came at the concept stage before Ackroyd arrived on the scene, and he chose a similar layout to three-time record holder Art Arfons, who placed a cockpit either side of a General Electric J79 turbojet in his highly successful if crude-looking Green Monster. Arfons' car later crashed at 600mph when a wheel bearing seized but the fact he survived with nothing worse than a headache and salt abrasions indicated the layout's suitability from the safety standpoint. Ackroyd endorsed the general plan, and set about the real design work. As Noble found more money he left Porsche and joined Thrust Cars fulltime, setting up his drawing office in the derelict house's kitchen. It was a lonely existence initially, and had him wondering about his general sanity at times, but the fact that he was working on the Isle of Wight, where he already lived, was an advantage. In the initial months he worked closely with Tube Investments' Ken Sprayson, John designing and Ken building the mammoth chassis. Sprayson is a superb welder, renowned as an ace motorcycle frame builder.The final design work began on May 1st 1978, and the first metal was cut by the end of June. Even so, money remained so tight Noble couldn't afford at one stage to let Ackroyd travel from the Island to Walsall to see the frame being built! There were other discomforts, too. Ackers became expert at hoarding 10p pieces and developed a precarious if quick waterside short-cut from his office to the nearest public telephone as Project Thrust couldn't afford the luxury of its own 'phone at that stage. The nearest photocopier was a six mile drive away and having drawings printed meant a fourteen mile drive across the East Cowes. The rest of the time, however, he used his "company car", a trusty black Hercules pushbike.

Meanwhile, Noble travelled the length and breadth of the mainland in his search for support, putting sponsorship proposals before managing directors, persuading other companies to contribute goods or services, giving lectures on the project to motor clubs – in short doing anything that he could to maintain that vital momentum. It was imperative that he kept up the level of interest and cash injection, for the design process was to be one of the most thorough in record history and Ackroyd was not one even to consider cutting corners.

Gradually the milestones mounted. The single most significant came in September 1978 after three weeks of low-speed wind tunnel testing of a one-tenth scale model at British Aerospace's Filton facility. Ackroyd had always felt that Thrust 2 had outright record potential and after the tests he and Noble calculated they could achieve 600mph on 10,000lbs of thrust. They concluded that they therefore ought to reach 630 on 15,000. Noble admitted, however: "At that stage we couldn't afford the transonic wind tunnel work, so all we could do was guess..." But from that moment Thrust 3 was quietly forgotten and Thrust 2, which had in any case been designed and built to the highest standards, became the record attempt vehicle. Suddenly Noble had a real ace in his hand.

In December 1978 the completed spaceframe, painted an anaemic shade of yellow, was put on public display on the Loctite stand at the Alexandra Palace Performance Car Show. That was where several of us learned by heart ninety-nine per cent of Tony Maylam's film *The Fastest Man on Earth* as we played it endlessly to a spellbound audience, losing count of the number of times an original-thinking individual would crack wise about Thrust 2's metal wheels. The spaceframe was temporarily mounted on small castors and had we received a pound for every comment about them being a bit small for the record attempt there would have been little need for further sponsorship.

By March 1979 the Avon 210 had been installed and the skeleton was transported from Tube Investments' Development Engineering Department in Walsall to Project Thrust's modest Isle of Wight headquarters at the Ranalagh Works in Fishbourne, on the banks of the Wootton Creek, for systems installations. On December 6th the part-completed vehicle, minus its complicated body panels which had yet to be constructed as the transonic wind tunnel testing was still to be done, was revealed on its wheels for the first time at a press reception at the Tower Hotel near London's Tower Bridge. That day Project Thrust was able to show its many sponsors immediate television coverage on ITN's lunchtime news slot.

Having lost his battle for a Lightning the first time, Noble tried again early in 1980, and this time he won permission to have a small team, comprising Project Thrust personnel and Supporters' Club members, strip vital parts from the hulk of an obsolete F2A on decoy duty at RAF Coningsby, on the proviso that the airframe wasn't damaged. That was where One-Take Watkins first came into the picture as he helped with the special tools needed and advised on methods of removal. After long, protracted negotiations with the Ministry of Defence at Harrogate, Noble succeeded in reducing the price from £16,000 to £450...

Friday, July 4th 1980 was a Red Letter day for the project, marking the first static test of the Avon 210 engine. As a tribute to its hardiness and the team's ability, ex-RAF men Tony Meston and Geoff Smee were able to tickle it into life after only minor difficulties, even though it hadn't run for years. And as team members clasped their hands over their ears at RAF Coningsby's tie-down area they saw for the first time the fifteen foot flame that signalled full reheat, complete with the sonic shockwaves. That was to become one of the most exciting sights during the project's life, but also one of the most troublesome areas.

By the end of the month Thrust 2 was finally ready in vestigial state to undertake its first test runs, just over two years since serious design work had begun. But the whole team was in for a rude awakening. Thrust was taken to RAF Leconfield's 7,000ft runway through the auspices of the Army School of Mechanical Transport, and was to be run on Dunlop aircraft wheels and tyres. Straight away Noble's introduction to piloting his new baby was rude. He had a lot of trouble driving it at any representative speed and a great deal of soul-searching ensued between driver and designer. After all the work he'd put in, was Noble really going to be up to his most important role?

It was only later that both he and Ackroyd came to appreciate just how unsuitable Leconfield had been for their purpose. "It had an appallingly bumpy surface and was used for training army drivers", Noble recalled. "The runway was littered with traffic signs which put me off, and I had to thread Thrust 2 through traffic lights at 180mph. Later we did our first airshow demonstration at HMS Daedalus and ran 200mph without difficulty".

There was a lighter side, which concerned Ackroyd's penchant for taking pictures of the Avon in full reheat during its static tests. When a television cameraman asked his advice on the best spot for filming it, Ackers went to considerable trouble to site him within the Avon's exhaust shock cone. That was fine during the static tests, but John overlooked that when Thrust 2 moved forward during a run the shock cone would also move. When Noble surged away both he and the hapless cameraman were blown to the ground.

The following month the team switched venue to RAF Greenham Common, then a tranquil far cry from the notoriety that would surround it when it became a British base for nuclear weaponry. Each time he made a run Noble learned more as a driver, steadily attuning himself to higher speeds until he began describing as boring runs made without a dab of reheat.

During the tests it was found that the Lucas-Girling disc brakes, which had been specially developed by quiet, train--obsessed Welshman Glynne Bowsher, were much more effective than anticipated. With the grip of the Dunlop tyres taken into account, Noble found Thrust 2 could be held at a standstill at Max Cold power, or 100 per cent of engine revs. Initially it had been expected 60 per cent would be the maximum before Thrust tried to drag its locked wheels along the tarmac. The result was that even better standing starts were possible and that reheat could be selected earlier.

Noble's procedure during demonstration runs was to build up to Max Cold while holding the car stationary on the wheel brakes, then select reheat and release the brakes the moment he felt its flame light. Thrust 2 would then accelerate to 100mph in two and a half seconds at 1.75G, and on to 200 in a further three seconds at 1.5G. It was a long way removed from the TR6.

As an indication of the challenge he faced at Greenham, he then had to deploy his parachute just five hundred feet from the end of the measured mile so it would mushroom and bite at exactly the right moment he cleared the timing traps. A moment too soon would rob him of vital speed; a moment too late and he could be in real trouble. His task was aided by brother Andrew, who positioned his VW camper at the designated spot with its headlights on main beam, but Noble wasn't facing a sinecure on those summer days as he travelled at four hundred and ten feet every second.

After the mile he then had a fraction over seven hundred yards in which to stop. Despite Bowsher's brakes and the ring-slot ten-foot diameter GQ parachutes produced by Brian Collings, safety and success could not be guaranteed. One slight error would have seen him speeding off course, and in that respect the runs were an excellent test of both man and machine. Eventually he was able to judge things so finely that he regularly pulled up with literally only feet to spare, but both car and driver passed their trials with flying colours. When the team felt ready, Noble went for his first significant speed marks.

During the weekend of September 24th and 25th 1980 he set six new British records, the most important being raising male clothing magnate Richard Horne's Flying Mile from 191.64mph to 248.87mph. His new figure also counted as the new British land speed record. The Flying Quarter Mile fell at 259.74mph and the Flying 500 Metres at 255.06, all impressive figures for a four-ton vehicle that was not designed as an out and out dragster. During the runs reheat was not employed. It would have taken the car to 400mph, and that would have been 150mph too much for safety in Greenham's tight confines.

The only real problem encountered throughout the two days was Noble's reluctance to adhere to Dunlop's stipulation that the tyres should not be taken to speeds in excess of 260mph – a speed he regularly peaked above during the runs.

Noble and Thrust 2 continued their airfield appearances during the year, and nothing typified the team's spirit more than the Coventry Air Display. "It was a very important day for us", Noble winced on reflection. "An engine fault cut out the reheat after one and a half seconds during a television demo we were doing. I was absolutely furious about it and we badgered for more time. We got the TV people back but they, of course, were dying to get their film off for the one o'clock news. Then our Palouste seized. It was a massive slog to get a new starter engine and get ourselves ready for the Air Display the next day, an appearance at RAF Alconbury on the Saturday and Coventry again on the Sunday. But we made it, and it all added to our credibility.

"Basically, we're paid to perform, we're in the public eye, and we don't let anybody down. So long as we don't risk the car we perform and move heaven and earth, because that's how to build credibility".

In his cockpit a Revtel speedometer was eventually fitted to monitor his velocity, but in the early days there were no such luxuries. "I used to race Tony Meston on his motorbike before we switched to radar, but radar guns are only calibrated to 200mph, so after a bit that too became useless. Then for Greenham we got the Revtel, which reads electronically from a small sensor in one of the rear wheel bearings. It's accurate to one mile an hour, so I know exactly what speed I'm doing even before I get my official figures".

Throughout the summer of 1980, before Project Thrust developed into the professional outfit that it became, Noble got firmly into the swing of driving the giant jet monster to the point where it became almost second nature. There was never any lingering spectre from the Thrust 1 accident, and he never felt any need to psyche himself for his task. The very suggestion could be relied on to bring a smirk to his face.

"Good Lord, no. I don't find any sort of mental problems arise. Certainly in the very early days when we were starting the Thrust 2 project I was very apprehensive about things, and if you've ever seen a Lightning fighter on take-off you'll appreciate why, because on full reheat they have one hell of a lot of power. I was aware of course that I'd have far more at my disposal than ever before. But we've always approached things gradually and positively, and after a bit everything clicked into place. I've tended to find my best performance is my first, which is interesting, and we've stopped bothering with warm-ups as a result and just get in and go. I don't understand it, but there you are".

If he did have a mental hang-up it concerned the *Nationwide* television news magazine programme. Where Donald Campbell had been intensely superstitious, Noble has no time for such indulgences, but even he admitted to a degree where the BBC programme was concerned.

"It's the only thing I am superstitious about, but it's a funny thing. Every British project that's been featured on *Nationwide* – the Atlantic balloonists, Barry Bowles' rocket car, Tony Fahey's jetboat – has run into some sort of trouble. We've been approached many times by the programme's people – they even resorted to sending cars to collect me – but we've always had to say 'Sorry, but you must understand why we don't feel we can appear'. It's an unfortunate thing but, you know, it's happened too often to be coincidence.

"I feel superstition is okay if it eases your mental consciousness but I think it suggests a fundamental fault in the sense that the driver is not satisfied with the design of his car or perhaps has not actually lived with the building of it, and therefore has come to it rather as somebody about to drive it on first acquaintance. With Thrust we've all lived through the building of the thing and John has always involved us in all the technical and design decisions, so I feel extremely confident. If I had any doubts or superstitions about Thrust I wouldn't be doing it. Simple as that. I can say though, that I'd have great doubts about driving anything that John *hadn't* designed. . ."

By 1981 Project Thrust was looking very serious. Thrust 2 was running well and had proved reliable during its preliminary trials. Since 1979 the outfit had been transported on a specially built Crane Fruehauf low-loader trailer towed by a Leyland Marathon tractor (later to become a T45 Roadtrain) which Noble's persuasive talking had won from Sir Michael Edwardes of British Leyland.

On the Isle of Wight Ackroyd concentrated in finalising the design of the aluminium wheels and overseeing transonic wind tunnel testing at British Aerospace in Weybridge. This time he used a special thirtieth-scale model machined from solid aluminium and duplicated from the wooden low-speed tenth-scale version via a three-to-one pantograph.

Throughout the build-up to these tests BA's men were extremely negative about the shape of Thrust 2, giving the distinct impression they felt its chunky, slab-sided design which had been developed with both cost of construction and aerodynamic efficiency in mind, had the slipperiness of a house brick.

The talk was all of high frontal areas and high drag coefficients. Ackroyd had the last laugh however, for when the tests were done and the calculations were in hand he received a telephone call from an amazed boffin.

"John, we don't know what the hell it is you've done with that shape, but our test results suggest Thrust 2 has a speed potential between 650 and 680mph!"

Work continued to progress on the car at the tiny Ranalagh Works, where Ackers' office was now at least a Portakabin. Things had become very much better since, in 1979, he had advertised for a second designer to ease his burgeoning workload. Eddie Elsom lived in nearby Ryde and had applied for the post.

"I saw Ackers in the kitchen in June or July 1979", Eddie recalls. "I had a job with Plessey at the time but joined Thrust fulltime in September. I had similar design qualifications to John although I had strayed from the drawing board to the management side in my career. I was recruited as assistant designer, but it was quite obvious to me there was only ever going to be one designer. It was John's car – he'd design it, build it and, if necessary, drive it!"

Instead, Elsom quickly realised that what was really needed was an Operations Manager, who could look after the day to day considerations as well as the complex task of organisation and progress chasing. Like many a Thruster, he virtually elected himself to his eventual role of Operations Director and would later be responsible as the team's Mr Fix-It for much of the detail planning of the record attempts as well as managing all the movements of Thrust 2 at home and abroad. It was one hell of a job, and one he handled brilliantly.

Meanwhile, with master craftsman Ron Benton, later to play a significant role of his own on the Black Rock Desert, worked expert panel wheelers Brian Ball and Norman Willis and gradually the mass of tubes, wires, bulkheads and bays became enclosed in a sleek aluminium shell. As one had come to expect it was finished to a superb, aircraft standard, with flush rivetting and quick release fasteners on the access panels which would have to be removed and refitted in a hurry between high-speed dashes. Noble estimated the cost of finishing Thrust 2 to record standard at £100,000 but it seemed worth every penny.

While the final work was being carried out the opportunity was taken to acquire a later mark of Avon engine, a 302, which was made available to the project. It was in excellent condition and came from a Lightning F6. Ever mindful of Leo Villa's advice to ensure he had more than enough power out on the salt, Noble now had 17,000lbs of thrust at his disposal. The move to the 302 was highly unpopular at Fishbourne as many of the car's systems had to be changed to accommodate it, but as history was to prove, Noble needed every one of those 17,000 pounds. The car was given a static engine test at RAF Wattisham once the work was completed and following painting by the Eric White Group of Ascot was readied for another Big Day.

At a stylish launch at Birmingham's Metropole Hotel on September 8th the finished car was finally unveiled to the press and with only one week left before the team was due to depart on the Great Bonneville Adventure Noble clinched the last sponsorship deal worth £40,000 with Fabergé. That topped up a £35,000 budget which he had succeeded in raising cold in a mere six weeks so he could get his team to America.

By the time it reached the salt Project Thrust's status had changed, almost imperceptibly. No longer could it be construed as a crackpot's dream, a paper project with little chance of getting off the ground. There were still plenty of detractors who gave Noble little chance of succeeding, but nobody could argue with the heavy financial commitments of a lot of hard-headed businessmen, nor with the technical integrity of the end product, even if the general consensus was that jets were old hat and rockets were the way to go. It was still the great adventure and everyone, Noble especially, oozed enthusiasm. He was still Don Quixote in a racing suit, but there was a really serious edge to things now. The pressure was on to justify the expense, just as it had always been on Campbell. There was also an unstated pressure on Noble to uphold national honour, since it was he who had decided to risk it in the first place. That came from the national press and the man in the street, for while everybody loves a British winner nobody likes a Briton who tries and loses. Richard Noble now really had to prove that after all the talking and chasing he could do what he'd always promised: drive a car faster than any other man in history.

This was the time when his character went under the microscope. How would this smooth-talking, Winchester-- educated pin-striper stack up when he donned his Nomex on Bonneville's hallowed salt?

It was easy to take him at face value, as a meticulously polite product of the British public school system, a suave executive with the right blend of articulate aggression to talk to company chairmen and managing directors in their own language, on their own level. But to accept his eloquence unquestioningly was perhaps to miss the incredible determination that lay so near the surface. The brand of determination that kept him working day and night on his project even when holding down fulltime employment elsewhere. The brand that actually saw GKN grant him an eighteen month secondment to go out and set the record. He didn't make it within that time and eventually left to work fulltime on Project Thrust, but the industrial giant's gesture was telling.

Where some might have given vent to their determination with aggressive outbursts and wild boasts, Noble simply let his flow with his enthusiasm, and what undoubtedly helped was his larger than life character; the way he would pump your hand as if you were the most important person he'd met that day, to the point where you began to fear for the safety of your limb. His booming voice with its cultured diction might just as easily if less interestingly have been employed in politics.

You couldn't forget his background as a salesman, for every- where about him was that salesman's practised certainty about things. Where Ackroyd might design a feature one way yet admit there were other possible methods, Noble would choose his route and stick with it, without ever admitting any other way was feasible. It was an intriguing contrast between an engineer and a saleman's ways of thinking, for neither man could ever be described as negative thinkers. Ackroyd simply remained open- -minded, while Noble preferred to charm dissenters round to his point of view.

The bubbling Biggles-like exterior, the enthusiasm he always radiated regardless of the setback, all contributed to his success in fund raising, and so did his almost electric energy. He is a man who simply cannot keep still for long. He has as much front as the Sears-Roebuck building, yet somehow those he charmed into contributing money, goods or services were left feeling they genuinely wanted to, not that they had been talked into it. It got to the point where one almost began to feel sorry for unsuspecting managing and marketing directors who were about to experience his charmingly forceful method of raising sponsorship. For while he was smooth he also did his homework very thoroughly, so he had answers to all manner of points that might be raised. Some probably never even knew what hit them.

His other asset is natural leadership, and that ability to motivate. With very few exceptions Project Thrust attracted sincere individuals right from the start, and though characters were many and varied and occasionally didn't mix, everyone on the team had a part of his or her personality invested in Noble's efforts, to the point where his dream became their own. Sometimes his boyish adventurism seemed a little too good to be true, almost a carefully rehearsed act. One such time was when he stood hands on hips and watched Thrust 2 and its trailer arrive at Bonneville's base camp for the first time.

"Incredible. All the way from the Isle of Wight". So far so good. Then: "But we mustn't get emotional about this. What we've got to do is get that record".

It smacked too much of a controlled throwaway line for his sponsors to pick up on when they saw the film that was being made as he spoke. But the incredible thing was that he sincerely meant every word! It was a bit like somebody going around saying 'Gosh, bally good show old fellow. I say, crikey, what a wheeze!' without intending to be humourous.

Throughout the Bonneville episode the usual stretched-vowel yaahs, faantastics and treemendouses peppered his speech, the same enthusiasm was apparent and on all but one occasion so was the same urbanity. But part of his cold-blooded approach became apparent in his attitude to the press, specialist or other-wise. Without publicity Project Thrust would most likely never have risen from the drawing board, yet the more he secured the backing he needed, the more his attitude towards the media seemed to change, as if he felt it had served its purpose and should now be placed on the backburner. By Bonneville, it seemed, it had become nothing more than a damned nuisance, even though in truth there were very few pressmen on site.

We'd known each other for three and a half years, quite well, when I travelled at *Motoring News'* expense to cover the Bonneville attempt, and I'd been involved with the project on several occasions. Yet there was a definite arms-length approach adopted to the press in Utah and on more than one occasion he exuded an air of resentment at any sort of media presence. The rest of the team seemed perfectly happy about it, but Watkins got a rollicking for his 'Reheat is a myth' notice outside the team's motorhome, into which the press was rarely invited, in case it gave anyone an inkling that things were not running smoothly.

Was Richard Noble the right man to drive Thrust 2? Behind the scenes that was one of the questions some crew members began asking themselves as this aspect of his character became more apparent, and a story began doing the rounds. It ran along the lines that the only time Thrust 2 seemed to run straight during the early runs was when Noble thought John Ackroyd was travelling with him in the left-hand side passenger cockpit. On one occasion, the story went, Ackroyd pretended to climb aboard but didn't at the last moment, when Noble was already strapped into his seat and couldn't tell. That time the car also ran straight. . .

It was one of those bitchy stories to which you rarely find a truthful answer. Noble himself had little to say on the matter at the time, but later provided a better understanding of his position and his own self-assessment.

"My problem in the early stages was that I had an unstable car with front wheels that were too narrow, the toe-in was incorrect so it would not run straight, and two big run-offs had left me with little confidence. The handling was appalling and the feel in the steering was non-existent. On top of that we also had a highly ambitious team, some of whom just couldn't believe there was anything that could possibly be wrong with the car. . .

"As far as my own driving is concerned, I don't have to psyche myself up. I don't believe in any massive personal preparation routine before we run the car. If you need to work yourself up into the right mental state just to get into the cockpit then you're quite the wrong man for the job, chum!"

The climax to the press business came the day after the flooding, and was one of the few times Noble ever let his public mask slip. Everyone had gathered at the Wendover airbase at which the plans to bomb Hiroshima were developed by Colonel Paul Tibbetts and his team in 1945, and as Noble strode towards the ramshackle building in which the team's summit meeting had been called I asked him what the plan would be for the next few days.

With barely a glance he snapped: "We're not telling the press anything", and marched on. He was under pressure, he'd carried the roles of team manager and driver for the past three weeks and he was facing a bitterly disappointing end to his campaign, but his response was arrogant and uncharacteristic. At the end of the day *Motoring News* had been the only specialist British publication that had thought his exploits sufficiently worthwhile to send a reporter six thousand miles to cover the story of a new land speed record. A long while later he expanded on his feelings at that moment. "I was suffering from Murphy's Law of Thermodynamics, I'm afraid. (Things get worse under pressure)!"

A week or so after everyone returned from Bonneville his attitude to the press appeared to yaw off in another direction, from resentment to paranoia over what sort of story was going to appear. I'd sent him a pre-publication copy to check for technical accuracy, something I don't normally do, and the relief in his voice when he called upon receipt the next day was telling. Without doubt he'd been afraid of a hatchet job which might create a lot of problems when it came to placating his sponsors. Had he stopped to think about it he'd have realised that was a remote possibility, but the fact that he didn't pause was an interesting indication of his lack of full trust in anybody. Former World Champion Jackie Stewart was once quoted as saying his success lay in the fact he never placed one hundred per cent trust in anybody, and Noble exhibited a similar trait. It wasn't something he did out of malice; in fact he was probably unaware of the impression he created. It was simply part of his nature. That's partly because he is a doer, and it's likely that given the chance he would have fulfilled every role on Project Thrust himself were it humanly possible, just so he had the extra peace of mind of knowing he'd attended to everything personally. Whatever, when he was running at Bonneville he really didn't appreciate having his on-site efforts monitored by anyone outside the immediate team.

To be fair, whenever he sought publicity it was never for self-aggrandisement, merely to progress the project. The man himself was always a reluctant hero. He once related a story how Donald Campbell's widow Tonia had expressed surprise at the way in which he tackled the Thrust programme, seeking so little personal publicity. And he was genuinely horrified when she told him how Campbell would deliberately go out and do something outrageous if his name slipped from the limelight for too long. Noble even looked slightly uncomfortable at times when one mentioned the other record Project Thrust made – an instrumental single written by 10CC keyboard man Duncan Mackay and released in 1981 on Steam records. . .

Another key to his Jekyll and Hyde 'media xenophobia' lay in the way he regarded developing Thrust 2 as akin to developing a new fighter aircraft. The latter was something he could never envisage the press being allowed to witness.


If Richard Noble had his occasional skirmishes with the media, he also had the odd run-in with his sponsors, even though his entire project was run on an exemplary system whereby regular meetings kept everyone informed of progress and requirements. One man after his head when he returned from Bonneville was Hugh Wickes, at that time Managing Director of Fabergé.

"Richard", he accused, "you promised us gold but you only brought back bronze".

His point was unarguable, its meaning undeniable. For Noble the fight was only temporarily postponed, but it was understandable that some sponsors would be dissatisfied with any excuses. To get any of them involved in the first place he'd had to make a lot of promises and whether he and his crew had been naive to expect to make up in one go all the ground lost to the Americans, while simultaneously learning about a new technology, was quite beside the main issue.

Wickes led a faction seeking to pull out of Project Thrust on purely commercial grounds, but ultimately Noble's persuasive manner won the day. By 1981 he had come a long way, and had certainly come much too far to throw in the towel at the first knockdown. And if he was going to carry on the fight, he expected his sponsors to stay in the ring as well.

On the credit side, morale was boosted when the team was awarded the Bluebird Trophy for British endeavour by the K7 Club, which was named after the racing registration of Donald Campbell's Bluebird jetboat.

By the end of the year it had become apparent to even the most callous sceptic that this man wasn't simply going to fade into oblivion. Whatever Fate might choose to throw at him along the way Richard Noble, Don Quixote in racing overalls, wasn't going to let go until he got precisely what he wanted. *"We mustn't get emotional about this. What we've got to do is get that record"*.

The show would go on.

# 5. Jeopardy

Wednesday, June 16th 1982 was one of those balmy sort of days that held the promise of the warm summer that followed. At its outset it was much like any other day in Project Thrust's recent life, except that there was the added bonus of Thrust 2 undergoing a series of tests at RAF Greenham Common, scene of its earlier triumphs.

Throughout the winter of 1981, as Noble chased the backing for another go, the car had been fully rebuilt, incorporating many minor changes to improve performance, enhance reliability and make it easier to maintain. By the 16th virtually everything had been given its final check and passed fit for the fresh attempt at Bonneville scheduled for August, in the height of the American summer. Only the microchip recorders had to be set up, and once that had been done there would be a couple of runs for press representatives and sponsors. Once I got back from covering the Le Mans 24 Hour race at the end of that week I was at last scheduled to occupy the passenger seat of the jetcar during the final day of runs. Only a week or so earlier I'd been in the driving seat of a rocket-propelled dragster owned by American Sammy Miller, who was thought to be one of Richard's most likely rivals for the big record once his own car was finished. So far it hasn't materialised as a completed product, but in December 1983 Noble admitted Miller was the rival he had most feared.

"All through the life of Project Thrust he was a threat. I was always worried I'd wake up one day to hear Sammy had broken the record and upped the ante beyond Thrust 2's capability".

On a scorching day at Santa Pod Raceway Miller's dragster Vanishing Point had given me the ride of a lifetime, accelerating from rest to over 200mph in a ridiculous two seconds. The two machines were of widely differing concepts. One was a full-blown record contender designed not so much for outright acceleration but to sustain its speed throughout a measured mile, and be able to make at least two such runs within an allotted hour. The other was a quarter mile drag racing machine where all that mattered was clipping vital fractions of a second from its elapsed time. On paper it was a fascinating contrast but sadly not one I was destined to experience firsthand. It would have made a superb comparison feature. . .

Kathy Ager, then in charge of *Motoring News'* photographic department London Art Tech, was the first to break the news when she arrived at our hotel in Le Mans. "Your holiday in the States looks off this year. Your mate has just smashed his car".

The 16th, which had started so normally, had swerved violently into one of Project Thrust's blackest days, in which its very existence was to be threatened and then questioned time and again.


As Noble was strapped into the cockpit of Thrust 2 that Wednesday he was merely preparing to do what he had by then done a hundred times. To the layman his task might have seemed incredible, but to him it was no more daunting than a leisurely run down to the shops in his road car.

This time it was to be Mike 'The Chute' Barrett's turn to ride shotgun, but as he in turn was strapped into the confines of the passenger cockpit he could never have envisaged just what a ride he was about to get. As events were to prove however, Noble could not have had a better man aboard.

Initially the run started well, as Thrust blasted off the line up to its 230mph target. But then Noble made a small yet disastrous error, whose effects were cruelly magnified. "It was my fault entirely," he later admitted candidly. "I kept the engine on a fraction too long and went over the maximum intended speed".

As he deployed the low-speed parachute so carefully prepared by Barrett himself only a short while earlier, it streamed out on its long line but failed to open. Thrust was simply going too fast for its capacity. Up to the British land speed record runs in 1980 the team had used GQ 'chutes, switching to Irvin GBs for

Bonneville onwards. However, on this occasion, to save the Irvins for the new Bonneville effort, Noble was using second grade military 'chutes and with his excessive speed this one failed.

As horror began to register on the faces of spectating crew members, a frantic rush began for support vehicles to chase the errant jetcar down the all too short runway. Greenham was restricted enough as it was, and as Noble for the second time in his life faced losing control of a jet-engined car he made the only decision he could. If Thrust piled headfirst off the runway the consequences at best could be severe damage to the car. At worst there might be serious injury to the occupants. That left a high-speed swerve as the only realistic course and in less time than it takes to read his options he assessed the situation and at 180mph put the big gold car into a one hundred and fifty foot left arc and slammed on the brakes. Thrust 2 skidded with locked wheels for some four thousand feet, arcing further left across the runway in a four-wheel slide that seared the front tyres right through to the canvass and left a stench of burnt rubber hanging over the telltale skidmarks. It hit the grass verge at 125mph and then careened across the rough terrain in a series of lengthy hops. Each landing gouged the lip of the air intake into the soft turf and threw clumps of debris directly into the precious Avon 302.

When Thrust 2 finally slewed to a halt, Noble and Barrett evacuated themselves from their cockpits and scrambled to safety as the emergency crews moved in, both shaken but otherwise totally unharmed. Project Thrust had just received another body blow, but some of the accusations and recriminations that were to follow were to be far more serious than the shaking Richard received during his inadvertent crash test.


As Elsom urged all but the fire crews to keep well clear of the tattered machine which lay forlorn, its contracting hot metal clicking ominously on the grass, Noble was joined by Richard Aston, then managing director of Loctite.

"She's a little bit bent", Noble observed with resigned understatement. Aston, as ever enthusiastic about the project into which his company had invested so much, was quick to offer consolation.

"We'll put it right. No problem".

He was one of the few intimately involved with the team to spend more than a cursory few moments talking to the crestfallen driver. Most were too distraught at the sight of Thrust 2's damage to speak. There was now absolutely no chance of meeting the August 10th deadline to run at Bonneville.


In a state of delayed shock the team craned Thrust on to its trailer and transported it to a nearby hangar, whereupon immediate inspection of the damage was carried out. It was highly likely that the engine had been ruined, its innards scoured by the ingested debris, and as if conducting a post-mortem, the shattered crew set about removing the unit and arranging for it to be transported to RAF Binbrook, Watkins' base, to have the unhappy diagnosis confirmed.

As far as the chassis was concerned the omens were more favourable, for the damage looked repairable. The brake discs and pads showed signs of an enormous workload, yet incredibly still continued to work perfectly when tested. All four tyres had been shredded, the left front having suffered so much torture it had actually punctured, and there was severe damage to the front suspension. However, Thrust 2 had performed exactly as Ackroyd had intended it to in such an emergency. The front end of the car ahead of the front wheels had been designed to crush progressively to absorb impact, and had done just that, while the front suspension had twisted but not sheared, also as intended. While several components in the car had been dislocated, none had broken. In fact, it had withstood its crash test remarkably well. Its inherent strength and Ackroyd's preoccupation with primary safety had been fully justified, for had the suspension broken Thrust 2 could easily have rolled during the high-speed swerve, with unpleasant consequences for driver and passenger. Likewise the secondary safety features emerged well, for neither suffered much discomfort. Neither was even bruised during the ordeal and they remained restrained and fully supported in their seats throughout.

While he might have been angry at the damage his brainchild had sustained, and the manner in which it had been inflicted, Ackroyd could still view the situation in a dispassionate light, picking out the positive points.

"There was no rollover, despite the high G turn. There was no fire and all three onboard extinguishers performed exactly as they should, both during and after the accident. There were no critical failures in either the structure or the suspension, and the front end collapsed progressively in the sacrificial manner intended. Most important of all, Richard and Mike weren't injured at all and both escaped from the wreck very quickly. We've put all our safety theories to the test – the hard way".

The onboard monitoring equipment later revealed a 7.8G deceleration, plus 4G and minus 1G vertical, which was bad enough. As Ackroyd was quick to point out, the values experienced at the front end of the car must have been even greater, for the equipment was mounted towards the middle. In total, it was estimated that one tiny driving error had caused £22,000 worth of damage.


What was far less easy to quantify, yet even more serious, was the damage to the Thrust team's morale. Already, most of those involved had been working flat-out since the return from Bonneville the previous October, dismantling and painstakingly rebuilding a car they had spent so many months creating. These were not highly paid factory workers either, but skilled craftsmen performing a labour of love. The trauma of the accident, caused by a basic driving error, was incredibly hard for many of them to face, and all the worse because it had occurred on one of the last test runs before the car was due to be shipped to Bonneville. Everyone was thankful that Noble and Barrett were unharmed but as is human nature, once that fact had been established the recriminations had begun.

What the hell did Richard think he was playing at, risking so much with an error of judgement on a simple test run intended merely to check out the microchip recorders? How could he have been so lax in his cockpit discipline?

At Enbourne Grange Hotel near Greenham that night the

team, minus Noble, had a brief meeting. A week later, still shellshocked, everyone met again at the Bournemouth Flying Club at Hurn Airport. Immediately after the accident Noble had stood on the runway saying "We'll fix it. We'll fix it. I'll get the money". But the big thing was that the team had to believe it could be done, that it could get the car ready in time to run at Bonneville in September. The air was full of acrimony at first, but Noble bore the brunt of the criticism. The Bonneville doubts about his driving ability, swept away in the euphoria of the first full reheat run, came flooding back in some quarters. As Ken Norris was later to remark to Noble's embarrassment on *This Is Your Life*, "Most of the crew could have murdered him".

Ackroyd and Watkins probably felt the keenest sense of anguish bar Noble himself, but it was Barrett who might have been forgiven for being most critical since he had been obliged to share the greatest risk. Instead, he would pull the men on the Fishbourne shopfloor round, sort out the rates for the rebuild and actually handle half of the car himself, even though previously he had only built the gullwing doors. As Benton handled the starboard side, Mike looked after the port, with Ball wheeling new double curvature sections. As a result Barrett case-hardened the working relationship he had forged with Noble and its strength was illustrated after Project Thrust when he moved on to work with him at ARV.

Noble himself spoke for a long time at the meeting, outlining his determination, stressing again his uncompromising commitment to breaking the land speed record. It was not an easy meeting to address, given the feeling he had let down those who had stored so much faith in him, but at the end of the day he won back the respect and remotivated his team. Had he been rejected it would have been the end of Project Thrust, for he was such a pivotal figure – it was *his* project – that it could never have continued without him. Some crew members would still feel him to be on trial when the 1982 attempt finally got underway, but that day in June Project Thrust went through one of its most gruelling tests and emerged battered but intact. That in itself was a telling index of its inherent strength, borne purely of the personalities involved.

Ackroyd was the one who again saw the positive side of the

whole incident. "What Greenham taught us was that the team needed discipline. We knew after that that there was absolutely no room for people buggering about. That day Richard was chasing round after parachutes, talking to sponsors and passengers and all that sort of thing. About the one thing he really did do right was to swerve off. If he hadn't done that we'd probably have lost the car and the project.

"Greenham certainly put him under pressure, and though the meeting was very acrimonious we emerged a stronger team. At the time I suppose I felt more tired than angry, as you sometimes do in those kind of circumstances, but looking back you can say it was Fate again. We needed a lesson in discipline, and Greenham certainly gave us that".


As soon as the Avon 302 had been removed from Thrust's sorry carcass the chassis had been loaded back on the trailer and taken back to base at Fishbourne. There the first step in the restoration that would occupy the next twelve weeks was simply to wield hacksaws and cut off the entire front of the car, ahead of the front wheels. New sections of chassis were then welded on and once again the complex double curvature body panels were wheeled. The basic undertaking was far from straightforward, however. On June 16th the objective had been defined: to complete an intensive rebuild and have the car and engine ready for static and rolling tests by September 10th, less than three months away. Though time-consuming, the actual work involved in repairing Thrust 2 was something well within the team's capabilities, even on such a tight schedule. What was a more serious cause for concern was what to do about a new engine.

When he had purchased the original 302 Noble was aware he had been privileged to be offered it in the first place. Now, credibility dented after Greenham, he knew it was highly unlikely he'd be offered another. Buying either a new unit or even a secondhand one from Rolls-Royce was totally out of the question, while he once quoted the sum for a works rebuild at a cool £80,000. The 210 had been disposed of, and in any case would have had insufficient thrust. He was still threshing on the horns of the dilemma when he received a 'phone call from Watkins.

"Well Richard, what do you want us to do with this bloody engine?".

The question took him somewhat by surprise. Having concentrated so hard on finding a new power source he'd all but forgotten that the old one was still at Binbrook. In fact, he hadn't even wanted to send it there. Watkins' colleagues had asked for it in case there was anything they might learn for future reference from the extensive debris damage. It had meant forking out £200 that Project Thrust could ill afford to transport it to Binbrook, but Noble reasoned it was better to oblige than to risk offending good friends. As he collected his thoughts he replied that as far as he was concerned they could scrap it, but Watkins' response was totally unexpected.

"What the hell would we want to do that for? We've just spent the last ten days working nights rebuilding the damn thing. And the Queen has paid for the parts. . ."

Quite out of the blue, the Binbrook personnel had solved the engine crisis at a stroke. Against all expectations the unit had been stripped and fully refurbished. It was returned in better condition, too, for the opportunity had been taken to rebuild it to an upgraded standard. It was taken back to the Ranalagh Works for immediate installation. It is possible Richard Noble is still ignorant of the coarser messages the Binbrook boys left within the engine. Each man signed his name on the compressor blades, but if in centuries to come future generations ever strip the Avon it should provide an interesting insight into Anglo-Saxon humour, 1982 vintage. . .

Steadily the rebuild progressed and eventually the Thrust 2 which was rolled out from the workshop was indistinguishable from new. Three years later Ackroyd admitted: "We got it within a quarter inch when measuring the wheelbase either side!", but nevertheless the 1982 version of the car, with no fewer than twenty nine improvements incorporated prior to the rebuild, represented an even stronger contender than the 1981 model.

The most important changes centred on increased steering offset and castor angle to produce greater self-centring and make Thrust 2 easier to handle below 375mph. The new set-up was also designed to give Noble more feel after the deadness he had complained of at Bonneville. Hand in hand with this came new six inch wide front wheels to replace the four inch versions. These also had a different tread pattern, comprising circumferential grooves. The track was also slightly increased to enhance roll stability and a new heart-shaped link eliminated the offset action of each parachute drag line and thus made the car more stable under high-speed deceleration.

While the rebuild of car and engine had been underway, Elsom had faced a headache of a different kind as Project Thrust battled from cliffhanger to cliffhanger that summer. The moment Noble had overshot his speed target at Greenham the August 10th deadline for Bonneville had become redundant and to the resourceful Eddie now fell the unenviable task of rescheduling everything. Shipping and airfreight bookings had to be changed, air tickets revalidated, hotel bookings altered, holidays and personal arrangements for some thirty people modified. And all the time at the back of his mind was the fear that when everything possible finally had been done the weather might still create the ultimate cliffhanger to frustrate the project for another year.

As it was, American motorcycle land speed record ace Don Vesco had his own plans to launch an attempt on the wheeldriven car record at Bonneville in September, right about the time Project Thrust hoped to reschedule its effort. That potential problem was solved, however, when Vesco called Noble one night and offered to share his time on the salt. He intended to run on the regular BLM track, where Thrust would once again prepare its own track system comprising eight forty foot wide lanes of varying length to allow sixteen passes, two per track, in which to progress to record speed. It was only through the generosity of the publicity-shunning speed veteran that Thrust was able to contemplate launching a serious attempt at all that season.

In the middle of August Ackroyd flew to Bonneville to inspect the surface and report on the progress of track preparation, and in the meantime all support vehicles bar Thrust 2 itself were taken to Felixstowe for shipment to Los Angeles.

The rebuild work almost completed, Noble and Ken Norris now

took a long, hard look at the way in which Richard had run the 1981 attempt, and how he had prepared himself to drive Thrust 2. Already it had been decided that driving, managing the finances and managing the team was a combination that begged trouble. In February a press conference had announced that Ken, the most experienced man in Britain in the field of record breaking, had joined Project Thrust as team manager. A quiet, friendly man, it was Norris who had played such a vital role in Donald Campbell's record endeavour in Australia, over and above his responsibilities in designing Bluebird. It was he who had held divided factions together and poured oil on waters troubled by Campbell's occasional prickliness and a press growing restless at his lack of success, even though conditions were well beyond his control.

Again, Norris considered his four parameters: Man, Machine, Medium and Money. The machine was nearly ready as, it was hoped, was the medium. The money would always be a problem but there was almost sufficient in the kitty or in the pipeline to cover the attempt.

"It was only when we sat down and thought about it hard", Noble revealed, "that we realised just how little attention we'd paid to preparation of the man. Last year really was one hell of a fight, especially once we got to Bonneville. It was only through dear old Ken that we started to consider the problem more fully".

After Greenham Common Norris began to take a far more active role, outside the actual attempt itself, than had originally been envisaged, looking after all manner of trivial as well as major aspects. His first step was to cancel plans Noble was considering to take part in some Sports 2000 motor races, for small two-seater mid-engined racing sports cars with two-litre Ford engines. Instead, despite his driver's initial scepticism, he sent him to the Bournemouth Flying Club. It was a move that in every way would become as important to Richard as his father's decision all those years before to take that trip round Loch Ness. Suddenly, he had found a fresh interest, something that in the years to come would eventually supersede the land speed record in his order of priority.

Before long he had qualified for his Private Pilot's Licence (PPL) and later his IMC, the rating which qualifies pilots to fly with instruments only. And his initial scepticism had evaporated amid a welter of enthusiasm for the disciplines needed when flying. Campbell, another flying fanatic, had once said how the air was the one place he'd never be caught fooling around, and Noble echoed his sentiments.

Thrown in with his flying lessons was a spell with the Royal Military Police at Chichester. Initially it was something of a culture shock. When he was first examined he was given a C grade which, in RMP jargon, meant he was 'barely living'. But in his ten-day spell of swimming a kilometre before breakfast and doing six hours' circuit training and running ten miles a day, he passed out with an A grade.

As August ran into September and the threads of the 1982 project were slowly drawn together again, man and machine approached their big test in peak condition. But as everyone had feared, it was the medium which still proved reluctant to play the role in which it had been cast in the Great Bonneville Adventure 2.

When the Greenham accident occurred it was clear hopes of an early start to the 1982 campaign had been dashed, and that instead of running at Bonneville in high summer Thrust 2 would make its first runs nearer the onset of winter. That still left grounds for optimism, for Gabelich had set his record in October while Graham had run as late as December in 1959. Even before Ackroyd left for America, though, the signs were not good. At the time various theories were put forward to explain the awful weather that seemed to engulf parts of the globe against all reasonable forecasts. Some meteorologists put the freak conditions that had seen the Utah state flooded the previous year down to the Rage of El Nino, a particularly malignant weather cycle. Whatever, as he boarded his British Airways flight from Heathrow on September 18th he already knew that the salt flats were flooded. And when he stood on the causeway two days later he might just as well have been taken back to the previous October. Bonneville was again beneath five inches of water.

This time though, there was a difference. Again the local weather sages predicted a fast drying process if conditions remained stable, and this time they did. Though the situation was serious enough for the annual Speed Week, scheduled for the 19th to the 25th, to be cancelled for only the second time in history, there was an improvement. By the 22nd all but a three mile stretch of salt was above water, and the rest was drying fast. In fact, if the process continued there was every chance the track might just develop into its optimum condition, even though painstaking preparation work might be wasted.

Over the next few days the weather continued its game of cat and mouse as the fine, dry conditions tweaked hopes up by the hour. But as Noble arrived on the 26th, the day on which the schedule called for the pits complex to be established on the salt, the rain everyone had secretly expected came sweeping through, turning Wendover's streets into gushing canalways and dumping nine inches of water the length and breadth of the race track. By the causeway itself there was a good thirteen inches and Ackroyd and Noble actually went swimming on Bonneville the following day. All those thousands of dollars and four hundred and fifty man-hours of track work had been rendered utterly useless.

On the evening of September 28th over dinner at the Stateline Casino, Project Thrust was poised on the very brink of disaster. This wasn't just the ultimate cliffhanger; here was something that would stamp on Thrust's fingers and once and for all break its tenuous grip on what little hope it had left. After all that effort rebuilding the car and team over the winter, then further revamping both after Greenham, after all the Binbrook boys' secret refurbishment of the Avon, Noble's hours of flying, physical training and remorseless fund raising, and all Elsom's juggling with schedules and bookings, Thrust 2 wasn't even going to get the chance to turn a wheel under its own vast power. The ignominy and injustice of it all would have crushed a weaker team.

The general attitude of team members to the latest setback cast an interesting light on their dedication and determination. Sloshing home with their tails between their legs would have been an easy if unpalatable alternative, but it would surely have spelled the end of Project Thrust. Regardless of the validity of the reason for abandonment credibility would have plunged. Explanations would simply have been construed as weak-- sounding excuses by parties six thousand miles away who had not seen the watery battlefield for themselves. Norris had seen Campbell suffer so badly at Lake Eyre for similar, valid reasons. It was purported never to have rained there for nine years until the Bluebird equipe set foot on the salt, only to pour when the record attempt got underway. Norris knew only too well how distance and lack of understanding could twist even that sort of ill-luck into some sort of indictment of a determined man. The sole answer, incredible as it seemed, was to undertake a crash course in finding another location within the United States.

The project might be doomed but it wasn't going down without, to use Noble's favourite expression, "one *hell* of a fight".

That the team did eventually find an alternative venue raised a question in some cynical minds, mine included. If there was after all somewhere that was equal or even superior to Bonneville, or at least worthy of consideration, why on earth hadn't they discovered it earlier and chosen it in preference or at least as a back-up? After all, there had even been talk of a South African venue at one stage during the winter.

It was something to which Elsom provided a patient and plausible answer. Right from the start the obvious routines with global maps and atlases had been initiated and a shortlist of potential venues was drawn up. Besides adequate length – anything over eleven miles of flat, foliage-free track with sufficient run-off either end and either side – they had to have accessibility, physically, geographically and politically. That ruled out places in Russia, Iran and Chile. Ideally, the local weather patterns had to be stable. That tended to rule against the unpredictable Lake Eyre, which appeared to have done little since Campbell left but try to make up for lost time by soaking itself regularly. The latest intelligence reports suggested it was still under water. Then there was the advantage of English-- speaking alternatives, which heavily favoured America. Eventually the list was pared down, with particular emphasis being laid on places where other land speed record contenders had already run. That meant Bonneville, Alvord Desert in Oregon and Edwards Air Force Base in the Mojave Desert, formerly known as Muroc Dry Lake and once a favourite haunt of the Los Angeles drag racing fraternity. Pure budgetary considerations ruled out inspections of other potential American venues on which nobody had ever run, such as the Black Rock Desert or White Sands in New Mexico.

Over the Stateline dinner Alvord and Edwards were mulled over. Ackroyd knew a fair bit about the former. He'd been in touch with Bill Fredrick, who had designed and built the rocket-powered SMI Motivator which had run there briefly in 1976, and it seemed a likely alternative. Edwards was on the short side but Fredrick's Motivator successor, the Budweiser Rocket, had been run there in 1979 when an all-singing, all-dancing radar set-up had caught it at an alleged 739.666mph on a one-way run. This was totally unofficial although there were some who ballyhooed it as the breaking of the sound barrier on land. It was one of the shadows under which the Thrust project had had to labour. The Budweiser team had bypassed all the standard FISA rules of the game, as the Americans had been wont to do in the past, by opting for a flash reading of the projectile's peak speed, rather than trying to sustain it over a full mile or kilometre. The lance-like car had been designed accordingly, mainly due to its rocket engine which consumed its fuel so rapidly that it couldn't actually carry enough to last through the measured distance stipulated by the rules. Moreover, satisfying its appetite for solid and liquid fuel propellant took so long it couldn't be readied for the mandatory return run within the allotted hour, so again the rules were ignored. In public Noble would always praise the effort, while politely pointing out the different and unofficial nature of the Americans' approach. Ackroyd, predictably, saw it as a fine engineering achievement that simply chose to follow a less orthodox route. I think its maverick attitude appealed to his own free spirit type of nature.

The bottom line was that the British were unlikely to gain permission to run their car on *the* American air base in an attempt to beat the official American-held land speed record. I wouldn't have bet against Noble's chances of getting in there eventually, but it wouldn't have been possible in the limited time available.

During the debate one man sat assimilating the various arguments put forward. By pure chance he happened to be seated next to Norris. His name was Peter Moore and though British he lived in Belgium where he worked for the tax authorities. As conversations circulated the table he quietly asked Ken to repeat exactly what sort of requirements had to be satisfied.

"We need a miniumum of eleven miles of flat area which is dry, accessible and devoid of any plant life".

"Have you thought of the Black Rock Desert?".

"I believe it was an original suggestion in the very early days when we were looking for somewhere other than Bonneville", replied Norris, distinctively pronouncing it as Bonn-ville as he always does, rather than Bonny-ville like most others. "But with our budget we simply couldn't afford to make a physical investigation of every alternative. Is it suitable, do you think?".

Moore nodded. "I've camped there in the past. It seems to satisfy your criteria. I'd say it's worth a look".

He had just switched on the light at the end of the tunnel.

*The start of the dream: John Cobb and his jetboat Crusader on Loch Ness in September 1952. (Press Association)*

*Thrust 1 may have been a 'cathedral on wheels', but Britain's first pure-jet car spawned a remarkable project. (Project Thrust)*

*At RAF Fairford in March 1977 Thrust 1 met a sticky end after wheel bearing failure at 140 mph. Noble emerged unscathed — and undeterred. (Project Thrust)*

*The birth of Thrust 2: at Earls Court's Motorfair in October 1977 the Rolls-Royce Avon 210 (above) took pride of place. Initial wind tunnel tests were conducted on this wooden model (below). The canard fins proved unnecessary. (Project Thrust)*

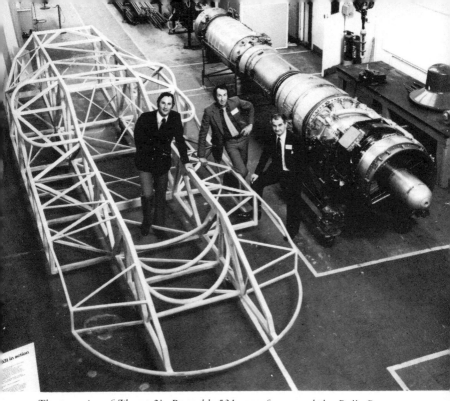

*The true size of Thrust 2's Reynolds 531 spaceframe and the Rolls-Royce Avon 210 become more apparent as Noble, Ackroyd and builder Ken Sprayson pose alongside at Walsall (above). It was transferred to Fishbourne after engine installation (below). (Project Thrust)*

*During aerodynamic studies on a one tenth scale model at British Aerospace in 1978, Noble and Ackroyd confirmed Thrust 2 had outright record potential. Meanwhile, the fullsize version was being fitted out on the Isle of Wight.*
*(Charles Noble)*

*Once ready to run, the part-completed jetcar was transported to shows on a special Crane Fruehauf trailer. In its vestigial form it first ran under power at RAF Leconfield in July 1980. (Charles Noble)*

*Noble initially found Thrust 2 a handful on the bumpy runway, but wherever it went the skinless monster attracted tremendous attention. (Charles Noble)*

*Major credibility breakthroughs came at RAF Greenham Common in September 1980 when, despite stopping with only feet to spare on every run, Noble smashed the British Land Speed Record at 248.87 mph. (Charles Noble)*

With the Greenham success under its belt, Project Thrust moved into the final construction phase by equipping the chassis with its aerodynamic bodyshell. Master craftsmen Brian Ball and Ron Benton played prominent roles. *(Charles Noble)*

*The road to nowhere. A battered line of cones was all that greeted visitors at Bonneville when the main causeway ran out, while at base camp John Watkins watches as Terry Hopkins prepares to unload Thrust 2.*

*Brutal and awesome, Thrust 2 awaits a run at Bonneville. The wooden panels in the jet intake protected the engine between spells of action. (Project Thrust)*

*Jim Deist, cigar as ever clamped unlit between his teeth, shares a joke with Ackroyd (above). (Project Thrust) At Bonneville black oil lines were used to guide Noble on his course (below). Thrust 2 is here lined up for the run to Floating Island.*

*Noble's other office (above). Salt build-up on the aluminium wheels is evident in this post-run shot (below). Every particle had to be scraped off before the next pass.*

Like a lady bidding farewell to her champion, Sally helps Noble kit up
*(above), while below her husband deploys his chute and begins to slow at the
end of Thrust 2's final run on the salt. (Project Thrust)*

*The damage caused by Thrust loosening the salt and digging ruts is clearly illustrated above, but it was Mother Nature's contribution (below) which finally killed the 1981 attempt. (Project Thrust)*

*In June 1982 Noble climbs aboard Thrust 2 for another routine test run at Greenham Common. This time, however, it was to have far-reaching consequences when he swerved off-course at 180 mph after parachute failure. (Charles Noble)*

*The team as well as the car was shattered by the accident. Repairs (above) delayed the schedule and by the time Project Thrust reached Bonneville it was flooded again. George maintains a silent vigil. (Charles Noble)*

*Such were the conditions, Ackroyd and Noble actually swam on the salt. The crisis prompted a frantic search for a new venue, but Ackers (below) found Alvord Desert unsuitable. (Charles Noble)*

*Incredibly, the team found the Black Rock Desert. Above, the jetcar arouses great interest on arrival in Gerlach and, below, is unloaded for its first trial at the new venue. (Charles Noble)*

*Thrust 2 is painstakingly prepared prior to its maiden run on the desert.*
*(Charles Noble)*

*Noble runs through his checklist prior to a run (above). Thrust 2 peaked as high as 615 mph this year, but ultimately the weather again killed the attempt.*
*(Charles Noble)*

At Hurn Airport in March 1983 the paint-stripped jetcar is given a static engine test. The new Davy McKee load cells indicated the Avon 302 was delivering maximum thrust with its full dancing diamonds reheat. (Charles Noble)

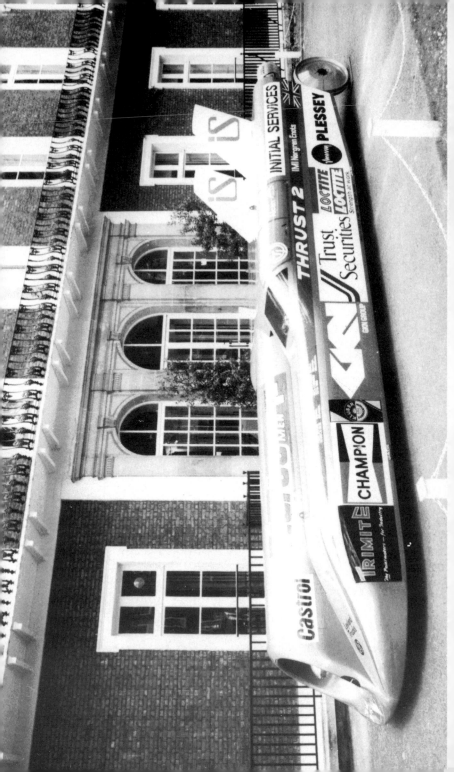

*The flags flew at Bruno's to celebrate the return of the British.*
*(Charles Noble). Mimi and Genny Noble are oblivious to the seriousness of*
*the situation as Thrust 2 is towed across the desert in its first crucial test of*
*the 1983 campaign.*

*Initially, runs were made in the cold of the early morning. In the foreground above is one of the Palouste starter engines, while below Noble gathers speed at the start of a run.*

*Bad day at Black Rock: Ball, Norris, Noble, Flux, Gabelich, Ackroyd and Palm gather round the jetcar after its flameout on Run 7, the day it seemed the project was doomed. The static test at Reno Airport, however, restored the Avon to rude health.*

*Pluming its distinctive roostertail of dust, Thrust 2 blasts across the Black Rock Desert at 650 mph on October 4 1983, on the run that cemented its 633.468 mph Land Speed Record. (Charles Noble)*

*Socialising in Gerlach often meant sumptuous feasts at the Miners' Club.
Benton's official portable toilet record, meanwhile had most locals scratching
their heads in disbelief.*

On its return to London Thrust 2 and the Project Thrust crew met with a rapturous reception during the Lord Mayor's Show. Noble (above) blended into the background by refusing to wear his distinctive driving overalls. Below, the remaining assets of the project are auctioned by Christies to help support redundant fulltime members. (Charles Noble)

# 6. *The show goes on*

On September 29th Ackroyd and Charles Noble left Wendover bound for Alvord. After the tedious run they'd stayed overnight with ranchers Karl and Omallee Thomas at their homestead on the edge of the playa, before venturing the next day to its centre. Ackroyd quite liked what he saw although the course was restricted and access poor. On more than one occasion he and Charles were grateful for Range Rover 'Rover Dover's' four--wheel-drive for the surface was wet and slick and his mental reservations centred on that stickiness and the fact that there was virtually no accommodation bar the Thomas' ranch.

The following day they drove back to Winnemucca to rendezvous with Noble and Moore. Then, again grateful for drive to all four wheels, the quartet tackled the dirt road that crosses from Winnemucca to the Black Rock Desert. It is considerably more hazardous than using Interstate Eighty but if the going is dry it can save time for travellers equipped with the right kind of transport. They picked their way through the tiny hamlets of Pronto, Jungo and Sulphur, and Noble's thoughts at the time can be imagined. If the Black Rock Desert was as wet as Alvord, a final thread of hope would be slashed. And that surely would spell the end of the 1982 attempt once and for all, assuming of course that they weren't in any case embarked on a wild goose chase. Maybe the desert would be totally unsuitable? Perhaps Moore had exaggerated, or misunderstood Ken's requirements? What if the surface proved too irregular?

His pioneering spirit was again roused as the trek evoked memories of his previous overland expeditions, and but for the nagging doubts in the back of his mind he was in his element, leading the scouting party through hostile environment. And when for the first time Rover Dover braked gently to a halt on the great playa, and he and Ackroyd took in the sight that confronted them, both felt an inward spurt of elation and relief. For miles in either direction stretched what appeared to be flat, dry desert, without a trace of sagebrush or sand mounds. Against all the odds, it seemed they really had found exactly what they had been hoping for.

Just as the Bonneville Salt Flats had once been a part of the Great Salt Lake, so the Black Rock Desert once lay five hundred feet beneath prehistoric Lake Lahontan in the Great Basin Desert. As Lahontan's level receded however, and the waters relinquished their one-time eight thousand square mile grip on the area, the Black Rock region evolved into one of the world's forty seven greatest deserts. Like Bonneville too it is still under water for much of the year, particularly when the Quinn River swells and flows down to its natural sink at the desert's southern end. As this happens, the interaction between water and wind gently pans the surface into perfect, smooth flatness, making it almost ideal for record breaking. With the summer sun's rays the water level evaporates and the flattened surface dries and cracks into distinctive, irregular-sized polygons of mud that can be crumbled beneath a boot heel. Beneath the thin mud crust lies a bed of silt from Lahontan, in some places more than a thousand feet thick. Locals tell various stories – apochryphal or not – of vehicles rashly taken on to the desert in the wrong conditions. According to lore they simply break through the crust before sinking remorselessly from sight, to rest forever in the primeval sludge.

With its lopsided Y shape the desert covers around a thousand square miles and at the base of its left fork to Soldier Meadows is the dark rock hill some four hundred feet high from which the area draws its name. The rock has acted as a travellers' guide for centuries, and would continue to do so even for one moving across the dusty floor at more than six hundred miles and hour.

The Black Rock Desert is one of the world's most beautiful places, desolate in the extreme yet possessed of a haunting charm. It is surrounded by purple-hued mountains ranging from seven to nine thousand feet and their very height seems to accentuate the flatness of the surface. Despite its barren appearance the region supports a wide range of wildlife, from rodents and toads to the Great Basin Rattlesnake. Towards the tail end of each year big game hunters flock into Gerlach in search of mule deer or pronghorn antelope, but to give the four-legged population a sporting chance each hunter is restricted to only two tags.

Saltbushes, grasses and sagebrush comprise the plant life, with a wide variety of trees of the most outstanding yellow, red and green hues, while thermal springs abound, their temperatures ranging from warm to scalding.

It is a place steeped in history, the legacy of the early north-west pioneers. In one or two locations it is still possible to find the mysterious stone crescents that still baffle archeologists, who cannot decide whether they are charm stones, fish gorges or arrow points fashioned by man. And just as Bonneville harbours the dark secret of the tragic Donner Party which made its ill-fated passage across the salt during its migration from Missouri, so the Black Rock Desert has its share of unhappy memories. Early pioneers suffered much hardship as a result of inaccurate information imparted by Californian explorer Peter Lassen. He advised travellers bound for California to use a route which later proved to be hundreds of miles longer than necessary. In the years that followed it was to become infamous as the Death Route.

For decades the canyons echoed to the cries of Indian tribes. In the main they were peaceful and respected by the white settlers, but in 1865 the Black Rock became the stronghold of notorious Indian leader Black Rock Tom who lead an uprising. After he was killed later that year the battle which ousted the last Indian raiders was fought in the bitter winter of January 1866, near the confluence of Queen's (now Quinn's) River and Fish Creek.

The public euphoria over that American triumph was soon superseded by something of far greater importance to the avaricious settlers: silver fever. James Allen Hardin had acted as a scout and hunter for an 1849 wagon train on the Lassen Trail and found an unusual metal lump in a water pool. He used it mainly to make musket balls but kept a sample which he later had assayed quite by chance in California. It was deemed to be silver. Ten years later Lassen himself attempted to locate Hardin's silver deposit, but was killed in mysterious circumstances. As the story developed, fanned by Californian and Nevadan newspapers, there was a silver stampede to rival the Klondike's Gold Rush. To this day nobody knows for sure if Hardin's silver find was a lie, a fluke or if a lode exposed at the time of discovery was subsequently buried again by one of the region's frequent cloudbursts or windstorms. Nobody has ever found the main vein.

Had Richard Noble known the story of the lost silver lode as he stood that day surveying the site on which he would eventually leave his own mark in history, it is doubtful he would have expressed much interest. Still ringing in his ears was Hugh Wickes' comment made after the aborted 1981 attempt. Noble had already won bronze; now it was not mere silver that he sought, but gold. . .

What happened next was unprecedented in the history of the land speed record. Noble, Norris and Ackroyd felt convinced they had found a lifeline, or as close to one as they were going to get; a location that offered their one slim chance of salvation. They lost little time. By October 1st Noble and Norris had inspected the desert again by ground and air and outlined a proposed eighteen mile course. Norris, who had intimate knowledge of Bonneville and Lake Eyre, and who had studied numerous other venues for Campbell when his 1960 attempt was originally planned, regarded the Black Rock Desert as the best record site he had ever seen.

Ackroyd, meanwhile, went back to Alvord to inspect it by air, just to confirm that they weren't backing the wrong horse. From the Thomases he learned how the environmentalist lobby in the region had logged protest after protest at the Motivator team's efforts until Fredrick had been forced to leave with a promise not to return. On top of that, although he felt the surface was of superior alkali make-up there was the fact that the run distance was insufficient. That clinched the issue and without further ado he drove back to Gerlach. His journey was to deteriorate into a harrowing ordeal as he covered the final eighty miles of deserted, isolated roads with his fuel running low and the warning light flashing its urgent message every minute. He admitted later his heart had been in his mouth most of the way, but when he did make it back to Gerlach a decision was made. Project Thrust would relocate without delay. The 1982 attempt was really on at last.

There were still myriad problems to overcome. The most pressing was to obtain permission to use the desert for record breaking purposes. Like Alvord and Bonneville, the Black Rock Desert is a Federal Bureau of Land Management holding, and as Noble swiftly put his charm to good use as he consulted Lynn Clemons at the BLM's Winnemucca office, team members packed up everything at Wendover and began the lengthy Interstate Eighty trek from Utah to Nevada. Bonneville, though wet, was at least something of a known quantity. Now they were moving into the unknown.

Elsom, meanwhile, sought out Gerlach businessman Bruno Selmi. The colourful Italian-American owned the town's sole motel and was naturally delighted at the sudden rise in business as Eddie rented every room. Bruno's Motel thus became official team headquarters, but he also owned a casino-café-saloon complex half a mile up Main Street and before long Bruno's Country Club became the social gathering point for the twenty three team members.

This was the sort of operation Project Thrust really handled superbly, even at that stage when all team personnel had yet to be welded by common adversity into the cohesive band of record seekers they became. Incredible as it seemed the entire project was established at Gerlach and ready for action by Monday October 4th, such speed due in part to the enormous help received from Gerlach School Vice President Walt Ashton and his Air Taxi service. Only six days after the decision to abandon Bonneville had been taken, Project Thrust was settled into its new venue. The triumph over logistical obstacles was phenomenal.

To get to the desert from Reno you head east on Interstate Eighty until you reach State Highway Thirty Four and the northbound turn signposted to Pyramid Lake. That takes you into Indian country, for Wadsworth and Nixon are part of the Paiute reservation on which the historically peaceful tribe now resides. Then, as the narrow tarmac road continues, you fork right at the base of the beautiful Pyramid Lake, famous for its pelicans, large cut-throat trout, the cui-ui fish which is only found in its waters, spectacular formations of tufa rock, and its occasionally treacherous moods.

It was here in 1959 that band leader Guy Lombardo and boat builder Lester Staudacher had first tested the jet hydroplane Tempo Alcoa in readiness for an attempt on Campbell's water speed record. The test ended badly when a freak swell sent Staudacher skimming ashore to come to rest with a damaged craft at Pelican Point, not far from the settlement of Sutcliffe on the western shore, but it provided a throwback link. The region Noble had chosen wasn't entirely devoid of speed record history.

The first time I made the trip that was a comforting thought as I headed north on the first day of my 1982 trek, past the wet mud expanse of the inappropriately named Winnemucca Dry Lake on the eastern side of the highway. From Pyramid Lake SH34 then stretches another sixty five miles before its reaches the next outpost of civilisation. Either side of the road hefty beef steers graze lazily; in the height of summer you can occasionally catch a glimpse of tarantulas crossing the road at the crest of a brow. Now and then a rattlesnake wriggles across seeking the warm of the tarmac. There are plenty of squashed reptiles on the road.

Finally, after what seems like hours, you pass through the tiny town of Empire, which signals you are near journey's end. On the left is the General Store, a petrol station and the vast gypsum plant which provides the majority of the region's non-agricultural employment, while further left beyond the town the Fox Range of mountains and the northern end of the San Ennido Desert shield Smoke Creek Desert from view. To the right is the impressive Selenite Range. The road acts as a natural boundary; Washoe County falls to the left, Pershing to the right. Too far ahead to see from either Empire or Gerlach, the Black Rock itself is sited on the border of Humboldt.

Gerlach is another seven miles north of Empire, the road almost a causeway across the desert floor. As it curves left into the town there is a level crossing for the railroad whose water requirements lead to Gerlach's foundation, while the first building is Cecil Courtney's petrol station to the right.

The trip itself and the limited size of the hamlets impresses on you just how demanding and unforgiving an environment it all is, and the inhabitants could easily be forgiven for lacking the social graces of softer town dwellers. But I hadn't been in the company of some of them more than a few minutes when an altogether different picture emerged.

Where the drive to Bonneville had been both tiring and exciting all those months earlier, the run to Gerlach had an extra edge. Typically, Noble had been very reluctant to impart to the outside world any information on the team's new whereabouts, and my only knowledge had been gleaned from GKN's Tony Jeeves, who himself had been given precious little detail beyond the fact that the team was now in a town called Gerlach which wasn't far from Winnemucca Dry Lake. I'd left Reno prepared if necessary to camp in my hire car for a couple of weeks, and had already gotten off to a bad start by assuming Winnemucca Dry Lake is close to Winnemucca itself. By some geographical aberration the two sites are separated by a good hundred and sixty miles of Interstate Eighty. Retracing my steps and spearing up into the unknown backwater of State Highway Thirty Four initially proved an eerie sensation.

By the time I ran uncertainly into Gerlach I was beginning to wonder where on earth I was and just what I'd let myself in for, when I discerned a red-tarpaulined shape outside the fading blue block that was Bruno's Motel. It could only have been Thrust 2. As Initial Services' Richard Chisnell came beaming out we fell into conversation about accommodation, and again he broke into an easy smile.

"I don't think you need worry too much about that. Everyone round here seems mad keen to see anyone British. They're crazy about adopting anyone who has anything to do with the project.

"I think the local sheriff has a spare room. Come up to the Country Club and I'll introduce you".

The Club wasn't quite the grandiose affair its name might suggest, but more a tidy little bar cum diner. When we located an iron-grey haired individual whose stocky frame wore an unmistakeable official green tunic, he was deep in discussion with Richard T. Briggs over the theft of the latter's generator. Both had an open bottle of Michelob to hand, which seemed promising. Similarly equipped, we joined them and within moments came my first experience of the Gerlach and Empire brand of hospitality. Dick West, the Deputy Sheriff of Washoe County, might have had the power of the law behind him and on his holster belt, but it still came as a major surprise when he casually dropped his keys on the table. Minutes earlier I'd been a total stranger. Now he simply said: "My place is back in Empire – on Third Street. Make yourself at home. There's plenty of beer in the icebox".

There was no worry about the length of my stay, even though he had relatives coming shortly for a hunting trip. It was an impressive introduction to a fine ambassador for a couple of extraordinary towns.


On October 5th Noble's official application for a permit to use the desert was presented to the BLM's Winnemucca office. Deliberating the matter would take time, but in the meantime the team was allowed to make a series of runs on the basis that the BLM offered no guarantee a permit would be forthcoming. In the circumstances, the only way to look was ahead. On the 6th the three-day course survey work began. Parts of the desert had ripples not wholly evident during the initial ground inspection, but the aerial reconnaisance had pin-pointed a half mile wide strip that was thirteen miles long and free from irregularities.

On the 7th, as survey work continued, Thrust 2 was acquainted with the desert for the first time. It had rained briefly overnight in Gerlach but the desert surface was unaffected and far from flying on the ground at six hundred miles and hour, Thrust's progress was far more sedate. Norris and Ackroyd wanted to test the dusty surface to assess its weight-bearing capability, so Thrust 2 was simply roped to Rover Dover and towed across a test section at a modest 30mph. The results were favourable, and proved two important points. The surface seemed quite happy with the four-ton jetcar; and the damage inflicted on it by the metal wheels seemed minimal. The latter would be an important factor in winning a BLM permit.

The weather deteriorated slightly that afternoon but the mood picked up again the following days as the surveying work was completed and Thrust 2 ran for the first time under its own power on the desert. Again, it was merely a test run, and Noble barely topped 100mph as he loafed along, but it was a significant advance and at last everyone felt the 1982 campaign had really begun. As the weather remained calm, clear and warm Noble worked closer to 200mph on the 9th and then achieved a 320mph blast the following day as the access road network was established. None of the runs was actually timed as the USAC timekeepers hadn't been called up yet, but the sense of optimism in the camp was almost tangible. Greenham Common and Bonneville were now literally miles behind, together with the endless hours of frustration. It was as if a new start had been made, and everyone was very aware that a fresh chapter of record breaking history was being opened. Now, at last, Project Thrust would get its crack at some glory.


As one of the conditions under which Thrust was allowed to make its initial trials, the BLM had stipulated that the desert surface could not be graded in any way, nor could oiled guidelines be laid as they were at Bonneville. Ackroyd and Norris, however, hit on a novel means of giving Richard something to follow during his high-speed bursts. Using the Jaguar Fire Chase, Ken patiently marked out each mile using the odometer, pink--ribboned stakes and a compass, then turned round and drove at speed past them all to leave his own wheeltracks as guidelines. This he did for every one of the track's sixteen lanes. His ability to drive arrow-straight lines with unerring accuracy was quite uncanny and was rivalled only by Thrust 2 itself.

Meanwhile, the remnants of United States Air Force combat

practice in the area had painstakingly to be located and removed by a willing band of helpers. All over the desert surface were strewn spent cartridges and all manner of debris, and on more than one occasion the entire junior population of Gerlach and Empire was given the day off school to help with the vital task. Norris called it defodding and although it was back-breaking work that actually caused one or two to start seeing double after so much bending in the sun, it was of crucial importance. If at high speed Thrust 2 struck any foreign objects – such as the natural rocks, rusted lengths of steel hawser or beer bottles that were found – the result could be disastrous. The standard of defodding became even more demanding when the first of many live shells was discovered. These two-point-seven five calibre rocket warheads were eventually detonated behind Bruno's Country Club by members of the military specially summoned for the job.

By the 12th the arrangements for ambulances had been finalised, the course work was almost complete as it was now fully marked out, and the desert surface was in pristine condition. Better still, the BLM's permit was ready for collection in Winnemucca. The past week might have been spent duplicating much of the preparation work wasted at Bonneville, but the effect on team spirits was inestimable. On the 13th Dave Petrali, Don McGregor, Buck Wetton, John Banks and Jess Tobey arrived to set up the USAC timing equipment and though a temporary hitch arose with the permit everything appeared sorted by the next day, when the start crews went through static drills in readiness for the first officially timed run on October 15th. That day dawned clear, bright and full of promise. By seven twenty Norris had started remarking sufficient tracks for four runs, a job which it took the conscientious engineer three hours to complete. By noon Petrali was satisfied with the complex timing gear and by twelve twenty Noble was away, slamming through the measured mile at 349.786mph in what was intended to be an exploratory run. Then the first of the day's problems arose.

Thrust 2 was always run at full throttle, Ackroyd controlling its speed through the measured distance by careful calculation of the run-up distance and the starting point. The closer Noble started to the timing traps, the lower would be his peak and average speeds, and vice versa. On that run he had allowed sufficient run-up for Thrust 2 to exceed 400mph, but the reheat failed to light up properly and it hit its peak beyond the measured mile. Then, as Noble deployed his braking parachute, split stitching in its carrying bag caused it to fail. Only partly opened, it failed to billow, wrapped itself around the rear suspension and was slightly damaged by the reheat. With so much room available and at such relatively low speed Richard was in no danger and when he deployed the back-up system of a cluster of three smaller 'chutes, known as the 'triple-ripple', Thrust 2 was brought safely to rest. The reheat and parachute problems were minor and presented no great difficulty to cure, but as the team trooped back to Gerlach a fresh bombshell was about to explode, and its repercussions were far more serious.

Since the 12th the team had been aware that a party of environmentalists objected to its activities on the desert, but it wasn't until the 15th that they really made their presence felt. Everyone was stunned to learn they had applied for and been granted, an injunction against Project Thrust, preventing further runs.

The instigator of the protest was a man called Charlie Watson, a former BLM employee and reputedly a great outdoorsman. In 1958 he'd formed the Nevada Outdoor Recreation Association (NORA) and to him Thrust's use of the desert was highly inappropriate. He enlisted the support of the Sierra Club and together they formed a powerful alliance, for each party had a history of being particularly outspoken in their condemnation of any type of off-road vehicle. Specifically, neither wanted the Black Rock Desert to become another world speedway, in the mould of Bonneville.

The original meeting to secure Project Thrust's BLM permit had been held with officials Bob Neary and Jerry Smith, but the protest obliged Noble to fight on several fronts. It was all a time-consuming interruption to the programme but this was just the sort of battle he relished. In Winnemucca he again sought out Lynn Clemons, the BLM recreation planner who has specific responsibility for dealing with anyone who wishes to use the desert. Lynn had seen most types of request in his time, and revealed an acute assessment of the situation.

"Basically", he explained, "the environmentalists want the east arm of the desert declared a wilderness area. That includes the playa itself and a wilderness area means no ORVers, or off-road vehicle users. Naturally, the ORVers don't want to be restricted in such a way when there's a great open space out there, and neither do all the rock hounds we get out here every year. At the same time the history buffs don't want anyone fooling with the scenic integrity of the area. We have places out here like the Applegate-Lassen Trail – the emigrant route to California and Oregon – which haven't changed at all since the gold and silver seekers used them back in 1849. These guys want us to continue protecting that sort of thing.

"But we also have to consider other things. Other potential users. We get an awful lot of requests for permits to explore the region from oil, natural gas and geothermal developers, all interested in digging out new energy sources. At the same time the local ranchers expect protection against that sort of thing. On top of all that, we get guys like you who want to try for world's records out here".

Clemons himself saw little reason to reject the British, but the BLM was legally obliged to observe protocol. Meanwhile, back in the desert, the local inhabitants had ideas of their own. To them the arrival of Project Thrust – "the British and their crayzee jetcar" – was one of the most important and exciting happenings in living memories and they weren't about to let it be snatched away "by a few spoilsports".

"Never mind Charlie Watson; he doesn't even live up here", was an opinion expressed on more than one occasion and by more than one individual. "It's our desert, we live on it, and we say Thrust should run".

They were prepared to stand and be counted on their conviction, too. Within a day of the permit's suspension, the entire populace of Empire and Gerlach had signed a petition of counter protest, demanding that the British get their chance. Joanne Irazoki and Kathy Mito, who worked in Bruno's Country Club, duly presented it to Jim Santini, at that time Nevada's Congressman in Washington DC. Santini was impressed, and added the bulging petition to the findings of his own representative Susan Linn, who had also done some exploration. She had been quite open in her personal opinions.

"I've been coming out here for the past ten years and I have to admit it's one of my favourite places on earth. I can tell you it is also one of Mr Santini's. My job is to represent him and the people of Gerlach and Empire, and to do what I can to help them. But on a purely personal level I feel about this thing quite strongly, too. I feel this is a very historic area and that there's history to be made here, so why not let Project Thrust go ahead?

"I can understand that the protesters are worried about traffic and the vulnerability of the desert to racers, but I haven't seen the kind of damage I'd expected. I'd say the protesters have no case bar the precedent set at Alvord a couple of years back. The damage is minimal and in any case the desert will rejuvenate itself when the rains flood it after the fall.

"As far as I'm concerned these guys are honourable people working very hard to anticipate the BLM's requirements. They're honest, first class people".

In the past the desert had faced significantly more serious threats than the marks left by the metal wheels of a high-speed vehicle propelled by an aircraft engine. In July 1967 a Reno newspaper had carried the story that it would become San Francisco's refuse dump, and that rightly set the environmentalists into a successful fight. Now, as he considered the Project Thrust case, Santini knew that Linn had a very strong point about the desert's ability to repair any damage it sustained when the winter rains came. Apart from the possibility of attracting ORVers the impact of Thrust 2's aluminium wheels seemed the only potential damaging factor, and that would only be of a temporary nature. Noble and his five hundred supporters had also made the highly relevant point that Project Thrust would actually leave the desert cleaner when it left than it had been when it arrived, thanks to the scrupulous defodding.

The debate raged for three days, during which a warm sun gently baked Thrust personnel as they continued with their track preparation work, confident that commonsense and freedom of action would eventually prevail. They were seated round the bar at Bruno's, glued to the television set, when CBS Evening News' Dan Rather broke the news that the permit had been reinstated and the objectors had finally been overcome. That night saw some hearty celebrations in Gerlach and Empire, for it seemed the final hurdle had been cleared. In reality though, the serious problems were only just beginning.

# 7. Acrimony and amusement

When Thrust 2 was lined up at the southern end of the track at nine o'clock on the crisp morning of Tuesday, October 19th, Project Thrust's 1982 attempt had an American life of twenty four days, with nothing better to show than an officially timed run of 349mph. There were some very pertinent reasons for those apparently unimpressive statistics, but nonetheless the pressure to start justifying the expense was now really beginning to mount.

It began to manifest itself in different ways. On the first run of the day cold power was down and then the reheat gave problems. Then on the second, Noble fried the front brake discs by inadvertently resting his left foot on the brake pedal as Thrust cruised to a 344mph pass. Sheepishly, like a schoolboy caught playing truant, he explained himself. "We had some new footrests made after the Greenham accident and the left one was erroneously fitted flush with the brake pedal. When I hit a small bump on the course at 430mph the jolt was enough to move my foot into fractional contact with the brake pedal and the steady build-up of heat through the remainder of the run was enough to overheat poor old Glynne's discs. . ."

Some team members were almost openly derisive of the explanation, for with the Greenham spectre still all too ready to haunt back into mind there were those who felt he had already thoroughly exhausted his error allowance. While Noble and Barrett had sorted things immediately after the airbase disaster, the overall situation remained one of a marriage patched up after one partner had been unfaithful enough for divorce to be considered. Such fresh mistakes out in the desert were enough to remind the injured party of the other's indiscretion and at times the wound began to ease open again.

With a best average of 370mph for the mile on the first run, neither Ackroyd nor Noble was happy with the power the Avon was producing, both feeling as did Watkins that it needed further tuning to suit the Black Rock Desert's altitude. The job of locating a site on which the jetcar could be lashed so its engine could be given a static test fell, as usual, to Elsom. He came up trumps. Just outside Reno is the US Navy's Fallon Air Base. Eddie reasoned that getting permission for the test might prove a time-consuming, red tape-cutting exercise, so his ploy was straightforward. Thrust 2 was loaded on the Fruehauf and sent on the road to Fallon, while a small advance party went on to argue Thrust's case with the base commander. Initially he proved a tough old bird who took plenty of persuading, but eventually he relented and grudgingly granted permission.

"Okay, you can do what you want. But you'll have to be quick. How soon can you get your car down here from Gerlach?".

Literally at that very moment Thrust's distinctive white tail fins hove into view outside his office window, as Elsom made a timely comment. "Well, I think that's her arriving right now. . ." Far from exploding with anger at the Britons' presumptuous cheek, the base commander seemed quietly amused.

While Bowsher fitted and balanced the spare front discs, Thrust 2 was tethered to the ground. Then, in test after test, it fought against its securing chains with Samson's ferocity as Noble ran the Avon to its full power. From eleven in the morning until dusk Watkins struggled to cure the reheat's reluctance to ignite properly. He reset the fuel injector nozzles for full power in the cold mode, without reheat, then reset them in their hot mode when the afterburner was employed. Still the giant flame erupted only intermittently from the tailpipe, and as darkness descended and the cool night air began to bite, One-Take's fluent curses kept the rest of the crew fully informed of progress. Then, just as hearts began sinking at the prospect of a serious engine problem, Noble tried again. This time that beautiful flame, complete with the 'rattler's tail' of sonic shock diamonds, lit up the tie-down area. The cries of relief raised a few American eyebrows but it was an emotional moment. Watkins received heartfelt congratulations, and as he headed back to Gerlach his face wore the expression of the bomber pilot who has successfully saved his crew by bringing his wounded craft home in one piece.

Now, surely, with full power, exactly the right type of reheat flame and an engine fully adjusted for altitude, the project could start making that much needed progress. The Thrust team had always been an optimistic bunch, taking their cue from Noble and his own amazing positive thinking, but gradually since Greenham an insidious fatigue had been creeping in. It had its rein when problems such as the overheated brakes arose, for in truth even at this stage many of the key members were in a punch drunk state after all the disasters and dramas they'd had to overcome, alternately exhausted by their own determination to do any job to their utmost and buoyed by their elation at any success. Watkins' efforts with the reheat were an immeasurable boost, but in this desert-based game of cat and mouse that Fate so enjoyed playing, another disappointment was just around the next corner. In typically cruel fashion, it followed right on the heels of that apparent fresh step forward.


By October 21st Thrust 2 was ready for further runs, the desert firm and dry, the weather, mercifully, holding up. With little apparent effort Noble blasted south to north at 465.296mph for the mile and a nerve-tingling 471.528 for the kilometre. On the return he achieved 462.071 and 466.416 respectively, the very ease at which Thrust bagged new British car and driver marks of 463.683mph and 468.972 for mile and kilo momentarily shocking the senses after all the previous troubles. After twenty six days the best from Bonneville had finally been eclipsed, convincingly, with the clear message from Ackroyd's onboard monitoring equipment that there was plenty more to come. As usual, he was progressing in stages, still determining Noble's top speed by the amount Thrust 2 was initially lined up from the start of the measured distance. On the surface, there was cause for celebration.

Beneath that calm veneer, however, there was further bad news. Noble complained of serious dust in the cockpit and once again he had made an error, for on each run he had fractionally misjudged the point at which he deployed the braking 'chutes, so they began to bite while Thrust 2 was still within the measured distance. There was no doubt he would have achieved even greater maximum and average speeds but for that aberration.

It was a simple mistake to make, particularly as he was adjusting to a new environment and especially as his total driving experience with the car on its solid wheels still amounted to less than thirty minutes. That was a point it was very easy to overlook at such moments, when his driving came under heavy criticism, for in the motor racing world one never really thinks how much experience a driver has had in his machine in terms of mere minutes. Hours, maybe. Laps and test sessions, and then actual races, more likely. As a parallel to what Noble faced, if you expected a total novice to climb straight into a 750bhp Grand Prix car, drive it at Silverstone for half an hour and then take it out in a race and win, you'd lose all credibility. Even if the driver had plenty of experience in lesser categories, you'd still lay yourself open to accusations of lack of appreciation of a racer's problems.

Moreover, Noble's wasn't one of twenty six or so machines contesting a race; instead he stood wholly on his own as far as observers judging his driving were concerned, and even the smallest mistake tended to get magnified out of proportion. Predictably his self-confidence remained, at least outwardly, unshaken. He gave a deprecatory shrug when anyone talked to him openly about things, as if he couldn't quite see what all the fuss was about.

"It's quite straightforward, really. We've replaced the old type of 'chute release button on the steering wheel and the new ones have hair triggers. With the old ones I'd let my thumbs hover just as I was getting to the marker flags signalling the end of the measured distance, but when I did the same thing with the new ones the slightest shake in the car around 500mph was enough to make my thumbs touch them and pop, out went the 'chute. It won't be a problem adjusting to them now I've identified the difference".

He was right, but what was the racing driver's equivalent of a harmless spin assumed greater importance to some, and once again there were almost guilty questions asked in some quarters whether or not Richard Noble really was the right man for the job, even if it was his car. It was nothing near as acrimonious as the questions asked of Campbell at Lake Eyre, and you sensed most of the questioners pondered more out of disappointment than anything else, but nonetheless the doubts were still lurking.

The fresh blow to morale was compounded when post-run inspection revealed damage to the front suspension after Noble had hit a ten foot long, four inch depression along the course on the second run. There would be no more runs that day, but just to make sure the departing team was chased inelegantly from the desert by a frighteningly violent dust storm.


It was bitter cold, the dark sky ominously clear of cloud. Every star was thrown into stark relief. Breath clouds streamed from mouths and hands beat against hips as cold men sought to maintain their circulation. It was twelve thirty on Saturday morning and still work went on rectifying the suspension damage as crew members worked in shifts to ready the jetcar for further action. It was a telling scene, for no matter what doubts anyone might harbour about Richard Noble's ability in the cockpit, everyone was absolutely determined to do his or her level best to have the giant car running again in the shortest possible time. At the back of most minds was the feeling that the weather, up to that point so good it was beginning to be taken for granted, was due to change shortly.

Though the final rebuild work was not completed until one that morning, the entire team was back on duty less than twelve hours later, and at ten minutes to two in the afternoon, twelve years to the day since Gabelich and the Blue Flame had been successful at Bonneville, Thrust 2 sat on the line ready for Run 6. Depressions in the track had been located and corrected the previous day and the high wind that had hampered that work had now subsided. Ackroyd and Norris bustled around doing their last minute checks and everything seemed perfect for the scheduled attempt to average 550mph, or more. This time, however, once the Palouste and the Avon had gone into their double act, Noble had shut off the bigger engine and reported over his radio that it had registered excessive revs. The Avon had overswung dangerously to 107 per cent of its permitted maximum. With such power units maximum thrust is measured at a certain percentage of the maximum revs, with 100 per cent as the baseline. However, in some cases and for short duration, units may be rated higher than that. Thrust's Avon could use an absolute maximum at that time of 104 but usually ran up to 102; had Noble run with 107 he risked serious damage.

It wasn't until four that Watkins managed to cure the problem once and for all, and though Noble peaked over 550mph on his northbound run his averages for mile and kilometre were disappointing: 518.507 and 513.175mph respectively. Then, just as he was about to embark on his return the wind began gusting beyond 5mph and further delays occurred when the team couldn't find the parachute launching projectile. The latter was simply fired from the back of the car when the 'chute was deployed, to ensure that it trailed out properly, but the missile always had to be located so Noble ran no risk of striking it during his return journey. Steadily the final minutes of the allotted hour between runs began their passage into history, and with them went the attempt to boost the British car and driver marks beyond the 500mph barrier. Noble, still strapped in the cockpit awaiting a fall in the wind strength, rose to the occasion well. Nobody could have known it at the time, but when he deployed his parachute prematurely on Run 5 he had made his last real driving error. Now, fed up with the interminable delay, and despite being troubled by the failing light, he took a bold decision and slammed back through the gathering gloom at five thirty, well outside the time limit. In the circumstances, with the all-important guideline wheeltracks ever more difficult to follow, 498.476 and 504.950mph for the Imperial and metric distances was a fine showing, especially as he crossed into the ruts from the previous run for a couple of miles and rode it out over 500. The team clearly thought so too, and later that night when the monitoring equipment was transcribed, there was further reason to celebrate. Thrust 2's spare cockpit never carried passengers after the Greenham drama, and on desert runs  housed instead a Sony Broadcast BVP110 camera. Its evidence revealed a peak speed during the first run of 575mph registering on the duplicate instruments. Bit by bit, despite the myriad problems, Project

Thrust was working closer to Gabelich's record and the bubble of spirit was once more being inflated.

That was when the weather began to deteriorate. The night I arrived in Gerlach I slept well after the long haul back to Reno to collect my things. That Sunday afternoon it had started to drizzle and that night I was lulled to sleep by the sound of much heavier rain rattling the boards on Dick's roof.


Over the next hours torrential rain developed from the initial showers and with more sweeping in on Monday and Tuesday the desert surface began to resemble a dirtier version of Bonneville as it threatened to disappear beneath an ugly liquid sheen. All about the town was a sense of controlled panic; *surely* the weather couldn't have followed the team from Utah? Every local's opinion on a likely forecast was solicited, and though they pendulumed from utter pessimism to total optimism one point was brutally apparent. The floods at Bonneville had indirectly led Thrust to the desert, which was held to be a better venue, but the delay induced by the shunt had put the project back into the bad weather time of year and it was becoming increasingly clear winter was already stalking around the Black Rock. Even if the weather cleared quickly, there was no disguising the need to get on with the programme. Almost imperceptibly the pressure was mounting even faster, bringing with it all the inherent dangers of haste.

The downtime was bad for morale, and exposed with ruthless harshness each individual's level of tolerance. It was also a bad time for those who bottled up their thoughts. The convivial relationship between Briggs and Thrust had curdled since Bonneville, for a variety of reasons. Briggs had been so captivated by his experiences the previous year he'd switched from being a fireman and now sought to establish his own public relations operation. He saw the Black Rock Desert's potential as a land speed record venue as a means of getting in on a deal at an early stage. Prior to the project's move from Bonneville he'd been a team member helping out with explosives permits and similar matters, but Noble didn't like his commercial attitude and steadily the two moved further apart. Noble certainly wasn't happy Briggs had followed the team out to the desert, but there was precious little he could do about it bar revoke his team status. For his part, Briggs was determined to stick it out, since he saw running some form of land speed record consultancy as his way ahead if a successful British endeavour spawned a wave of new American attempts. If he could promote sufficient credibility in that eventuality, he ought to be ideally placed to pick up a few lucrative contracts.

From a pressman's viewpoint, Noble seemed even more remote than he had in Bonneville, and it was eleven days from my arrival before we actually sat down to have a detailed discussion on progress to date. He would appear at meal times with Sally, Mimi and Genny, but was rarely in the bar or in the nearby Miners' Club during the evening socialising. He needed a good night's sleep so he daren't let his hair down too much; there was always the chance the morrow would dawn with conditions good enough for a run. Life for him at that time was at its most frustrating as the desert would be drying out by day, only to be doused again during the night.

I was angry that he withheld information for so long, yet it wasn't difficult to sympathise with his position. He'd already suffered one washed out attempt at Bonneville, had then damaged the car and delayed the subsequent effort after a minor driving error that had had far from minor consequences, and then Bonneville had washed him out again. And now that he'd performed an apparent miracle to transfer his team lock, stock and barrel to a new location, he'd run into numerous mechanical and human dramas and faced the distinct possibility of yet another washout. And all the time there was the nagging worry that the engine mightn't be producing sufficient power and the knowledge that the budget was fast running out.

Whatever happened, he had become the prisoner of his own dream, endlessly forced to pedal a record breaking treadmill of his own creation. To a certain extent that went for everyone else on site too, for the decision to join Project Thrust or to follow it had largely been taken by each individual that was now touched so tantalisingly by its tentacles. Most had literally forced themselves on Noble, such was their anxiety to become involved.

But beneath all that, Noble had a deep feeling of responsibility to them all, and that added up to yet another source of worry.

We finally talked in Bruno's dining area late one night, when the rest of the diners had moved next door to the bar. His continual stonewalling had me well fired up, but after an acrimonious start the conversation improved as we both mellowed out. Once I'd filled in some of the gaps, I began probing for a sign of what might happen if he failed to break the record this time around. He leaned back in his seat and twiddled with a table fork for a few moments before he replied, and I was slightly surprised when he didn't fire back his usual retort that Thrust would carry on until it was successful. Instead, he began to outline a plan, a skeleton plan at that, to resurrect Campbell's Bluebird CN7. For a moment I had the eerie feeling I'd ceased to be there and that he was simply thinking aloud.

"If we don't get the record this year I don't suppose we'll be able to carry on for another go, but there's always the old Bluebird and we might be able to get that for another run. After all, she never reached anything like her true potential on Lake Eyre".

It was an extraordinary moment, like a replay of Campbell in the darkest hours at Lake Eyre, plotting with Leo Villa to have another go at the water speed record. He paused suddenly, as if refocussing and realising he might have said too much, and added immediately: "I'd rather that stayed off the record for now. It wouldn't do any good confusing one issue with another".

Given how soon after that the 1982 campaign fell apart, and how he must have known it was virtually certain to, he must have felt right then that he was staring defeat in the face. Yet his manner remained outwardly assured, if a trifle defensive. In the days that followed he seemed no different, and maintained the usual confident air. The matter was never raised again.


It was small surprise Briggs and I felt a degree of mutual sympathy as 'outlaws', and we were joined in this by a lady called Val who'd come all the way out from the Isle of Wight at her own expense and impulse, simply because she wanted to see how the Isle-built jetcar would fare. For her enthusiasm and support she suffered the indignity of one senior fulltime Thrust member warning her to be careful how she conducted herself in case she gave the project a bad reputation. . .

There were brighter moments during that dreadful period, fortunately. Such as the time Briggs and I, in partnership with equally bored documentary film maker Neil Parker, borrowed a couple of guns and headed for the hills for some target practice. We soon tired of that and of searching fruitlessly for any live game, but Neil finally alleviated his feelings by shooting his car. He was extremely lucky to hit the rear door just by the double--skin of the wheelarch, for the bullet went clean through the doorskin itself. Had his aim been a fraction higher he would have shot his own very expensive video camera too, where it lay on the back seat.


The room was barely thirty feet long by twenty wide, and much of the available space was taken by a bar and a pool table. Both were used in almost equal measure by a rubber-faced local character who answered to the name of Whitey, and played a meaner game of pool than Paul Newman in the film The Hustler, regardless of how drunk he was. Yet the Miners' Club was frequently the most popular social gathering point in Gerlach. Within days of the first team members arriving, proprietors Bev and Arley Osborn took them to their hearts. On many occasions during our stay Bev would lay on full buffet suppers, to which all of the 'crazy English' were invited, and more than one American gaped open-mouthed at the manner in which their supposedly stiff-upper-lipped cousins could let their hair down.

The Miners' was always a good place to go to pass a wet evening, for plenty happened there. During one of the famous buffets 'Crazy Vic', a railroad worker whose enthusiasm for Thrust almost surpassed any team member's, provided the final proof. It started off when he insisted on revealing his extra-ordinary webbed toes, but he became appalled that he might in any way be responsible for bringing the project ill luck when Ken Norris' son John jokingly suggested the clouds on his favourite hat might be a bad weather omen. Before he could be stopped he set light to the offending garment and tossed it smouldering out the door, and his genuine gratitude was touching when Ken stepped in to recognise his sacrifice by presenting him with Gerlach's new answer to gold – a Thrust sweatshirt.

Another evening, after Barrett and Andrew Noble had softened up those gathered with their hysterical Hinge & Bracket double act and fanfared themselves with hunters' chukka-calling whistles, Bev met team member George. In his initial incarnation George was nothing more than a stuffed set of spare overalls topped with a handsome plastic face mask and a Union Jack bowler hat Barrett had left over from Bonneville, and he used to spend most of his time in a corner of the Miners'. It made a pleasant change from his previous duties on the Isle of Wight, where he was regularly left spreadeagled beneath Thrust 2 with only his legs visible. In that undignified position his role was to handle prying visitors who came by and asked too many questions.

Bev was so used to seeing George she'd even taken to saying good evening to him, so when she found him propped up at the bar one night, with a can of Budweiser for company, she gave her customary courteous greeting. This time however, she received the shock of her life when George responded by politely raising his hat. His mask and clothing had temporarily been borrowed by Intervideo film cameraman Alisdair 'Badger' Fortune. . .

It was that sort of occurrence that best typified the British team as it waited for the desert to dry, but the Americans proved equal to the occasion. A surprised Noble was tucking into a meal at Bruno's one evening when Dick West solemnly entered and declared him under arrest.

"Mr Richard James Anthony Noble? I hereby place you under arrest – for speeding on the desert!".

In the mock trial that ensued Noble was further indicted for impeding traffic by going too slowly. Said West: "I had to arrest the guy for going 500mph, but I figured it was only fair to charge him for failing to top 600 as well".

Noble loves that sort of thing and immediately entered into the spirit of it with schoolboyish humour. "I could see him coming up in my rearview mirror when we were running over 500", he offered in mitigation. "There was nothing I could do but move over!".

As he pleaded guilty to both charges, West sternly offered him the alternative of a night in jail or promising to set a new land speed record. As Noble went to bed that night, with the weather still inhospitable, he must already have been pondering his chances of being granted a year's bail.

# 8. Failure in the desert

It was after a nightcap at the Miners' that Tom Palm, who had again trekked all the way out west from Minnesota to act as a team member, took five years off my life. As we left the bar in the early hours and began beating our arms against the bitter cold, he suddenly leaped into the air and let out a fearful whoop of delight that scared the hell out of me.

"You know what this means, don't you? You know what this means?". A cloud of breath fanned from his mouth as he gesticulated. "Just look how clear the sky is, man! It's getting real frosty and that means we're gonna start losing the rain! Hell, I bet you!".

He was right, too. Day by day conditions began to improve. On the 29th and 30th it rained again on the desert, but not too much, and by the 31st the surface had begun to dry really well. It was a heartening indication of just how fast conditions could change. Ironically, it was a part of the desert called Nobles' Trail, named after prospector William Nobles in 1851, that was steadfastly refusing to dry sufficiently to allow access for Thrust's trailer, but Ackroyd and Norris were able to try the main track surface in Rover Dover and found it drying rapidly. By November 1st things were promising enough for Ackroyd to order some adjustments to the front suspension in readiness for runs the following day.

That Monday however, much time was lost pandering to television film crews which had suddenly arrived in Gerlach. The suspension work didn't get underway until the team had gone through the lengthy rigmarole of transporting the car to the desert and unloading it and loading it again to satisfy the television people. After the last four full runs Ackroyd had become convinced that the rake of the car was still too steep, and that it was still creating too much downforce and running slower as a result. He was already sure that the desert surface created more rolling drag than had Bonneville's harder salt, for the playa was altogether more flaky. That meant every extra little bit of momentum was going to count. Dropping the rear of the car by screwing in the locating eyes of the rear suspension struts, the adjustment that had been tried at Bonneville, would have lowered the car too much, the reduction in ground clearance then damming air beneath it and risking it flipping over backwards at high speed. Thus Gordon Flux and his men were obliged to resort to altering the ride height of the front suspension, an altogether more complex job. There were token grumbles that Ackers was going by the book as the components were dismantled, but in his own mind John was pretty sure he had identified the reason for a front ride height that was lower than intended. He explained it with typical thoroughness.

"I'm ninety nine per cent sure that when Richard overheated the brakes during Run 3 the temperatures within the front wheelbays must have risen so high that the rubber springs in the suspension were literally fried for a couple of minutes. They must have been subjected to some 700 degrees in that time. That meant that the rubber became recured in a higher downforce condition and that the front ride height sagged as the rubber settled with the weight of the car as the heat began to dissipate once Richard stopped.

"That's the real reason why we can't simply lower the rear end, which is admittedly a far easier alternative on paper".

The real puzzle was why it had taken the team all its downtime to decide that the suspension required attention, so that work on it ate greedily into the fine weather. The same had applied to repairs to damage to the underbody strakes which had been inflicted on Run 5 when Thrust 2 had hit the depression. They were finally carried out at the same time. It seemed ludicrous that work which could easily have been carried out during the bad spell, should be delayed so long.

It was an organisational flaw which ensured it was not until lunchtime that Tuesday that Thrust was once again ready to be taken to the desert. However, the day had already seen some record breaking activity. John Griffiths had stripped Fire Chase of its roof lights and firefighting equipment and in deference to Jaguar's wishes had hurled the bright red XJ12 across the playa to achieve an average of 129.7mph, a new officially recognised record for fire engines. Griff, who in the early hours of that morning had celebrated continuous success on one of Bruno's slot machines by hurling all his small change through the window of my car as he said goodnight, was his usual deadpan self when he described the first outright record yielded by the Black Rock Desert as "quite uneventful", although he felt he could have bettered 130mph but for the altitude and the softness of the course.

By the time Thrust 2 had been unloaded and towed to its starting position the sun was beginning to dip and the team began to pay one of the penalties for taking so long to alter the suspension. It was not until four o'clock that the jetcar began to move under its own power, and then Noble made only a loafing run at 280mph to check out the front ride height.

Immediately afterwards came one of the waiting spells that was to characterise the team from an outsider's standpoint that year. To many it seemed light enough for a couple of serious runs, but the team hashed and dished the idea for so long that tempers became frayed. Noble, more than anyone else, was qualified to make the decision for he alone was the one who had to guide £1.75M worth of car down the smooth brown course at speeds nearing 550mph, and he alone knew just how difficult and disorientating it could be in tricky light conditions. The pressure might be on to make the most of the remaining good weather but he wasn't about to indulge in an ill-advised response to critics, that might lead to further damage to the car. That he was right became apparent later, when Intervideo boss Tim Inman confirmed that during his last spell of filming at the end of the test run he had been obliged to stop down to an F2 exposure, rather than his normal F22...


As we trooped back down State Highway Thirty Four towards Bruno's and a welcome meal, a fresh development came to light. Far into the evening the search for more thrust became even more earnest. The afternoon's test run had proved that the reheat was now working satisfactorily on initial acceleration but wasn't staying lit throughout the duration of a run. Then there was the fact that by Ackroyd's estimate the Avon was at least 4,000lbs down on thrust, and that would make a colossal difference to the car's performance. Worse still, he also felt the engine had been thirty per cent down on power during every fast run up to that point, although Watkins was adamant it was in perfect mechanical condition. As events were to prove, both of them were right.

From that point on the debate over the engine output would intensify, exacerbated by the fact that even if the car was taken back to Fallon – which would more than likely prove very difficult to arrange a second time – there was still no means at hand to measure the exact thrust. The problem polarised. Either the Avon was significantly down on power even though mechanically it was sound and had checked out okay in its static test, or its full 17,000lbs of thrust simply weren't going to be enough after all to beat the record.

As the latter point etched itself on everyone's minds the mood in Bruno's became steadily less convivial, and added fresh edge to the 575 and 600mph average runs planned for the next day. As far as Thrust matters were concerned, tempers were short and answers elusive. You either played pool at the Miners' or Bruno's, or you went straight to bed that night.

Just as we were about to leave a well-meaning local imparted the news that the weather forecast for the end of the week was snow. Already it had fallen on the surrounding mountain ranges and was creeping down below five thousand feet. Gerlach itself is about four thousand five hundred above sea level, so time was running out. By now everyone had become inured to bad news; it simply seemed an appropriate way to end a dark day.

The change in atmosphere at Bruno's the following morning was quite amazing, a testimony to the benefits of sleeping on a problem as well as to the underlying determination to succeed of all parties involved. Over eggs, bacon and coffee spirits were high and everyone was keyed up for a successful day in which it would be the elements' turn for a beating. Outside, the dawn was crisp, cold yet clear, the sign it would be warm by midday.

Out on the desert, Thrust 2 was the recipient of more loving care than ever before. Every wheel was scrupulously scraped clean of the mud that had adhered during the short tow from trailer to starting position. On the previous run Barrett had hit on the idea of polishing each rim with talcum powder to act as an inhibitor to mud build-up during initial acceleration, and now the process was repeated.

Ackroyd bustled round, pausing to rub some of the desert's fine dust between his fingers, with the wry comment: "This stuff's just like very fine cement". Bowsher, meanwhile, was the attention of the film crew as he put everything into polishing the bodywork. "We've decided to give it two coats so it'll go supersonic", he grinned. Ball was busying himself with cleaning the wheels, and the idea of using talcum powder clearly tickled his sense of humour. "Who'd have thought a car trying for the land speed record would end up being dusted down with baby's bum powder?".

Twenty minutes later, just before noon, everything had been finished and the gleaming jetcar sat at the one mile marker, allowing Noble a run-up of four miles prior to entering the time trap. In a Bonneville echo he joked again about Howard Hughes' obsession with cleanliness as he painstakingly wiped the driver's cockpit screen, and ten minutes later he was strapped in his seat working through his copious check list. Fire Chase and Air Plane, the emergency air ambulance, left for their positions further up the course and as the Palouste whined into life you could have cut the atmosphere even with a blunt knife. At four minutes past twelve, in forty two degree ambient temperature, Noble began his ninth timed run, aiming solidly for 575mph.

Of all the runs to date that was probably the most exciting; certainly it was the most efficient, despite speedometer problems. Noble performed superbly and smacked his target right on the nose with 575.44mph for the mile and 572.837 for the kilo, which in any case the team had never deemed to have the same importance as the Imperial distance. A solid return run would cement some excellent, highly encouraging progress. We didn't know it at the time from our vantage point midway down the course, however, but the day was instead about to turn into a shambles.

Watches were consulted a thousand times as the precious remaining minutes of the allotted hour between runs began to ebb remorselessly away. Yet still there came no word across the airwaves, no suggestion that the return run was imminent. At the northern end of the track the situation had become shambolic. Thrust 2 had been towed into the wrong starting position once it had been turned round. A miscalculation had seen it lined up a mile closer to the measured distance than Ackroyd had planned. While that was being rectified the towline had snapped, creating further delay. Suddenly, as the hour began to draw to its close, time stopped walking by on tiptoe and began a desperate sprint.

It was Sally who commanded the greatest sympathy during the ordeal. For a while she paced the pit area nervously, before she could bear it no longer. "Why don't they *do* something?", she demanded angrily, before stalking off to the caravan. Moments later she could be heard screaming for action of any sort, and gradually a crowd began to gather outside its open door, sensing the human drama. I slammed it shut from the outside and dispersed the congregation, but moments later Thrust Cars' Company Secretary David Brinn inadvertently had it open again from the inside. It seemed Sally Noble's agitation was to be public after all.

It was brought to an abrupt end as Noble's voice suddenly crackled on to the air. Already there was the faint hint of an edge to it.

"Speedy One to Control. Can I go, over?".

There was no answer.

"Speedy One to Control. Can I *go*, over?". The edge was now pronounced.

Still there came no answer, no clearance to begin the run. In the end it was Norris who gave Noble a visual signal to get on with it after his radio had developed a glitch, and he got away with literally only moments to spare. Such was the level of disorganisation that Air Plane and Fire Chase were both at least four miles short of their positions, and one of the team's strictest safety rules had been broken.

The speeds, when they came through, were greeted with whoops of delight that made a dramatic contrast to the earlier tension. The mile at 575.539mph, the kilo at 578.467. That gave respective averages of 575.489 and 575.652 and another new British car and driver best. In terms of performance the day, after all, was a major success, even though there had been a four second delay before the reheat lit.

As far as the team's organisation between turnrounds was concerned, however, it had been an unmitigated disaster that could easily have risked driver and car.

Noble himself looked haggard after his efforts, and confessed to feeling completely shattered. Thrust 2 had leaped and slewed from damp patch to damp patch, giving him an awful ride and demanding every ounce of concentration he could muster.

"The surface was just bloody awful", was all he could say afterwards, too drained to contemplate any further runs. Chisnell, in America as overall representative of all the eleven major sponsors as well as looking after Initial Services' interests, was distinctly unhappy about that, but while he kept his full feelings to himself he nonetheless wore a worried expression for the remainder of the day.

The ritual analysis of performance brought a much-needed injection of fresh hope that offset the growing realisation that the course simply wasn't long enough, the power was insufficient and the weather was just waiting for its chance to move in and shut things down for good. Ackroyd's equipment revealed that for the first time the car had actually gone transonic, shock waves racing across the cockpit screens and changing the internal pressure quite markedly. If that caused Noble some discomfort, it was deemed a small price to pay. Structurally Thrust 2 exhibited no signs of adverse reaction to the new speed threshold, which in the past had caused problems for Breedlove's Spirit of America – Sonic 1 by buckling its body panels. Better still, it had actually brushed through the 600mph barrier at its peak, with a speed of 610. Now that the speeds were edging closer to the region of Gabelich's record everyone sensed a major breakthrough had been achieved. Thrust was becoming a highly respectable performer and the British were making up ground in leaps and bounds.

Although November 3rd was in retrospect Project Thrust's blackest day on the desert that year, in terms of organisation, it also marked a watershed. For all that his ride was uncomfortable and exhausting, Noble did an excellent job, for Thrust 2's wheeltracks ran die-straight down the course on both runs. And he had proved himself capable of maintaining his composure under real pressure in the period between them. After that day I never heard a single team member raise any further points of criticism about their leader's driving ability.


The 610mph peak undoubtedly raised some false hopes, for Gabelich's peak during his record runs had been much closer to 650. However you dressed it up, there was no disguising the fact that Thrust needed another 40mph, at the very least. Despite that, it was felt there might just be an outside chance of the record the following day, especially if the weather was really hot. At a meeting in the back room of Bruno's that evening, Norris carefully outlined the gameplan.

"What we've seen today is that we are in with a very, very slight chance of the record tomorrow, and we have to take that chance. If we can lose some weight in the car, give it an extra polish and pull the elastic back as far as possible, we might just do it".

Accordingly, he and Ackroyd decided to risk running Thrust 2 a mile further back at the southern end, even though that meant starting the south to north run on the damp patch that was stubbornly refusing to dry fully. They also discussed the possibility with Watkins of giving the Avon an extra tweak for that precious increase in power, but nobody was under any illusion; Project Thrust had its back to the wall. If the 4th was going to be the last chance in 1982, they were going to seize it with both hands.


If Richard Noble felt that the big day had finally arrived, after all the years of dreaming, planning, persuading and suffering, his face gave no sign of it as he sat over breakfast the following morning. Instead, he seemed relaxed yet anxious to be getting on with the job, as if he wanted to know as soon as possible if he would have to start thinking about the possibility of another attempt in 1983.

Even as it sat on the Fruehauf on the desert, Thrust 2 was subjected to the minute polishing routine, but this time Ball was also at work with wet and dry paper, vandalising the carefully applied sponsorship signwriting and smoothing every detectable paint chip. To reduce boundary layer drag to a minimum and boost maximum velocity, everything had to be as smooth as possible. The very fact that a millimetre of paint was deemed a potential penalty was an indication of how close to the edge things had become. Particular attention was paid to the bulge of the front wings and the area round the cockpit screens, where airflow was already reaching supersonic speed, and once again the wheels were carefully scraped and dusted with talcum powder. By ten fifteen the team was ready to go.

It was at that point that the true paradox of the chosen course was really brought home. For while the northern end was flaky and friable because it was almost too dry, the southern end was still too damp. In accordance with Ackroyd's plan the car was rolled down to the mile zero marker, but even before it came to rest the deposits of mud clinging to its powdered wheels told the story. With the run-up distance so crucial in determining the overall average speed through the mile and kilometre, the all too apparent unsuitability of the final section of the southern end left only one alternative. If the end of the track couldn't be extended the only other way to achieve the same effect and stretch the elastic, was to move the measured distance a mile further north.

That in itself was a major undertaking, for the track crew had spent days erecting the giant mile marker flags, while Petrali and his USAC boys would have the unenviable task of resiting the timing equipment. The beams operate by shining a light through a lens on one side of the track to another on the opposite side. Thrust's tracks were so wide that siting the second lens in daylight was an intricate affair as locating the original light source was so difficult. Petrali had actually set up the lights originally in the dark, yet now he and his team were asked to perform the task not just in daylight but in strong sunlight. With them now rested the responsibility of giving the Thrust team its final chance. Dave, Mac, John, Buck and Jess responded magnificently to the challenge, and earned universal respect by carrying out the operation within ninety minutes.

Still the false starts continued, however, for when Thrust was finally lined up ready for departure at one twenty an American film crew ignored the rules prohibiting any traffic movement during a run by flying their helicopter into the pit area. When that little drama had been enacted the jetcar was at last cleared for a start, and just before the half hour Speedy One was rolling up to the famous Black Rock, pluming its orangey brown roostertail of dust.

The speeds were good. Very good. In fact they were the best Noble and Thrust 2 had ever achieved. But as they were revealed we all knew the attempt on Gabelich's record had failed, unless the start from the northern end produced something quite exceptional – and that was highly unlikely.

Noble had achieved 596.421mph through the mile and 594.612 through the kilometre, while the overlap between the two was the best of the lot at a tantalising 599.414. But, once again, the reheat had only lit after a four second delay, and even then the light-up was so explosive it had momentarily shoved Noble and Thrust forward with violent 5.1G acceleration.

On the return the friable northern end proved even worse than hoped and slowed initial acceleration markedly. In fact, it was in such poor condition that Griffiths hadn't been able to coax the Jaguar above 96mph and at one stage under braking had ploughed right through the crumbly crust. "It was like running in porridge in the first part of the run", said Ackroyd mournfully. The reheat hiccoughed again too, further stealing speed. Afterwards Noble sat atop the giant gold monster awaiting his speeds. Griff and Hearn had pulled up in Fire Chase and their silver fireproof suits gave the desert's landscape an almost lunar quality. At 584.975 and 587.121mph respectively the second run mile and kilo figures were well out of the newly created ballpark. Ackroyd said only two words when he heard them: "Oh, *shit*!".

The average of 590.551mph for the mile brought Project

Thrust its third new British car and driver mark of the year, but the deflated team was nonetheless bitterly disappointed. Noble, besieged by the local people and television crews, sat almost nonchalantly on the side of Thrust 2's cockpit and maintained his public image even in adversity.

"So, we have an interesting situation", he began. "What we want is a hotter day, a drier course and a little bit more power". His manner was precise, matter of fact. In no sense bitter. He handled himself beautifully. He didn't look or sound like a man tasting ultimate defeat.

"Anyhow, the speed through the distance was 599mph so I think we can satisfy ourselves we've just scratched the 600. The problem is the time of year. The southern end is too wet, the northern end is too dry. And the temperature is very low, which means that transonic drag comes in much earlier. We'd really planned to run this car in the hottest part of the day when we'd got temperatures nearer eighty degrees".

The wind tugged gently at his hair and as Sally approached he gave her a cheerful smile. "Hallo, my love. Your husband is safe at the other end!".


Once again the back room at Bruno's was busy that evening, and the meeting held was the most crucial of the 1982 attempt. Refreshed only partly by hot baths and food since arriving back from the desert, team members wore resigned expressions, as if they knew their fate long before it was finally confirmed. As everyone sat round the square of tables team manager Norris addressed them. He looked spruce and bright, and of all those present probably understood best how frustrated Noble must be feeling.

"The meeting has started, but I don't know when we are going to finish this one because we might have to make a decision separately, having got some ideas from the various members of the team", he opened in his measured, engineer's tone.

"We might well have been here tonight saying well, we've done it. Unfortunately, we haven't done it. We went out there with the intention of doing it today; we thought we had enough power to do it; we had a driver who put his foot right through the floorboard, right the way through. He did exactly what he was told. And we ended up with a 590mph average.

"From the traces we've got, we are indicating about 615mph maximum on the first run, and 610 on the second. We also have evidence from Tim on the video that we did go transonic over the windscreen and the intake, so we know that we have a vehicle that can do the job, and all we have to do is have a long enough track and a big enough boot up the backside. So what can we do?".

He paused momentarily to let his words sink in, before continuing.

"The alternatives are fairly straightforward; the decision is very difficult. We could say alright, let's defy the weather again, let's take the vehicle to a tethering point, let's tweak up the engine in a proper manner, let's measure the thrust, decide when we have enough, and come back and have another go. If we do that we have to be sure that we have got enough team members left with us in order to do it. If we have no further rain, we have got to have the bottom of the track drying out. At the moment it is showing some signs of drying out, but very, very slowly. So we may be in for a long stay. On the other hand, we may retain the eight miles of good track and about three miles of not such good track which caused considerable difficulties in the early part of the run from the north to the south, and we might, with the tweaked up power, even get a record on that eleven miles.

"The other alternative is to say okay, we will not have the team. John Watkins will have to go back whatever, even though he is laughing at the moment. He may have to go back soon and we do need a first-class engine man. We have got one here with us and we do need him to stay. If we could not get him to stay, then we would not have a chance of the alternative.

"Next year, if we do decide to come back, then we have the opportunity with our figures that we produced, of coming back here provided a) we get a BLM permit, and Steve (Till) is around here cringing in the background. Okay, if we get a BLM permit then we need b) to get the engine home on the test bed, and to make sure that we have the thrust necessary to do the job. We need to come back with the team. We possibly need also to elevate our sights on the record that we may have to break, on the speed we may have to achieve. We have a 660 maximum that we were hoping for, a 630 record minimum that we were hoping for. This is what we had this year, that was our target. We might find next year that the target might have to be elevated, and it may be because somebody else has got a machine that is more powerful than our transonic Thrust. So we have to consider that too".

All around the table a sea of faces, each individual mulling over his or her own thoughts, watched him carefully. A few wraiths of cigarette smoke coiled noiselessly towards the ceiling, and nobody spoke as Norris went on.

"On the BLM front, we can apply for a permit and we would have to wait for an answer until maybe April or May next year. In that case, we may find that the sponsors, if we have any when we get back, will decide that they can put aside a budget, which they would allocate if we get the permit, and then again we would be able to go on.

"The weather situation is an important factor, because although it has stopped us so far in having a reasonable track we may have a little problem in not really being washed out. We may have queered our pitch to a certain extent by trying hard to break the record, to continue despite what others might have considered to be a wash-out at Bonneville – which it certainly was – and another wash-out at the Black Rock Desert. But we have, I think, carried out our bargain with the insurers by at least trying to mitigate the fees they would have to pay if we had given up earlier. The fact is that we have been determined, we have gone on and I think should be entitled to a complete insurance claim, even if we pack up now. The fact that we have not got a course long enough is really because the weather did pack in, and did in fact wash us out. Richard here is very concerned that maybe that would not be good enough, and that we really do have to have the wash-out which is inevitable if we stay here long enough.

"So, there are the factors. What we would like from every team member is a considered opinion whether to stay or to go. So can we have feelings from various members?".

It was Noble himself who broke the immediate hiatus after Norris' untypically long speech. Like all the others gathered in that small room, his expression was deadly serious. He had sat throughout stroking his chin and listening intently to Ken's points, although he must have known them all by heart. Now he coughed once and addressed the roomful of people who were there purely because each and every one of them believed wholly in his great dream.

"One has to face facts. What is the *actual* situation? The actual situation is that the car has the stability and design to do the job, but unfortunately we don't have the length of track available in which to do it. If we can get some more power output – and I think it has to be quite a substantial boost – then we can probably do it on the limited track available. If we *don't* get that power", he paused for dramatic effect, "then we haven't got a chance in hell".

While Noble was, predictably, in favour of trying to tweak the Avon on site, Ackroyd took a different view. He immediately punctured one myth.

"I must make the point that we are not looking for a few miles an hour. You cannot compare our *peak* performance with someone else's measured mile *average* performance. We are looking for another 40mph, even 50mph. I must make this *absolutely* clear. You must compare peak to peak or measured mile to measured mile". Sentence by sentence his words became more pronounced as he gave them extra effect. "And the measured mile record is 622 and we need to beat it by an official one per cent, which means we need 630. And we did 590. . ."

He, like Norris and Noble, paused to let his points sink in, before continuing: "I would like to pass this on to Rolls-Royce and its development engineers and do the thing in laboratory-type conditions where we know exactly what we have and exactly what we can get for a short life engine. And I'm not sure we are going to do it on the edge of a cliff". His final remark indicated beyond doubt how close to the bone he felt the project had become. At this point, Petrali leant his weight to those in favour of abandonment.

"I would agree with John. Unless you would find you're only getting 8,000 pounds of thrust out of the car instead of 17,000.

Somewhere along the line you've got to come up with a *lot* of thrust".

Putting forward a point of view shared by many of the fulltime team members who'd rebuilt the car after the Greenham Common accident, chief engineer Gordon Flux raised another issue in his rolling west country accent.

"We've been here eight weeks. We've accomplished four excellent runs and proved the technical ability of the car and that Richard is a good driver, especially on the last run today. Can't we be satisfied with what we've got now and put the car in a better *technical* condition so when we can come back it is ready for what John has said is the hump at the end? It's only a 50 to 60mph hump but it's the one that's going to give us the works. At least then we know we're on the right track".

At that point Ackroyd interrupted him.

"I would only disagree with Gordon on one point, and that is that he has *totally* underestimated the length of the time which this team has been under strain. It started in an *intense* manner before Greenham – with the build-up to the Greenham run – *and it hasn't let off for one day since*".

Tired and very clearly emotional, Ackers added the rider: "And personally, I've *had* it".

There was an uncomfortable hiatus and silence fell as he looked away, unable to speak further. Everyone in that room felt for him, for other than Noble no-one else had put quite so much into the project as he had. This time, it was Chisnell who stepped in.

"Are we so near yet so far?" he enquired. "Are we near enough to push a little bit harder, notwithstanding the fact that you are drained of emotional energy after a very successful day and a very hard and outstanding few weeks in achieving what you've done so far? Are we not denying ourselves that final opportunity or are we facing reality and saying no, we can't do it? I don't know.

"We have to consider: will the sponsors be prepared to invest £X00,000 or whatever it costs – presumably much less than this year because of the Bonneville preparation budget? Will they feel that's a good commercial risk? Will there be lots of new sponsors lining up ready to take over? That's what one has to ask oneself. Will the existing sponsors be keen to carry on, having got this far?".

Noble's response was brief and to the point as he sat with elbows on the table and the tips of his fingers touching one another as if in prayer, but the quiet manner in which he made it was redolent of his determination.

"If we decide to go home and try and enlist Rolls-Royce's help I will get the money. It's as simple as that".

"What we have to remember is that the team has performed magnificently", continued Chisnell. "The car has performed magnificently, the *driver* has performed magnificently. The driver's *wife* has performed magnificently, and I don't think Sally should be forgotten in this".

That won the interruption of a chorus of 'hear, hear' around the table, as Chisnell summarised the general feeling. "We just have to see what we can do. We just have to live to fight another day. . ."


Much later that same evening the decision was finally taken to abandon, return to Britain and regroup for a fresh attempt in 1983. There was no celebration that the strain had at last been lifted, and certainly no consolation party. The emotions were too drained for that. I stayed talking for a couple of hours to Flux and Watkins, then headed back to Reno and home. Saying goodbye to newfound friends such as Bev Osborn, Dick West and Bruno's daughter Lena was particularly hard, and about the only easy thing about leaving Gerlach that night was the knowledge that somehow I'd be back the next year.

Two days after I got home I learned sandstorms had struck the desert on November 6th. On the 7th the winter snow had arrived. . .

# 9. The crossroads

Two attempts, two failures. Those were the inescapable if unpalatable facts as Richard Noble once more headed back to Britain to court continued sponsorship and industry support. He had done much better than bronze this time; he had won the silver. But still only gold would do. Had he been an entrant in the America's Cup, where participation against other boats brings at least reflected glory, he might have been regarded as more newsworthy by the mass media. Had he been an athlete, no doubt his exploits would have been splashed all over the daily tabloids. Instead, he'd got a couple of short spells on television news and the usual paragraphs on progress. Nothing more. He knew, however, that this time his achievements were far more solid, the progress far more tangible. And constantly spurring him on was the knowledge that if he, and he alone, couldn't keep the financial ball rolling, Thrust 2 would simply end up another land speed record failure despite his absolute conviction it could do the job.

Like everyone concerned with the project, he was adamant that its success was something that was impossible to measure definitely until it was irrevocably finished. In terms of hard results, in early December 1982, Project Thrust had broken the mark for a British car and driver four times, but those were unofficial accolades that mattered little without the overall record. The uncharitable regarded it as a failure. At that point, though, the story was far from over. Noble anticipated one final chance the following year; if, twelve months later, the record was still in American hands, that was when talk of failure would finally be justified. And failure, as ever, was the furthest thing from his mind.

In many ways the 1982 attempt was so extraordinary that the countless cliffhangers tended to obscure exactly what the team had achieved. First there had been the endless hours spent preparing the car after Bonneville and incorporating Ackroyd's modifications. Then there had been the Greenham Common accident followed by twelve intensive weeks of rebuilding on a very tight schedule. Then Bonneville had flooded and the fairy tale relocation to a hitherto completely unknown site at Gerlach had been accomplished in mere days, at a stage when lesser organisations would already have thrown in the towel. Then there had been the battle with Charlie Watson's faction to win a permit to use the desert, and when that had finally been restored and the team had at last reached the point at which it had started at Bonneville the previous year, it had become besieged by all of the usual record breaking frustrations such as human and mechanical dramas and unsettled weather. Looking retrospectively, outright success in 1982 had been doomed the moment Thrust 2 had crashed at Greenham, but the team had done one hell of a salvage job, as those new British marks and three runs peaking above 600mph testified.

Thrust's critics frequently indulged in selective amnesia. It was often suggested that only the Americans had the flair and ability to go out to Bonneville one week and run at record speeds the next, as if to suggest that such undertakings were best left to other nations. If that was the case, went the argument that was usually propounded by other Britons, why couldn't Noble stop embarrassing the nation's pride and reputation and either do the same or do the decent thing and get out?

In a memorable bout of land-based jet warfare in the mid sixties, Donald Campbell's hard-won 403mph record, set in full accordance with the FIA's wheeldriven regulations extant at the time of its design, was annihilated by the new breed of pure jet-thrust American machines. Even before his eventual success Breedlove had cocked a snook at the authorities by clocking 407.45mph in two runs in August 1963 and although that was unofficial the FIA was subsequently obliged to capitulate and recognise a new class for jet or rocket cars. The moment it was ratified it was axiomatic it would be the class from which the outright record holders of the future would come. Without all the drama of finding traction, of having tyres designed that could transmit a car's fantastic power to the track, and with far more power available from their Air Force surplus turbojets, such cars immediately took over to establish speeds a car driven through its wheels could never hope to achieve.

Less than three months after Campbell set his record, which was 4mph slower than Breedlove's first jet mark, an Illinois engineer called Tom Green beat both officially with 413mph in Walt Arfons' Wingfoot Express jet. Less than a *week* later, Walt's estranged brother Art took that away with 434 and in an incredible battle with Breedlove won the year's round in his Thrust-inspiring Green Monster with an eventual 536mph. In his wake Breedlove had managed a 526mph best before that ride into a lake after parachute failure. By the end of 1965 Breedlove had regained his crown and remained king with 600mph until Gary Gabelich took over five years later. Conveniently, few remembered – or even knew – how much frustration and technical trouble Gabelich had to endure before he was successful.

The 400mph barrier had first been cracked one-way by Cobb in 1947, but had resisted all two-way efforts until Campbell's in 1964. Now, in less than eighteen months, the American jet jockeys had shown the decadent British just how to do the job. The ante had been kicked up not just by one hundred miles an hour, but two. So why couldn't we respond? Why was it the British always seemed to make such a meal of things? Was Noble scared? Or. worse, was he stringing it out year by year so he made some real money out of it?

There were several facts the critics chose not to consider. When Breedlove and Arfons had fought their High Noon at Bonneville, conditions could scarcely have been better, for the salt was in good shape and the weather favourable. Neither ever had to wait around much, and both had shaken many of the bugs out of their cars in previous runs. Moreover, neither ran them flat out, with full power, on every run. With jets it is possible to govern the percentage of overall power below 100 per cent, just as it is to adjust it above, as Thrust had done. Apart from the last series of runs in 1965, as both drew a serious bead on 600mph, neither Breedlove nor Arfons regularly ran 100+ per cent on their General Electric J79 turbojets, and neither always used their afterburners throughout a run, but only in quick spurts. Usually, canny as they were, they kept something in hand.

Had only one of them been running for the record it is likely the pace would have developed much less dramatically. Then it would probably have been edged up deliberately each year to provide an income and give the sponsors a little fresh publicity each time out. That was virtually what Campbell had done with his boat in the fifties as he edged closer to 300mph, and why not?

Project Thrust, by contrast, didn't have a choice. Noble wasn't making his fortune out of the endeavour. Sponsors weren't queueing up in their droves to shower him with money. Instead every inch of progress and every pound of backing had to be fought for, and that was reflected in the manner in which Thrust 2 was run. Time spent in foreign locations chasing land speed records is horrendously expensive and partly for that reason and partly because it allowed him to gather far more significant data about the car's performance, Ackroyd stipulated it should always be run at its maximum power. That was why he altered the run-up distance to modify the entry speed to the measured mile. That denied Noble any luxury of keeping some power in hand or of using the afterburner only in brief spurts. There was no gainsaying what Craig and Art had achieved in their careers, and nobody suggested theirs was anything but a laudable jet duel, but Thrust's method put some of it into perspective.

The Americans also had the advantage of birth, of course. With Bonneville effectively on their doorstep they could always trail back to base to make modifications, and then go back to the salt for another try the same year, maybe even the same month. The British could only afford one attempt a year, given the logistics involved and the hurtful expense.

While the weather was the ultimate culprit in closing down the project for a second year in November 1982, it was not wholly to blame for delays in progress. The series of cliffhangers in the desert acted like Magnaflux to reveal cracks in Project Thrust's organisation on several occasions, and quite a few times the substitute for action was seemingly endless discussion and counter-discussion that would have been the death of any race team, before decisions were finally made. On its 1982 showing, if Thrust had been entered for the Indianapolis 500, held on Memorial Day at the end of May every year, it would have been ready to roll by June. The delay in the decision to change the front ride height was a telling example, for had it been taken earlier in a week of inactivity the job could have been completed in plenty of time for a brace of runs on the 2nd. Instead the work was only begun the previous day and ate into valuable fine weather. It was the sort of delay that could ultimately mean the difference between success or failure.

As Ackroyd had stressed, however, it had been a team under intense pressure for several months, so perhaps it was understandable. Every lesson it learned was something no amount of theorising and forecast could prepare it for back home; the desert had to be the crucible. That Noble had gathered about him a basically strong, highly dedicated band was never in question. It was simply a matter of learning the hard way. And if there was something the team did to perfection it was learn from its mistakes. Where Gabelich himself had had to quell a near mutiny during his salt time with the Blue Flame, Noble's crew never looked remotely like quitting and the final decision to await a third chance in 1983 was the product of logical argument rather than any desire on individuals' behalfs to throw in the towel. As 1983 was to prove, it was a good thing they did retire to regroup.


In the months that followed the most important single question concerned the missing thrust, and it was a two-fold problem. *Was* the engine down on power, or was 17,000lbs of thrust, after all, insufficient for the job?

Watkins provided a few clues when we spoke in Bruno's the night before I left for home. A typical Forces character, he still smoked with almost surreptitious stealth, sneaking a quick drag before standing with arms behind his back and his cigarette hidden in the cup of one hand. He is a slightly cynical, almost dour individual, although the latter aspect is really only a cloak which is dropped once you pass a few of his stringent assessment tests. Then a mischievous sense of humour emerges, and from then on nobody's dignity is sacred. Above all, John knows jet engines in general, and the Avon in particular, inside out.

"One of the biggest problems, that has haunted us right through, is that we never knew just how much bloody thrust we *did* have", he began, banging a fist into his palm to stress the feeling of frustration he felt at being denied that vital piece of knowledge. "We had no baseline from which to make any comparison. After the cock-up at Greenham and all the work on the engine, there just wasn't time to get the thing on a load cell somewhere and measure the thrust before it was time to ship the bloody car to Bonneville. When we went down to Fallon all we could really do was establish why the reheat wasn't working and make sure we fixed that problem. We went in at such short notice and they were so busy in any case, that there was never any real chance of organising a load cell there, either. And really, we would have needed ten ground runs there to tweak the engine properly for the altitude.

"We knew, though, that the operating temperatures, the fuel flow and the rpm were within acceptable limits and, generally speaking, if that's the case the thrust figure should check out as well".

He leaned back in his chair, swilling a draught of beer and taking a quick drag before continuing his battle with the din in the smoky bar.

"In the whole time I've worked with Avons I've only ever known one out of literally thousands to be rejected for insufficient power". His eyes lit with humour as he fixed me with a meaningful glare and added dryly: "And although our engine is pretty damn old, I'd say it's bloody unlikely we've got number two!".

"So why wasn't there enough thrust?", I asked again.

"I don't think we were ever actually *down* on thrust. I think it was more a matter of what power we had was taking too long to make itself felt. Look, the ratios of air in a jet engine have to be stabilised before reheat will select. You've seen the car running and you know that Richard sits with one foot on the brake pedal as he winds up the engine on cold power, then takes his foot off and Thrust begins to roll forward. That's when he selects reheat and away we really go. Our problem has been that the reheat was often taking three or four seconds to select, especially on those last two runs. The runs are over quickly enough at the best of times, so a delay of four seconds robs you of a lot of acceleration and therefore top speed in the measured mile. . ."

Back in Britain the theory was developed further. When the engine was tested statically on cold power prior to reheat selection, its air pressure ratios would be balanced and the reheat functioned correctly. However, once Thrust 2 was in motion air crammed into its intake unbalanced the air/fuel ratios with the result that reheat could not immediately be selected. As video films of the runs revealed, the hotshot which ignites the fuel introduced into the tailpipe by the injectors, was working properly, but until the air/fuel ratio stabilised – it took anything up to nine seconds into a sixty second run – the reheat wouldn't operate efficiently.

Consideration was given to adopting a revised running technique, with Noble getting Thrust 2 fully underway on cold power before selecting reheat at a point at which the ratios would be stabilised, but that might prove something of a luxury that would depend entirely on the length of hard track that might eventually be available.


On other fronts there was cause for considerable optimism over the project's achievements. A lot of ballyhoo about the 615mph peak speed on the penultimate run tended to obscure the need to find at least another 40mph, as Ackroyd had pointed out to the meeting, but in some ways despite Noble's irritation the fallacy that Thrust 2 was within 7mph of the record helped convince some of his backers to stay aboard for just one last try. What complicated the issue was that he had always chosen Gabelich's 622.407mph mile record as the figure at which to aim, for that was the figure put out by the FIA and FISA. However, Gabelich also held the kilometre figure at 630.388mph. Where the same car and driver hold both marks FISA tends to choose that made over the greater distance as the outright record, mainly because that's how the land speed record began, but it wasn't difficult to foresee problems if Noble was to achieve a mile record that beat Gabelich's yet which fell short of his kilometre mark. To become the fastest man on earth officially in 1983, Noble had to set his sights firmly on anything above Gary's kilo record.

There were a lot of people, especially in the motor racing world, prepared to deny that Thrust 2 had any hope of such speed. The most popular criticism was that the shape of the nose intake was all wrong. A significant number of enthusiasts and quasi-experts around that time were sure the car would simply run into such a ball of air over 600mph that the intake would block and starve the engine.

The fallacy of that wasn't too hard to spot, for Thrust 2 had shown no sign of such a problem at 615 and was now easily the second fastest jet-engined car of all time and the third fastest car ever built. Arfons' Green Monster, on which Noble had based Thrust's concept, had set its last record at 576mph and been destroyed at a speed just over 600 in an accident attempting Breedlove's 600.601mph record set in November 1965. The Monster had used a large pointed probe in its intake to dispel any shockwaves, but though Ackroyd didn't feel one was necessary for Thrust it was encouraging to know that Arfons had survived with barely a scratch in the world's fastest land accident. It was also encouraging and comforting to know that thanks to Kluber and British Timken, Thrust 2 was unlikely to suffer the seized wheel bearing problem that had caused Arfons to crash. A new grease called Isoflex Topas NB52, based on products the former had developed for Concorde, guaranteed that each of the latter's bearings could be held at its maximum rotation for minutes on end without any sign of its temperature reaching danger limits. That sort of mechanical peace of mind was invaluable to driver and team alike, and the general manner in which the car had performed on the desert, engine problems apart, gave everyone concerned genuine faith and confidence for 1983. Once the low-speed yawing from Bonneville had been alleviated with the toe-in adjustments and the six inch wide front wheels, the car always ran with arrow truth, without the slightest hint of any aerodynamic instability.

Immediately after the final runs at Black Rock in 1982 Ackroyd had grabbed my arm and led me away from the group surrounding the car. As the sun set behind us we peered into the gloom that was slowly descending over the course. Despite the limited visibility Noble's wheeltracks were still very clear, stretching for miles to the distant horizon. As we walked a way down them John turned, a look of excitement on his face.

"You see what these tracks mean? See how shallow the ruts are? That spells low rolling drag because the car isn't grinding right into the surface, and that means there is less resistance to the car moving forward. They also say high stability. See how there are only small pockmarks in each track? That's the effect of the reheat blowing away the dust, and nothing to worry about. It's the same thing we found at Bonneville. You know, these tracks are actually straighter than the surveyor's course lines, and that's exactly what we're looking for. They show the car is safe and stable and that we can go on adding power to it and taking longer run-ups when the desert allows us to".

In stark contrast, Breedlove had admitted his Spirit of America – Sonic 1 was right at its limit at similar speed, even though it had originally been designed to go supersonic. Film shot during his time at Bonneville reveals how the front wheels had lifted clear of the salt on more than one occasion beyond 575mph as the venturi between the spats of the closely-spaced front wheels choked the airflow and broke down the downforce. When he made his record bid for 600 he actually had the angles of his car's front aerofoils altered between runs to provide the extra downforce necessary to keep the car from flying. In his auto-biography written with Bill Neely he admitted: "I got in the car and felt good. I knew this would be the last run in Sonic 1. It would never go any faster because we had reached the point beyond which all of the negative lift in the world wouldn't keep the car on the ground".

Breedlove had also run into a lot of trouble with high speeds buckling the bodywork and heat from the J79's afterburner causing further ripples, and he had been obliged to incorporate a whole series of drag inducing louvres to alleviate the problems. On Thrust 2 Ackroyd had cunningly devised simple cooling ducts comprising triangular openings alongside the cockpits which ran the full length of the Avon's reheat pipe, and the bodywork never developed the slightest hint of a ripple in its smoothly crafted surface.

While the machine had proved it had the basic potential to do its job, albeit with some improvements incorporated, the man had also proved a lot. By the end of the 1982 attempt Richard Noble's driving experience with Thrust 2 amounted still to less than an hour, as far as the car in its full record specification was concerned. Handing over the team management responsibilities to such a capable figure as Ken Norris had proved a major benefit and there was less worry about financial matters at first, although much of that relief was cancelled by the flooding at Bonneville and the need to locate and approve the Black Rock Desert before transferring to it. The battle with Charlie Watson was a further drag on emotional resources, yet he still thrived on the challenge. Because he drove Thrust 2 for longer and considerably faster than he had been able to at Bonneville there were naturally more opportunities for him to make errors and the overheated disc brake and prematurely deployed parachute episodes were to be expected, irritating though they were to the team. In truth, had it not been for the interruption and psychological blow of the Greenham accident, his driving errors would probably have raised much less caustic comment.

Quite the most extraordinary thing about his personal development was the manner in which he improved the faster he drove. When he had set up the project the driving had always been the very last factor to master, and there are those who criticise his road driving very heavily, but once he got into and beyond the 500mph bracket he obeyed his instructions from Ackroyd and Norris to the letter, and his eventual skill in deploying his parachute at exactly the right moment saved valuable minutes during the turnrounds.

"The technique is quite simply, really", he explained the day after our pow-wow in Bruno's. "The most dangerous part of any run is when I back off the throttle once I've completed the mile. It has to be done gently so Thrust is not destabilised. At that point I could deploy the main parachute, but that's been so effective with its 24,000lbs of drag and 6G deceleration that I'd stop far too quickly. Don't forget, if it was the first run of the day I'd have to begin the second from a predetermined point to get the right run-up and speed. Because the main 'chute is so effective I can inadvertently stop a long way short of the intended run two starting point, especially on faster runs when I get a lot of run-up distance.

"Once I come out of the mile I reduce engine speed to eighty five per cent for two point five seconds. The car is on tiptoes at this point with all the drag transferred up front. Then I cut the engine, watch the speed down to 500mph and pull 'chute one. That gives a deceleration of 4G. Then I use the wheelbrakes at 100mph to prevent the 'chute dragging. When we pull the 'chutes over 600mph I get at least 5G deceleration and that disturbs the inner ear because you are losing 100mph per second. It seems as if the world is tipping over!"

As he related his story his face became more animated, as if the schoolboy within was vying for control of his expression with the deadpan test pilot character he tended to adopt when describing his driving processes.

"Once we get the speed down to 400mph I just let the car roll and lose speed but once we get to around the ton I use the disc brakes to stop as close to the next starting point as possible to minimise the amount of towing we have to do".

The fact that he was prepared to undertake only two high-speed runs in a day did not meet with universal approval. I often got the impression Ackroyd, Norris and Chisnell would have been far happier with four or even six, for both engineers naturally wanted as much run data as possible, and Chisnell equally naturally wanted success as soon as possible. Noble, however, was adamant.

"The problem is one of mental tiredness. It's nothing physical, because at really high speed the car is beautifully behaved. No, it's just totally mental. Driving Thrust 2 down that course is just a very, very high pressure minute. It's absolutely knackering, believe me!"

By the time the final four 1982 runs were made everyone on the team was solidly behind him again; the early bickering had ceased and the Greenham spectre had finally been exorcised. As the threads of experience were slowly drawn together, the nucleus of the team that would reap success the following year, which had been forming slowly over the past years, was about to reach its final maturity. By the end of the attempt nobody doubted Noble's suitability nor his ability, and certainly his courage was beyond question. Chief engineer Gordon Flux summarised the team's views on the latter as we sat discussing the thrust problems with Watkins on the evening of the 4th. Bruno's bar was a seething mass of people and Gordo had to raise his soft voice at times to make himself heard. Every so often nerves were set jangling as Bruno indulged in his ever-unexpected trick of raising a beer bottle emptied after serving a customer, and smashing it mercilessly into a plastic container behind the bar already full of the fragments of bottles which had met a similar end. That rarely failed to create a hiatus in any conversation until heart and pulse rates settled once again.

"You know the amazing thing about Richard?", he asked as he leaned forward in his seat. "There he is, with less than one hour of driving experience on deserts, or on metal wheels, in a car worth a million pounds. And when we get to him at the end of one of the runs the other day, and raise the cockpit hatch, there he is calm as you like, filling in his run log. I mean, a man who's frightened of what he's doing doesn't sit there afterwards writing, does he?".


If the areas in which the car could be improved had been identified, and the driver could be said to be at his peak, the real problem facing the team continued to be the medium.

"Under better conditions we would have had a considerably better chance than we had today", Ackroyd had said guardedly during an American television interview after the final run. "If we had been able to run in much higher temperatures we would have had a better chance simply because letting the temperature go up postpones the point at which transonic drag builds up, and so lets your car go faster".

With higher temperatures and a longer run-up either end of the course, it seemed possible at the time that Thrust 2 might have had an outside chance of the record, but it was an academic argument since neither weather nor desert had improved. But as far as 1983 was concerned, the weather was going to be one of the real keys to significant progress. There was little chance of expanding the course at the southern end, as the road to Sulphur and Trego cut right across the desert just beyond mile zero and created a surface dip severe enough to act as the southern limit. However, if the southern end at least dried out fully, and the northern end was in slightly better shape, Noble might get his longer course. Much, however, would still depend on the Bureau of Land Management's verdict on the level of damage inflicted on the desert's surface by Thrust 2's metal wheels. The likelihood was that the winter rain would expunge any evidence, but nobody could be certain and the BLM was definitely holding the other key to any proposed new attempt at the venue. Furthermore, there was also the probability that Charlie Watson would regroup his forces to fight any new permit.

In the very first interview I did with Noble it became apparent very quickly just how much enjoyment he got out of the cockpit.

"It's not only the driving of the car, which of course is the ultimate thing, but also the apparent impossibility of building a high technology vehicle against all odds and on a minimal capital base, with a very small but very enthusiastic staff. It's been very addictive and, believe me, we all fight like hell to keep it going".

Now he was back in the role, chasing the support to keep his long-held dream alive. In 1974, when he'd first started, nobody had been interested, and one of the most sustaining things then had been the challenge of conversion. He called it taking on the impossible.

"You've got to change people's attitudes – a whole industry's attitudes – in order to pull it off", he had counselled. Now, with the 1982 achievements under his belt, the dream was much less impossible. As far as the money side was concerned, he was true to his word and immediately set about placating or encouraging his sponsors, depending on their level of understanding of the difficulties he had faced, and following up fresh avenues. The prospect of going over so much old, familiar ground all over again, when he had hoped to return in triumph, might have daunted a less resilient character, but to Noble it was all simply part of the game. You got knocked down, you just had to get right back up again. As he had said all those years before: "It was one hell of an uphill struggle to get people turned round, to get them to have a go at it. But I get a tremendous kick from working with a very small, very, very efficient and effective team. It's almost like a sort of David and Goliath thing. It's much more fun being part of a small team taking on the impossible, fighting endless battles with would-be sponsors. We've had situations where we've been back and back six, seven, eight, nine times with new suggestions, new ideas. Eventually it gets to the point where they say 'Richard, we never want to see you again' or 'For God's sake, we give up. How much do you want?'.

"And that really is terribly satisfying, it really is. But the thing with it is that you've got to progress all the time. It's a funny game, because you're not competing with anyone else. You're competing against yourself and therefore if anything you tend to be much more competitive".

The man who from the very start had observed the credo that his team should be a paragon of credibility, to the point where every evening after work for GKN was spent ensuring that letter writers received a reply by return post, most certainly wasn't going to be daunted or swayed from his ultimate goal by a few setbacks.

As soon as he had returned from America he had leapt back into the swing of things, for while in any case it is not in his nature to wait for things to happen, he knew how crucial the project's credibility was. Now, more than ever, he could not afford to pause at the crossroads at which he found himself. Instead, momentum had to be maintained at all costs. On the debit side of the balance sheet was the second failure; on the credit side was a nonetheless impressive list of achievements against the odds, real proof that nothing worthwhile is ever won easily. If Project Thrust had again failed to bring home the promised gold, Noble could at least hold his head up and explain exactly why without any fear that his team's dedication could be called into question.

There was further urgency in his actions, for the point in the year at which many companies allocate their budgets for the coming season had already long passed. And while there was little left in the kitty after the American campaign, overheads still had to be met. On the Isle of Wight Ackroyd and the fulltimers were already planning for 1983, and any delay now would translate directly into further delay when the 1983 project was supposed to be ready for action. Noble knew only too well the repercussions of delays that pushed land speed record attempts beyond the American summer and into the callous clutches of a hard Nevadan winter.

The second major feature report on a Project Thrust record attempt was published in *Motoring News* on Wednesday, December 15th 1982. The previous day, having received our office copies direct from the printers, I'd gone over to Richard's house in Twickenham with an armful, intent on making a point and some plain speaking. The front door was of the stable type, split into two halves. As the upper swung open in response to the bell Sally Noble stood in the doorway, a smile on her face.

"Talk of the devil! We'd just been discussing you".

I walked into the living room, and as her husband pumped fearfully on my hand she disappeared into the kitchen to make coffee. Noble grabbed a copy of the paper and as he eagerly swept through to the centrespread I steeled myself to be ruder than I wanted to be, rather as he had done in Gerlach earlier that year. He was back home now, and his usual affable self, but there were things that needed to be said and I made sure they were, heavily criticising his press relations. Throughout he nodded, his face registering the nearest thing to an abashed expression he can manage. Given his ebullient manner, it isn't much. Finally, he cut me short as Sally brought the coffee in and sat down beside him on the arm of the chair.

"You have a point; we're weak in that area. Just before you arrived Sally and I were discussing the problem and we've hit on an idea. How would you feel about handling that end of things for 1983?".

I asked him for a day or so to think it over, but by the time I'd gone fast enough to hit fifth gear going home I'd already made my decision.

# 10. Getting through the gate

Norris, his fawn raincoat flapping in the breeze, clapped both hands to his head. Ackroyd simply let the deafening roar wash over him. Elsom and Andrew Noble protected their ears with blue plastic defenders. A hundred yards away groups of spectators, huddled tight against a piercing wind, watched agog as the giant orange-red flame of Thrust 2's reheated Avon seared from the tailpipe.

It was a bitter cold Saturday, the 23rd of April 1983. For the first time since the previous November the jetcar was on display publicly, although this was ostensibly a private test session at Hurn Airport near Bournemouth, where once a visiting Arfons had gunned his Green Monster. The plan was to conduct a static engine trial. Thrust was looking more brutal than ever, its paint stripped back to bare aluminium save for the glass-fibre nose intake cowling. Devoid of its sponsors' identification and several of its access panels, it looked even more awesome, like some giant primeval beast.

Beneath its shell there were a lot of changes. As everyone had expected, Noble had finally been able to talk Rolls-Royce into readjusting the Avon 302 to provide more power, and Ackroyd talked of 3,000lbs more usable thrust. The attention of the famous engine manufacturer was crucial, and marked just how seriously the motor industry Establishment now took the project. Twice in the past it had turned him down flat; now for the first time since George Eyston's Thunderbolt in the thirties, the Crewe company had a vehicle capable of breaking the record with one of its powerplants.

From all of Thrust's previous runs Ackroyd had more than enough data to plot exactly how much drag it encountered, measured aerodynamically and in terms of its resistance to rolling. Once both types of drag build up there comes a point where the power required finally equals the power available, and that is when the vehicle ceases to accelerate and instead reaches its maximum speed. Considerations such as ambient temperature aside, he knew Thrust's 1982 thrust/drag ratio yielded a peak speed of 615mph on the eleven mile track on the Black Rock Desert, and his plan was straightforward.

"What we have set out to do this year is improve the thrust/drag ratio by boosting available power and by making the car even more slippery", he outlined during one of the quiet spells that morning.

Rolls had reset the angles of the inlet guide vanes, which duct air into the Avon's compressor and thus exert a considerable influence on its performance. At the new angles another 1,400lbs of thrust were said to be usable at the critical speed of 600mph and beyond, while work on the reheat system had realised another 1,600. The nozzles injecting raw fuel into the tailpipe, to ignite the unburnt oxygen in the exhaust gases, had been opened up and a brand new fuel system driven by a fueldraulic two-stage booster pump was incorporated to restore the fuel pressure and ensure that the engine's expected extra thirst for fuel could be satisfied. If all that meant the car could now produce its correct power output, Ackroyd had not been prepared to leave it at that. To reduce drag, and thus effectively give the car further usable power, he took a long look beneath the chassis and set about smoothing the underside.

"The problem is, the faster a car goes, the faster is the airflow beneath it", he explained. "When you're running at a venue such as the Black Rock Desert it is axiomatic that the air is going to be laden with dust, and that it will impinge on anything that gets in its path. And that is going to kick up the drag".

To alleviate the problem the entire floorpan had been removed so that the external stiffening ribs could be deleted. Instead they were incorporated inside the car, leaving the bottom completely smooth. Fairings had also been added to the suspension arms front and rear, and the openings in the front wheelbays, through which the wheels themselves protruded, had been reduced to a bare minimum. That way less dust would get in and less drag would be created.

While the prime objective had been to improve the performance envelope, he had also paid a lot of attention to improving the reliability and reducing the complexity of the onboard monitoring equipment. Previously the braking system had relied on an engine-driven pump, but because it was of much greater capacity than necessary it took some power from the engine. Due to its location it also required time-consuming priming before every run. Now in its place was a simple electric pump located beneath the reservoir tank, and the need for priming had been removed.

The twin fuel tanks were now linked through the boost pump, and to save time could be refuelled from one side only, while the sensors for the Revtel speedometer had been swapped for units of greater output to enhance speedometer and recorder response. At the same time a Plessey Doppler system of speed monitoring had been installed to provide a useful independent back-up.

To give more stability to the ride height settings new rubber springs had been fitted all round, and for the first time coil helper springs were fitted to one of the two front dampers on either side to relieve the static load the rubber had to bear and to prevent it sagging. There were other minor changes, and even a cursory glance down Ackroyd's list of improvements was sufficient to confirm that no stone had been left unturned in the search for positive benefits.

Once Thrust 2 had been rolled out of its temporary hangar that day at Hurn, it was towed across the airfield behind the Range Rover, followed by a vast thirty-car crocodile that seemed like Hampshire's answer to the Indianapolis parade. Well away from the main airport buildings, Thrust was tethered beneath giant apparatus used for static engine tests of jet airliners. Huge twin silencer cones are normally used to deaden the noise, but as Thrust sat lower than any aircraft they simply towered above, and its scream was to go unabated. Stout steel hawsers were used to shackle the car to iron rings set in concrete, and for the first time Ackroyd was able to use his latest toy – a pair of load cells provided by Davy McKee of Sheffield. These were bolted to the back of the car to provide the attachment point for the hawsers and for the very first time with the engine installed in the chassis, he would be able to measure precisely the amount of static thrust developed. The cells were exactly what the team had needed so sorely in America the previous year, and would again play a crucial role in the 1983 attempt. Had they been available in 1982 Ackroyd could have determined at Fallon exactly how much power the Avon was producing, and the situation would have been markedly less confusing and inconclusive.

In a series of tests. one aborted until a minor problem with a sticking throttle was rectified, Noble sat kitted up in the cockpit and ran the Avon to its maximum cold and reheat power. With the latter the spurting exhaust flame leaped for well over thirty feet, its dancing shockwaves and accompanying diamonds dazzling the eyes as raw power belched from the jet. Stout trees two hundred yards behind were bent like saplings in a hurricane under the seven and a half ton blast, eardrums were assaulted and large chunks of loose tarmac were spewed angrily into the distance. Visually it was an impressive experience, and though it was impossible to know whether it was better or worse than the last static run at Fallon, the load cells told a healthy story. Ackroyd and Norris didn't try to hide their delight.

"Naturally we can't achieve any drag measurements in a static test", began the former cautiously, "but we've been able to satisfy ourselves that the new fuel system, which we designed to boost our performance when we get into that tricky 600mph range, works every bit as well as we'd hoped. And those load cells are terrific! For the first time with Thrust 2 we know the static thrust with the engine mounted in the car rather than on the test bench. And that gives us such a valuable datum with which we can compare any figures we obtain in America when One-Take tunes the Avon to allow for difference in altitude".

That day the team left Hurn with its tail up, and Thrust headed off to a British Aerospace hangar to have its paint applied before Loynes went to work to apply the sponsors' signwriting. That lead to a confrontation with the two freelance painters sponsor Trimite had contracted to apply its specially formulated gold basecoat. The end result was a complete disaster, with runs, sags and overspray everywhere, as well as shade differences between panels and evidence of faulty preparation with dust beneath the final coat. When one of British Aerospace's experts saw the workmanship he was openly derisive.

"This paint'll stay on this car even if it goes 750mph", countered one sprayer aggressively.

"Then you must have a bloody funny idea of speed", retorted his critic. "Look".

With that he walked round to the passenger cockpit, over which airflow had gone supersonic on the fastest runs in 1982, and blew as hard as he could. The paint around the top of the screen began to lift. . .

In this pitiful state Thrust 2 was run at low speed at HMS Daedalus in Portsmouth so Plessey could calibrate its Doppler radar speedometer, and then Brian Ball rose to the occasion and arranged for his former colleagues at BA to strip the offending paint coats and begin again, this time with a proper etching primer and suitable pride. The car was due again at Daedalus shortly afterwards for publicity photographs and it was touch and go for a while whether or not it would make its deadline, but fortunately the British Aerospace boys did the business. Properly applied, Trimite's paint stayed on without the slightest problem, even at a subsequent Mach 1.4 over the screens, intake and wheelbays.


Working with Richard Noble proved, as I had expected, demanding, rewarding and eye opening. With motor racing teams I'd become used to blasé attitudes towards the sponsors who paid the bills, and several team owners in the sport talk as if the moneymen have absolutely no right to details of expenditure. With Noble things were different, and the sponsors were treated the way a business would treat its investors.

I was often asked by sceptical colleagues just how much he was making out of 'Project No Hope', as if he had committed himself to such a time-consuming venture simply for the financial rewards. John Cobb once said "If anyone tells you you can make money from record breaking, he is a liar", and from him that was quite a mouthful. I never did know all the monetary details, except that he was paid a salary by Thrust Cars like every other fulltime member, and that it was the same as Ackroyd's. Even if he broke the record there was no cash bonus scheme built in to his agreements with the eleven 1983 sponsors – Castrol, Champion, Fabergé, GKN, IMI Norgren Enots, Initial Services, Kluber, Loctite, Plessey, Trimite and Trust Securities. I asked him once about that idea, which seemed a reasonable suggestion given the risks he was taking, and his expression was almost comical, he looked so surprised.

"Good Lord, no. We're in this to get that record, not to make money".

Certainly, he had a very open and honest manner of dealing with sponsors. Throughout the early months of 1983 there were regular meetings to which all of them were invited to send representatives so they could all be kept fully appraised of the latest developments. Each meeting would take place at a different sponsor's premises and full information on budgets and expenditure, as well as technical and publicity progress, was freely divulged. It often seemed to me a lot of the points Noble had to justify to these men were things he really shouldn't have had to explain, yet he answered each one fully, and with, where necessary, logical argument. It certainly wasn't management by committee, for he was far too strong a personality to allow that, but there was no excuse for any sponsor to feel his company was getting a rough deal. As it had been right from the start, Project Thrust was run on exemplary business lines.

By May a tentative schedule had been circulated for a new attempt in July, and the welcome news had come through at last that the Bureau of Land Management saw no problem granting a fresh permit to use the desert. However, that right had not been won without another fight, as anticipated, with Charlie Watson and the Sierra Club conservationists. One of Thrust's strongest allies in this had been Bruno Selmi. At Gerlach in early May the BLM held a meeting attended by sixty four locals, and Watson. It showed a brief film and outlined Project Thrust's viewpoint, and then threw things open for discussion. It then became apparent that Watson had some strong political allies as he tried to exert power and legislation from high places, but Selmi too had done his homework, soliciting letters of encouragement and consent from luminaries such as US Senator Paul

Laxalt and Chic Hecht of the US Senate Committee on energy and natural resources. Nevada State Governor Richard H. Bryan was also enthusiastic, writing: 'I hope that the Black Rock Desert near Gerlach will be the site where you will realise a new land speed record'.

Charlie Watson's proved a lone voice of dissent, but his Right Wing manner so annoyed the locals, who felt he paid no heed at all to their interests or feelings, that many of them attended a second meeting, a 240 mile round trip away in Reno. There Watson was supported numerically by Glenn Miller and Roger and Margaret Schnell from the Toyabe Chapter of the Sierra Club, although there was no sign of any support from NORA. Most of the environmentalists were pleased to see the BLM's evidence that Project Thrust had left no negative impact on the desert, and readily acknowledged it had inflicted no damage. Their main concern was that wheeldriven cars weren't attracted to the region. When the meeting was put to the vote Watson went down again, the decision overwhelmingly in Project Thrust's favour.

On the 18th everyone was summoned to Daedalus so Charles Noble could shoot the official photographs for the forthcoming press conference, which thanks to the Society of Motor Manufacturers and Traders' generosity, was being held at its headquarters at Forbes House in Halkin Street, just off Hyde Park Corner. Since this was my show, and Project Thrust instilled a strong desire in everyone not to screw up, I'd done a belt and braces job. From initial talks with John Weinthal, then SMMT's Head of Press and Public Relations and someone I'd known for some time, the only aspect of the venue which caused any worry was the width of the entrance gates, as it was imperative we could display Thrust 2 in the semi-circular drive right outside the imposing building. Thrust 2 is eight feet four inches wide, and on its trailer closer to eight feet eight, and because it weighed four tons it was obviously going to be a lot easier if we could back the trailer up the drive and then offload, rather than having to unload in the street and push the jetcar into position. If I seemed distracted as John and I talked the first time we discussed details it was because I had to know exactly how wide the entrance was. He was cheerfully adamant it was wide enough, but despite his assurances I insisted we actually measure it. Thus we went out on hands and knees with a one-foot ruler and grovelled by the gates. John was right; it was exactly nine feet.

Come the big day I was still apprehensive, even though Andrew Noble had also cheerfully informed me beforehand that nine feet would be ample despite cramped access. We had to bend the odd one-way street sign to clear the Roadtrain's mirrors, and the Fruehauf's tyres took one hell of a lot of distortion in the tight manouevres, but thanks to Andy's skill and patience we were eventually able to squeeze through with little more than half an inch either side. . .


There was a sponsors' meeting at the SMMT immediately after the conference, and at last David Brinn was able to report that a long running dispute with the insurance company, relating to the 1982 attempt and subsequent claim, had been settled. The problem stemmed from the fact that the insurers deemed the November 4th runs as a record attempt, in which case they didn't feel bound to pay a sizeable claim figure since Thrust had only been insured against inability to make attempts for reasons such as bad weather, not inability to succeed in them. As Norris had pointed out at the final meeting, the team's insistence in carrying on after Bonneville's second flooding, had actually worked against it, even though such dogged persistence was way above the requirement of a due diligence clause in the policy. The insurers deemed his remarks at the meeting evidence that Thrust felt it had made an official attempt on the 4th, even though Ken's comments followed on from what was said at the November 3rd meeting, where it was agreed to go for the record on the 4th if the track had dried out enough to yield the extra mile necessary at the southern end. As it was the track hadn't dried out anything like enough and under FISA's rules November 4th's runs were far from a record attempt. The rule in question states: 'Until a run has been made in one direction at a speed which exceeds the existing record by one per cent or is at such a speed to make a second run technically possible for the record to be broken, then no attempt has been made'.

The settlement took the better part of seven months.

The day after the conference Thrust 2 went on display at the National Motor Museum at Beaulieu for a fortnight while the remainder of the vehicles and equipment were shipped to Los Angeles aboard the MV Columbia Star. Thrust would join them via Flying Tigers Jumbo in the middle of June with the rest of the team following a week later. By July 15th it was hoped the first runs would be made. When I wrote the newsletter copy to that effect I added a rider that the one thing we could be sure of was some dates changing because of the weather. What we didn't realise was just how much they would change.

Ackroyd spent literally weeks in Gerlach as the project's weather scout. All through the winter months Bev and Lena had kept Richard informed of the weather and the desert's condition, but for months after the winter snow melted the region remained under water, and when it finally began to recede the wait for the surface to dry to its full hardness became agonising. Week after week dragged by, with little positive news. And as each passed so came the dreadful suspicion that the 1983 attempt might actually be damned before it had even really begun. Incredibly, after the troublefree start to the year, the situation remained the same as July became August; it was still too damp to justify pressing the go button.

For John life in Gerlach and the surrounding countryside took on a special meaning in the lull before the storm, and with his easy style he blended fully into the society as he took the trouble to strengthen friendships from the previous year. He is the type with time for everyone. A cross between an urban cowboy, with a cowboy's restlessness, and a desert rat, with the latter's ability to merge in anywhere, he became captivated so much by the area he even spoke of staying on for a while once Thrust had achieved its goal.

Back in Britain it was easy to imagine the responsiblity on his shoulders getting heavier with the delay, for if he made the wrong decision, if he didn't second-guess the desert correctly and gave the go-ahead only to have the weather stand the team down again once everyone had arrived in Gerlach, he might single-handedly bring about another strung-out failure. He had to be certain conditions were right, yet daren't observe favourable signs too long without taking apposite action in case his delay wasted good weather.

In fact, the responsibility didn't bother him at all, and he later disclosed it was no different from deciding whether or not to run for the record on October 3rd or the 4th.

"I've never had a sleepless night through the project", he remarked. "I've never worried about a wheel falling off or anything like that. The only real problem I ever had was the cumulative effect of working under pressure for so long, particularly in 1982, which was the tiredness". He went on to explain why the responsibility had been no bother, and his reason wasn't at all what I'd expected from a  man who spent most of his life dealing with cold scientific facts.

"As the days went on I began to feel more and more remote. There was a time in Wendover when I went up into the hills and looked down over the salt flats, and I began to think just how insignificant man and his pursuits were. It put things in a different perspective, probably because as I looked down all I could see were little dots, not people.

"During those days waiting in Gerlach for the desert to dry I almost began to forget about the car we'd worked so hard on, waiting back home on the Island".

His study of the desert had yielded a fifteen mile track, a significant improvement on 1982, and it was nicely free of the inevitable humps and sinks. From the previous year he knew fifty feet was an adequate lane width and with sixteen lanes, sufficient to allow the desired number of test and record runs, the track itself measured eight hundred feet in width. Either side a quarter mile safety zone was allowed, and the entire grid was boundaried by the east and west service tracks. At the southern end the road to Sulphur and Trego still acted as the natural boundary, while to the north the limit was soft, damp mud. As in 1982, access was by one of two routes off State Highway Thirty Four, to the western side via Nobles' Trail to Soldier Meadow and the ninety degree right turn partway along which allowed access to the pits. These were again stationed along the west service track overlooking the measured mile. The latter was once again located in the middle of the course and when it became clear only thirteen miles of track would be dry enough, Noble was effectively left with a six mile run-up to the timing zone from either direction. That was a valuable mile each way better than the previous year.

One of the main problems with the course was a sump roughly halfway down. "When the winter snow finally melted and our proposed track was under water, this natural sump developed partway down and that's what has really created the major delay", said Ackroyd. "The rest of the desert was drying out quite nicely and the ambient temperature was just what we wanted, but that wretched section was far too damp to allow Thrust to run".

Finally by mid-August, a good five weeks later than planned, he felt confident at last and gave the rest of the team the green light. Suddenly, after the false alarms and weeks of waiting, all systems were go. Ackers' decision initiated Day One of a twenty six day countdown to Thrust 2's first scheduled runs, and in that time the course had to be surveyed fully and the six foot marker flags had to be erected at every mile interval. The entire track surface had again to be defodded and all team vehicles, equipment and personnel had to be transported to the site. A week after Day One rain spattered the desert, causing a few heart-stopping moments, but this time it was a minor storm which did the course little harm. Noble viewed it calmly without letting it bother him, his manner more relaxed and confident of success than ever.


In marked contrast to my last journey up State Highway Thirty Four, the drive up to Gerlach in early September was a snap. My hired Oldsmobile had the wings of a bird and the four of us in it – myself and my wife Trish, out for her first glimpse of Thrust 2 in action, Benton and Plessey's Simon Walmsley – were in high spirits. An orange sun boiled in the cloudless sky and it was one of those days on which it feels really good to be alive. As soon as we hit Empire we got a taste of the welcome we could expect.

'The British Are Coming!'

The signs were everywhere. A Union Jack and the Stars and Stripes, crossed on a pale blue background above that logo, greeted us the minute we stopped for supplies at the General Store, and when we parked at Gerlach and walked into Bruno's

Country Club old friends offered warm greetings in a touching display that made you swallow hard a couple of times. Bar one obvious sign of its new affluence, the town hadn't changed a bit. There was the level crossing guarding the entry to Main Street; Cecil's petrol station, in which Thrust 2 would this year be garaged; the Miners' Club; the general post office, which was a wooden affair with an ageing safe, a row of mail boxes and stacks of old American pulp magazines for those with time on their hands. There was the Mexican restaurant where the road begins to curve right on the way to Cedarville, and Norm's Cozy Corner shop. On one of its walls, in white paint brushed on so thick it had run in places, was the legend: 'Where the pavement ends and the west begins'. It was the truth. Less than twenty five miles further north the tarmac surface gives way to dirt for another thirty miles before the run into Cedarville.

Past Norm's were the hot pools, while on the opposite side of Main Street, tucked away on the curve, was the compound in which Dick West now lived with his girlfriend Leslie Weingartner and their mad Alsatian Brutus. In typical style Dick had invited us both to stay in his spare room, away from the inevitable hubbub of Bruno's Motel. The latter was the only part of Gerlach that had changed, for in front of the old building now stood a proud new block of rooms. Clearly the profits from Project Thrust's last visit had been ploughed straight back into the business.

By mid-afternoon we'd checked out the small room at the motel from which the on-site press and public relations would be run, and had a short briefing of the following day's schedule. That evening we dined at Bruno's and after a near ten month wait I savoured again one of his delicious clam chowders. That alone was worth the return visit. Meeting Bev again later at the Miners' was like seeing your favourite aunt after months of separation, and she couldn't have made Trish more welcome. When Whitey came rolling in 'schmuckered' for his usual game of pool it was as if we'd never been away.

We retired early to catch up on things with Dick and Leslie and shortly before turning in I read through the papers Eddie had distributed at the briefing. Mostly they covered rules for driving on the desert, and they'd been very carefully thought through. 'Richard's only guidelines are the tyre tracks left by the Jaguar along the course lanes', one section began. 'It is vital that no other tracks are left on the course, so do not drive on it'. The first part of the sentence was typed in capitals, as Ackroyd stressed the importance of letting Noble have as simple a course guide to follow at 630mph as possible. It reminded me how easy it was to lose all sense of direction out on the playa, and it made sense as much for one's own wellbeing as for Richard's. 'Stick to established roads where possible. If it is necessary to drive off the roads, do so very slowly and marks will be minimal. Approach roads at ninety degree angles so your tracks do not create diversions'. Far from just designing Thrust 2, John Ackroyd had also done a masterful job of designing so much of the infrastructure of the record attempt itself.

There were some further guidance notes, including one which forbade anyone to reverse up to the jetcar just in case the million pound streamliner was accidentally damaged, and all team members were advised to carry water and a torch aboard their cars. It was the note concerning preparations for solo trips which most caught my attention. 'Notify someone who can raise the alarm if you are not back within half an hour of your eta in Gerlach at the end of the day', it read. After the excitement of returning to the town it was a timely reminder that while the inhabitants were hospitality exemplified, the Black Rock Desert region itself could be a dangerous and unpredictable trap for the unwary.


On Friday, September 16th, Thrust 2 was taken out to the desert for the first time in the 1983 campaign and this was to be the first time it had turned a wheel for any real distance since its final run on November 4th the previous year. Besides the changes to the car, many other aspects were different. Most important was the weather, for now there was a healthy sun high in the lightly clouded Nevadan sky, and the forecast was for a relatively settled period over the coming week. The team, too, had changed, although the difference was one you had to look very closely to detect. By that day everyone of the thirty six members was a dyed-in-the-wool believer in the project and any doubts anyone might have harboured about Richard Noble's ability to drive Thrust 2 to a new record had been chased away months earlier. But there was also something else, detectable only in their bearing and the look in their eyes whenever we talked about success. All trace of the battle weariness from the previous November had gone, naturally, but these seasoned soldiers of speed had also lost their slightly guarded approach, the what-if-we-don't-make-it look. By 1983 the Thrust team looked like a bunch of winners, and their mien suggested they expected to be nothing else. It was quiet and it was very understated, and maybe it was only apparent if you knew what they had been like before, but in their heart everyone knew this was going to be the year. In the past Fate and Mother Nature had won most of the real battles, but this year Project Thrust radiated the warning that enough was enough. If Fate and Mother Nature chose to play dirty pool yet again – well, they had better just be prepared to step aside. . .

In true Thrust style, the crucial importance of the day was well masked by the external expressions on the faces of Noble, Ackroyd and Norris, but in its own way the day was going to be make or break, and they knew it. Just as they had done in 1982, they intended to tow Thrust behind Rover Dover to form an assessment of the load bearing strength of the worst section of track, between mile seven and mile eight. Ackers in particular pulled no punches as we stood talking while Thrust was unloaded. He had a faraway look on his face, and it was easy to guess the thoughts running through his head. If the surface proved to have inadequate bearing strength the jetcar couldn't run until it had dried out more.

"In retrospect we might find this test the most crucial point of the whole attempt", he remarked quietly, almost as if he was thinking aloud. "We've got to find out if the desert really is in good enough condition simply to let us make a run, let alone try for a record. It's like learning to walk before you can run properly. We've got to find out whether or not we can get through the gate first; never mind yet whether we can get through the barn door".

Watching his creation being towed behind the Range Rover also clearly upset him, and as we watched as Barrett accelerated gently up to speed with Thrust 2 a tow rope's length astern he muttered, again almost sotto voce: "This is the worst treatment we ever give the damn car".

He was right, too. According to the onboard monitors the car endured vertical accelerations of 0.5G when transported on its trailer, and that was not dissimilar to the towing process. During the record run itself the vertical acceleration, despite the speed, was only 0.1G!

For all his anxiety he needn't have worried. When I caught up with him again he was deep in conversation with Ken, and they both appeared relieved, even if Ken did begin with a frown.

"I'm not so happy with the high level of surface drag in the middle of the test section. That's certainly going to slow Richard at that point. But I think we've got a surface here that is at least hard enough to allow us to run the car, and it should give less drag once the sun begins to dry it out more".

Ackroyd nodded in agreement, before making the suggestion: "I think we might shift the measured mile a bit, Ken. It should give Richard a better chance if we shift it a mile south, at least for the initial series of powered runs".

They continued their discussion and I wandered over to check the depth of the car's ruts. They weren't too deep, although they were naturally a lot worse than those made when it was in action the previous November, but there was still a telltale build-up of mud on both the smooth front wheels and the ridged rears. A hump had been crested, though. The 1983 attempt could now move into its final phase. The inevitable flipside that always seemed to accompany good news for Thrust was that there was still no guarantee the full course would ever dry out sufficiently to yield a new record. Like Donald Campbell, Richard Noble was simply going to have to soldier on as best he could.


From the Canon Checklist booklets with which we had all been equipped, and from team briefings, we knew Ackroyd planned eight high-speed runs to capture the record. Now that the tow test had given the course the green light a wave of anticipation swept through Gerlach with the announcement that the following day would see the start of the powered run programme.

Run 1 was to be relatively simple. Ackroyd wanted to see

300mph as Thrust 2 entered the time trap, heading north with a three-quarter mile run-up, with a maximum speed of 375mph. The multi-purpose test would be used to prove the car's systems and establish a run routine, and was the only one intended to evaluate the low-speed 'triple ripple' cluster of three seven and a half foot diameter parachutes.

At six thirty that Saturday morning Bruno's dining room was alive with the clatter of cutlery and the rattle of coffee cups, and the speed with which people ate and the manner in which they spoke illustrated just how keen everyone was to get to grips with the desert for another round. Half an hour later the first vehicles in a lengthy convoy had started the fifteen mile trek to the starting point, the morning air crisp and chilly, the sky turning paler by the minute. Those mornings were always excrutiatingly beautiful as the orange ball that was the sun climbed slowly from the blue-misted horizon, and that one was one of the best.

As the sun rose higher the early chill was steadily chased away and when the Palouste was wound into action minutes before eight fifty the desert was a cool, tranquil backdrop to the human endeavour. The Avon fired perfectly amd moments later we were all choking in the gathering brown dust cloud and laughing with the sheer exhilaration as Noble and Thrust 2 vanished down the track. Compared to the previous year's cloud, this one seemed significantly larger, and as we rushed to our cars and headed north everyone felt that was a good omen, for it suggested the course was drier.

By the time we reached the point at which Thrust had been brought to rest, and sprinted the remainder of the transverse distance to Lane 1, Noble was out of the car and chortling with unconcealed pleasure. As further indication of his delight his gestures were becoming almost caricaturish again, a sure sign he was excited.

"That was really fantastic!", he was telling anyone within earshot. "She felt really tremendous. She's definitely got more power than last year, that's for sure, and she feels an awful lot more responsive. She's much crisper in response to the throttle".

Bud Moore, who'd been aloft in Air Plane through the run, had landed by then and came running over with a big grin on his face. He too seemed anxious to communicate with anybody who'd listen.

"Boy, he just left me for dead! Like I was painted to the flats! I felt so slow I damn near got out to see what was wrong!"

When the official speed came through it was greeted with whoops of delight. Noble had sped through the mile in a shade over nine seconds and his average speed was 394.477mph. There were times in the project's history when such speed would have been met with derision, but with a three-quarter mile run-up that was impressive and encouraging. Better still, the peak speed was 460mph, achieved in a mere twenty seven seconds.

As moves were made to prepare for Run 2 the wind, which had been sidling above USAC's safety limit, sprang more boldly to around 10mph, but with spirits sky-high there was little disappointment as we headed back to Gerlach. Just after lunch I solicited Ackroyd's view of the morning's success, and found him as ever several steps ahead of the obvious.

"It was a pretty important run", he began with his usual understatement. "And, yes, it was pretty promising, too. But I'm still worried about the state of the track. We're approaching another cliffhanger really, because the big question is going to be whether or not it'll dry enough to allow Thrust to plane over the surface, or whether she'll be forced to plough. That difference is going to be crucial to the attempt.

"As you know, Thrust 2 is designed to get up and plane on the keels of the rear wheels above 250mph, and she rises a little bit more over 550 too, but she won't be able to do that if the track is too soft, because all she'll do then is plough and increase her rolling resistance.

"What we really need to determine now is just how hard the track needs to be. We need to identify the threshold above which she'll plane and below which she'll plough". He paused for a moment, and again that preoccupied look came across his face.

"If we plane we could get the record. Because of the rolling drag, I'm just not sure we'll get it if we plough. . ."

The worries about the surface ran over into Sunday. The choice facing the team was quite straightforward. Either it could sit it out, waiting for the sump to dry fully yet wasting the benefits of reasonable weather or, as Ken put it, "We can suck it and see if we can do the job with the tools we have". Most tended towards the latter, especially as nobody was inclined to turn their backs on good weather when it was available. Besides that there were signs that other parts of the course were actually improved since 1982. Noble was adamant that the southern end was a major improvement, devoid of any bumps and nicely dry, and as proof of the latter the front wheels didn't pick up any mud as he was towed to his starting position on Run 1, while the keeled rears only picked up a light coating that could be wiped away with finger pressure.

The surface of the Black Rock Desert is well suited to metal-wheeled projectiles in many ways, and because of the manner in which its soft substrata behaves Ackroyd likened it to a giant Dunlopillo mattress. Thrust 2 has an inch and a half suspension movement, which is rare by land speed record car standards, yet its ride was further enhanced by the way in which the mud beneath the desert's crust acted as a suspension medium on its own.

By half past seven on Sunday morning the jetcar was back on the crumbly polygons, but it was positioned a mile and a half from the southern entrance to the timing traps. Just then the tranquility was destroyed as the wind gusted above 20mph. Reluctantly the decision was taken to load it back on its trailer and an hour later it was unloaded at the same position at the more placid northern end. As we drove to our position the wind was barely a murmur sufficient to flick the pink tape at the top of every service road marker pole, and even then only occasionally, but on this day the desert was again being playful. Literally as the Palouste was cranked over the wind picked up dramatically as it rolled up from the south, gusting on and off until eleven fifteen. As it continued to blow the length of the course, and showed no sign of abating, the day's activities were cancelled.

Long after that decision was taken – and it was a good thing it was long after – the desert was engulfed in a spectacular windstorm that brought a total whiteout to the course. As an illustration of what nature could do in that region it was a breathtaking warning. As a morale bruiser it was ineffectual.

The latter point was made abundantly clear at the day's debriefing, when every mention of wind brought forth a stream of childish *doubles entendres*.

To use Don MacGregor's expression, Project Thrust was once again caught in a hurry up and wait situation, one of the desert's favourite traps, but even the wind had a positive benefit for every gust went some way towards drying out the mid-course sump. At the meeting another positive emerged. Barrett noted that Thrust was slightly easier to tow behind Rover Dover and that the jetcar hadn't bedded in as much as it had the previous day. Perhaps, after all, the desert was actually trying to help.

# 11. The last cliffhangers

The wind continued until Monday, creating an ironic paradox. While the rest of the conditions were perfect, Thrust 2 was unable to run because of the 10mph gusts. The day, however, was not wasted. A different kind of record was set before the sun faded behind the mountains.

Had any of Noble's potential rivals – Craig Breedlove, Gary Gabelich or Sammy Miller – arrived on the desert that afternoon it's highly likely they would have left bemused yet relieved, for what they would have seen might well have convinced them the British had either been out in the sun too long or were less than serious about their task.

The Project Thrust team was making a film of Ron Benton – setting a new record for portable toilets.

The moment the idea had been mooted, to provide a spot of humour to while away the downtime, it was picked up on by so many imaginative and agile minds that by the time the team had assembled on the desert creativity was running high. It really was the most extraordinary scene, which had those Americans present, and who felt they were getting to know the British, scratching their heads and wondering why on earth they went so crazy every so often.

The star, of course, was Benton. As Ackroyd had once remarked, Ron was fated to become involved in Project Thrust. His list of accomplishments during an outstanding career as a master craftsman included the design of the first hovercraft with Sir Christopher Cockerill, for which he still claims he did not receive his due credit or recognition. His standard of workmanship is the highest and he can turn his hand to working any material. While he was frequently the butt of jokes about his motorcycling days at Brooklands racetrack, he was no slouch when it came to the witty rejoinder. On one occasion, as we sat lazily sunning ourselves on the verandah of Bruno's Motel, we discussed the building of the famous concrete oval track in 1907, and a part Ron's father played in the effort. Brian Ball interrupted with the quip: "I suppose you were there as well, weren't you Ron?".

Without batting an eyelid Benton, who celebrated his 67th birthday during the campaign, slipped out the response: "I was there in liquid form", and the group cracked up.

When Ron 'Liquid Form' Benton stepped on to the desert that Monday yet another of his talents became evident. He was dressed as ever in his blue Thrust overalls, but now somebody had wound him a scarf of white toilet paper and he had borrowed Charles Noble's brown leather flying helmet and a pair of goggles. He looked for all the world like George Eyston, about to attempt the land speed record at Bonneville in the late thirties. Had Eyston's giant eight-wheeled Thunderbolt suddenly rolled on to the scene few would have been surprised.

One of the hired portable toilets had been lashed to a small trailer hitched to the track team's red Dodge pick-up, and as Benton revealed just what an accomplished ham actor he can be, he was piped aboard his missile by Barrett and Andrew Noble, yet again employing their chukka calls and sink plungers. Mere moments later the mobile restroom sped on its way across the desert. In less than ten minutes Benton had achieved his goal: 56.477mph for the mile, 57.070 for the kilometre. The times and speeds were official averages, recorded and ratified by USAC. What Petrali and his boys thought was never really made clear.

As the hilarious charade continued, Benton emerged from his capsule to wave his arms aloft in triumph, as his colleagues doubled up with helpless laughter. Rob Widdows of TVS stepped forward with his microphone. Why had he done it?

"It's like mountains, you know", replied Ron in his slightly wistful tones. "They just happen to be there".

And future ambitions? The question brought a serious look to his face as he replied, deadpan: "I should like to break the sound barrier. . ."

His sheer aplomb had grown men wriggling with laughter,

and tears flooding. Noble, daughter Genny perched atop his shoulders, laughed loudest of them all.

In previous years such a juvenile exploit would have been unthinkable, but in its way it was just another further indication of the underlying confidence that September. Any team that could horse around like that either lacked any kind of serious approach to the job of record breaking, or else was so serious it knew it could afford to because every variable within its control was indeed under it. Project Thrust fell straight into the latter category, and the following day underlined it.

As we clambered into warm clothing to fight off the dawn chill, and struggled over to Bruno's for breakfast at the ungodly hour of five o'clock, all of Gerlach echoed to the rattling of screen doors as the wind ripped up Main Street. Another day lost to the elements? It certainly seemed likely. There was no haste as we ate, as if everyone had mentally detuned themselves. Talk, while necessarily limited at that time of day, centred on Benton's bravado and the post-run realisation that there were few of the five hundred inhabitants of Gerlach and Empire that he didn't seem to know personally. That, and how likely it was the wind was even stronger out on the desert.

John Norris and Ian Robinson, who was at that time working for the National Motor Museum at Beaulieu, were in charge of track maintenance. In high winds it was their unenviable task to brave desert conditions and roll up the flags which marked each mile of the course, to prevent them acting as sails and being torn away altogether. That morning they had gone out as usual to check them, and returned breathlessly with the news that the desert was as still as a morgue. Whatever the wind was doing in Gerlach, it wasn't repeating a few miles north.

The scramble to get out to the desert was rapid but controlled and as we stood beating our circulation into action, Richard wore one of his heartiest grins. As Thrust 2 went through its unloading process he danced gently from foot to foot, his breath visible as it clouded his face.

"This temperature is absolutely ideal. It's great for the air, you know. It lets the old engine breathe much better because it's denser, and that means more power. And visibility down the course is much better. Just the thing for this type of run".

He was less pleased when the timing apparatus suffered a temporary glitch as a result of the previous day's wind, but just after eight he was ready to go and the wind was still non-existent. Then, anti-climactically, the Avon's deep rumble ceased and the stillness that descended was broken only by the distinctive rattle of its compressor blades as they windmilled to a halt. The throttle pedal was operating stiffly, and Noble had aborted the start. Ten minutes later the problem was eradicated and the start-up recommenced, and when Run 2 finally got under way it was a good one. With one and a half miles run-up he peaked at 570mph after only thirty six seconds and whisked a mile average of 488.465mph, with the kilo at a faster still 503.020. The third run called for double the run-up distance, and seemed better still. This time Noble averaged a whopping 588.712mph for the mile, with 580.870 for the kilo, figures almost as good as the runs from November 4th, but with much less run-up. The only drama came when he pressed his 'chute button only once, instead of the recommended twice, and the 'chute failed to deploy. What might have presented a moment at Bonneville, with its restricted space either end of the course, translated into nothing more than a minor irritation at Black Rock, Thrust 2 simply running on further before rolling drag and Noble's foot on the brake pedal brought it to a gentle halt. It was a minor driving error which nobody criticised, mindful that the previous year the driver had been rebuked for firing his 'chute mortars prematurely.

On the face of it, significant progress had been made, for on a mere three runs Thrust 2 had achieved what it had taken thirteen to accomplish the previous year. But something in Ackroyd's manner alerted my suspicions, and before long it transpired all was not what it seemed on the surface, as was so often the case with Project Thrust. Many times it was like an iceberg; what you saw on the surface was really only thirty or so per cent of what was really going on. Despite the doubled run-up on Run 3 the peak speed was only 590mph, a mere 20 better than Run 2's. Its peak was also close enough to the run's average to suggest that the engine settings already needed further adjustment for the desert's altitude. With John Watkins on site that would have been little problem. However, recent promotion had kept him back at RAF Binbrook and prevented him joining the team until the 24th at the earliest. His absence was to have a significant effect, and by the time he eventually flew out to Gerlach the project would have reached crisis point.

Despite the temperature's beneficial effect, Noble had complained of disorientation at times during the day's two runs, and that afternoon Norris and Robinson doubled up the flags at the entry to the measured mile. That began at mile six, and as the flags also bore the same number the timed zone thereafter was nicknamed Route 66.

At the evening debriefing Ken paid due tribute to John and Ian's diligence. When they had taken their initial wind readings at the southernmost part of the track the result had suggested the course would be unusable. However, they had persisted and taken measurements at the northern end as well, with the discovery that it was calm enough. Without that, two solid runs wouldn't have been possible. Ken made a further point.

"We've learned a good lesson today. We've learned that we can get a run even when we don't expect to, so it's absolutely vital we are ready to capitalise on any breaks we get. We're in the same position as we were last year. We've got to find our window in the weather and, just as important, we've got to recognise it when it comes and take fullest advantage of it".

Once again Wednesday's dawn saw perfect weather conditions out on the desert, and once again there was to be an early delay. This time a parachute mortar electrical lead required soldering, and electrician Gordon Biles was despatched from his position with Start Team 2 at the southern end. Nobody knew it then, but Gordie was to perform a simiiar, even more desperate rescue dash on the day of the record itself.

Biles' work brought a wide grin to Ackroyd's face as he sprinted back to his own start position, close to Elsom in the Control car. "That's whack-a-moled another little sucker," he laughed with relish, referring to a mole hunting video game that had captivated team members the previous year in Reno. "I just wonder what the next one's going to be?". It wouldn't be long before he got his answer.

As Noble rumbled off down the course on Run 4 there was no sign of the familiar reheat flame, and its blast as the dust cloud obscured progress down the course suggested it was only establishing intermittently. With presence of mind Noble let the car roll to a halt without deploying the parachute and without completing the full distance. That saved Barrett the task of repacking the 'chute and towing the car further than necessary, and as Richard fired Thrust 2 and cruised it down to its starting position for a fresh run at the southern end Ackroyd suggested that the reheat had failed to establish properly because the Avon had not been fully stabilised on take-off. "The engine reached only ninety nine per cent instead of its normal one oh two. She should be alright this time".

She was, but Thrust 2 had now reached a stage where its performance was like the curate's egg: good in parts. It looked a really good run, although the optical warp created partly by the heat haze and partly by having to observe from a vantage point at least a quarter mile from the action, always meant that accurate visual judgements of the car's speed were impossible. This time Noble had started at the harder southern end of the course, and he achieved his best speeds ever. The kilometre yielded 606.215mph, but even better was the mile figure: 608.416, from a four and a half mile run-up. For the record runs it was planned to use a six mile run-up, so the air of optimism that greeted the figures was understandable. Once again Thrust 2 had peaked over 600mph, matching its previous best of 615 and this time reaching that figure in a dazzling forty nine seconds. Noble had simply to repeat the performance on his second run to erase Breedlove's 600.601mph mark as the all-time record for jet-powered cars.

The FIA regulations stipulate that a record is only officially broken if it is exceeded by a margin of one per cent. That meant Noble had to average better than 606.607mph for his two runs. As we made our calculations during the turnround that didn't seem too much to ask, given the way in which car and driver seemed to be performing and the added bonus for Run 6 of an extra half mile run-up.

When Thrust 2 rolled to a halt after that run, and the dust cloud kicked up by its passage still hung along the course, the tension within the pits area was almost tangible. Every second dragged by with the slothfulness of a cinema interval, and as figures huddled round the radio set in Brinn's car the atmosphere was alleviated only by Mimi Noble's insistence that Genny lie down on a colourful plastic mat to act as her baby.

When the speeds were finally made public they brought a moment of numbed silence, and disappointment. 604.534mph for the mile, 602.297 for the kilometre. Fractions of a mile an hour slower than required. The irony was that though Noble had averaged 606.469mph for the mile, 6mph faster than the jetcar record, it wasn't quite fast enough to satisfy the one per cent rule. In cold terms it was a gut-wrenching 0.138mph too slow. Any disappointment Richard felt was not evident in his face as he stood by the car, now bathed in warm sunshine as the day drew on.

"It's no problem", he offered with a nonchalant shrug. "No problem at all. We'll get it tomorrow".


The meeting later that day was to echo that sentiment, as Ackroyd and Norris put forward possible answers to the only question that mattered: Why had Run 6 been slower than Run 5, even with a half mile longer run-up?

"It's possible", advanced John, "that Richard either lifted off a fraction too soon as he left the mile, so that Thrust was slowing before she cleared the exit flags, or maybe he deployed the parachute a fraction of a second too soon".

Noble accepted the possibility with equanimity, admitting: "It's possible I popped the 'chute one point one seconds too soon".

It seemed the most logical reason for the disappointment, and it was an answer of sorts. Only later would events prove that he hadn't in fact made any such error, and that something far more serious was lurking in the background.


Even though Thrust 2 could not claim the jetcar record, it was beginning to move into territory uncharted by any other turbojet-powered land vehicle, and by the day as that happened the technical side of the attempt became ever more fascinating. The further the car probed the transonic speed range, the more important became several factors. The most significant now was the effect of ambient temperature. As Noble had observed, when the air is denser a jet engine breathes better and therefore develops more thrust. While there is a mechanical advantage, however, there is an aerodynamic penalty, for with the thicker air there is greater drag. When the ambient temperature is higher the engine breathes less efficiently but the speed of sound – Mach 1 – is also higher. That means the transonic barrier occurs higher up the speed range so the velocity-sapping effects of its drag have less impact at the sort of speeds Project Thrust sought. Ackroyd and Noble had always been aware of this, and from September 21st, now that Thrust was running over 600mph, considered changing their tack. They planned to abandon the early morning runs in favour of seeking the hottest part of the day. Opinions as to when this change should be made were divided, as some felt power was more important than drag at that stage, but as events were to prove Ackroyd's desire to "catch the sun and forget the cold" was timed about right.

Another complication was revealed at the meeting, and centred on the effect of air being rammed into Thrust's intake at such high speeds. From the onboard telemetry equipment Ackroyd produced a graph of the Avon's power curve, which revealed a drop in thrust around the 600mph mark and a further boost due to this ram effect closer to 620. With a peak of 617 on Run 6 it was felt Thrust 2 might just have failed to reach the threshold at which ram effect contributed the extra boost. With the full six mile run-up, it was hypothesised, the situation might change with significant effect.

To give an added edge to the evening, current record holder Gabelich arrived in Gerlach shortly after the meeting ended. Before long he began telling Ackroyd and Noble about his plans for a new car, effectively to be a Mark Two version of the Blue Flame. I'd met him earlier in the year during the Long Beach GP meeting, and at that time he'd seemed tired and on the verge of calling it a day for his project. Now, as news of the British going over 600mph reached him, he had decided it was time to check them out. His old enthusiasm had clearly returned, and like Breedlove who would come to Gerlach later, he seemed genuinely eager that his record should be broken. It reminded me of what his father had said in Bonneville two years earlier.

At one stage in his career, after setting the land speed record, he had nearly lost his left hand in a dragster accident; that night however, the left-handed Californian proved he had lost none of his dexterity as he and his friend Van beat the pants off Noble and Tremayne in an Anglo-American game of pool at the Miners'.

The following day he was on the desert to witness firsthand what the competition could achieve. To provide a datum with the previous day's runs it was decided the first run should be made around the same time, rather than at the hotter period, so once again everyone gathered early in Bruno's. Out on the desert Gabelich took up position at the timing stand with his old friend Petrali, wondering perhaps if his reign as the Fastest Man on Earth was nearing its end after thirteen years. At the northern end, with the elastic stretched back to its six mile maximum, Thrust 2 was positioned ready to catapult down the dusty course, but twice it refused to start. On the third attempt it finally blasted away, only to falter within seconds. Barrett was despatched to tow it back, and as the Range Rover and its strange partner edged north at a steady pace his voice across the airwaves brought some levity. "We're doing a staggering 25mph Richard. Are you okay with the G forces or shall I slow down a bit?"

It was past ten before Thrust finally began its southward charge, and already concern was mounting as there were visible signs of bad weather moving in over Gerlach. Even as Noble sped down the course a brief rain shower fell at the southern base, and with the bad news that was to follow it somehow seemed apposite that the desert had finally exhausted its new-found patience. Privately Noble complained that the engine seemed to lack thrust, and the speeds were again disappointing: 607.903mph in the mile, 602.459 in the kilometre. Today's best was actually a fraction slower than yesterday's, despite the extra half mile run-up. The subtle suggestion from the previous day that the team was in trouble, had now sprung boldly into the open.

At the southern end crowds gathered round Noble and Thrust, but the manner was casual. Even those to whom the run looked fast could sense the mood. To a team chasing ultimates, calloused by all the previous runs, Run 7 had been bad news. As Ackroyd and his crew conferred, Gabelich sauntered across the see Thrust 2 in close-up for the first time. There was a spring in his step.

"Nice run, Rich. Nice run".

Noble, for once, was curt and dismissive. "Not really, Gary. We could have done it a hell of a sight better".

This time there was no emphasis on the word hell, as there usually is when he wants to put his point over forcefully. Instead he was almost deadpan. Given the slow speed and the fact that the idea of a second run had clearly been abandoned, my ears pricked up when I heard his comment and the manner in which he made it. It spelled trouble. A few minutes later he called me over and we convened a quick press conference on the desert, there and then. That in itself was unusual, and wasn't something that could wholly be accounted for by the presence of several important television crews, including the BBC outfit fronted by Martin Bell. Richard sketched out a few notes and paced gently from foot to foot as he read the prepared statement.

"We have got a problem", he disclosed, pausing very slightly between each word as if anxious to check what he actually revealed. "Basically, that run was only two miles an hour better than yesterday. . . We have aborted our run today. We don't think we have a serious problem but we are hoping our engine specialist John Watkins will be able to come out very shortly".

How much that bald statement represented only the tip of the iceberg was to become apparent later that day. At that moment, however, I showed Gary round Thrust 2 and took photographs for him of him standing alongside it with his friends Van and Ida, a likeable middle-aged couple. Gary's wife Rae was expecting their first child and hadn't made the trip. Outwardly he seemed quite impressed by what he saw, although like Richard I got the impression he thought the car had gone as fast as it ever would.

As Noble left for Gerlach and what turned out to be a crisis meeting with Ackroyd and Norris, the film crews turned their attention to Gary as he strolled round Thrust. "Nice car", he offered. "This is the first time I've seen it. No, I don't think I'd change much – except to make it left-hand drive!".

Showman that he was, he rose to the occasion and as the rest of the team left the desert he was threatening to turn the whole situation into a personal commercial. Despite that, I liked him a lot. He was a straightforward dragster of the old school, and he'd proved he had what it took countless times. Within four months he would be dead, killed when his motorcycle collided with a truck in Los Angeles in January 1984. Gary wasn't wearing a helmet and died immediately. It seemed a sad, stupid way for that kind of man to go.

That afternoon, in an irritating drizzle, we ran Birgit Ackroyd up to the General Store in Empire for supplies. At the level crossing on our return we met Hearn and Noble in Mike's Range Rover. He flashed his lights and as we drew alongside it became obvious from Noble's expression that something was very wrong.

"Dave, we've got a major problem on our hands. We think we need a new engine and we've got to start setting things in motion right away. We need you back at the office".

A new engine? At this stage of the project? What the hell had gone wrong? The news brought a wave of alarm, for almost certainly a new engine really meant the end of Project Thrust. I didn't doubt Richard's ability to conjure one up from somewhere, even after the trouble he'd experienced after Greenham in 1982, nor did I doubt the team's ability to get it transported to Gerlach and installed in Thrust 2. But the chances of doing all that before the weather closed in for the winter looked distinctly remote. We were all very quiet and thoughtful as we drove back to the press office.

There, Noble outlined the situation. On the desert he had glibly given out a story of fuel feed troubles, and had theorised that the engine's governor was preventing it running as it should. Now as we crammed into the small room, he lay his cards on the table. He and John believed the engine had possibly surged and sustained crippling internal damage. Our immediate task was to get some expert help into Gerlach any way we could, and that meant two things. It was no longer merely desirable to have

Watkins on site; it was crucial to the chances of success. More, Noble wanted Rolls-Royce to send out a representative as well. Thus we began to exert some subtle pressure. As Noble set about contacting Watkins and Rolls-Royce again, I began preparing a series of 'situation critical' press releases which were transmitted by facsimile machine to our London press office for distribution. As I worked I gathered from Richard's conversations that the damage really might be as serious as feared.

When a jet engine surges the reason is usually that it inhales more air than the compressor blades can handle at that moment. It gulps in more than it can digest. It's a bit like drinking too much. Excessive pressure is created in the rearmost section of the compressor – the Avon has a fifteen-stage system – until, like electricity, the air seeks the easiest escape route. Then the engine behaves like the unhappy drunk and vomits its excesses. Along the way it has a nasty habit of inflicting severe damage on the compressor blades and thereby wrecking the engine.

On Run 7 Thrust 2 had accelerated beautifully up to 580mph, but had hiccoughed once, recovered after losing about 20mph, then hiccoughed again in the middle of the measured mile. It had recovered a second time but by then the exhaust temperature was up to 1,000 degrees, way above the advised maximum of between 840 and 850, and that had finally caused the engine to flame-out, or extinguish itself.

The bottom line at the end of that day was that  testing, shipping and installing a new engine – assuming that one could be located in the first place – would take a minimum of two weeks. That was more than enough to set the project right back to the point where ambient temperatures remained low enough even during the hottest part of the day to jeopardise any record chance. It was the worst day of the 1983 campaign, without doubt. In retrospect, it was probably the worst day of any of Project Thrust's three American sorties.


The telephone calls to Britain went on all afternoon and well into the night, further complicated by the eight hour time difference. Gordon Flux conducted as much inspection as practicable without dismantling the engine, and Noble relayed his findings to Watkins or Rolls. During the course of the conversations Rolls revealed it had altered the angles of the inlet guide vanes to an Avon 301's settings in search of more thrust, but though that was known to present a slightly higher risk of surge its technicians were confident it had not been the cause of the apparent problem. Watkins actually felt that, though the engine might have surged, it might have sustained less damage than feared. As the day drew to a close he held out the hope that it might still be possible to continue with the trusty 302, and advised how best it might be inspected.

The following day thus saw Flux's portly form inserted head--first into the jetpipe, as Gordo clutched a powerful torch. He was looking specifically for any sign of aluminium spatter, which would indicate surge damage, but he found none. Similar deft probing with the torch down the inlet guide vanes revealed no sign of damage, and everyone began to breath the first of several tentative sighs of relief.

For all that, Project Thrust was still not clear of the wilderness, but Noble's continual cajoling had won him what he wanted. Watkins finally rolled into Gerlach on October 24th, while Rolls-Royce's man from Atlanta, George Webb, had arrived the day before. The situation was interesting. At times in 1981 and '82 the outspoken Watkins had felt his advice ignored as he was overruled by Ackroyd and Noble, and quite how he would react to the belt and braces approach of having two engine specialists on site remained to be seen. Rightly, he came into his own. Webb was an equally outspoken Lancastrian, and the two hit it off together immediately. George fitted into the project as if a berth had permanently been on hold for him, and by Monday, September 26th, both were convinced the engine was in basically good health. Instead of running over the cliff, Project Thrust was still just gripping the edge with its fingertips.

Avon engines are used in all kinds of dynamic and static applications throughout the world, and Webb has seen an awful lot of them. Like Watkins, he knows them inside out and, again like John, he has a very dry sense of humour. "I've seen these babies surge and literally blow away three inch thick doors", he grinned, with deliberate pause for effect. "I think you can safely say you'd have known all about it if this one had surged".

So what had gone wrong during the fateful Run 7? The hot theory was a combination of fuel starvation and a weak mixture, but during an inspection another crucial discovery was made. The reheat selector would only operate to two-thirds of its full movement. That hadn't manifested itself when the engine was on winter test at Rolls-Royce as the incorrectly adjusted quadrant was a fitting on the car. Suddenly, it became apparent just where all the missing 1982 thrust had gone and why Thrust 2 had appeared to reach a 608mph performance plateau in 1983. It looked as if the reasons for the hiccoughs, the flame-out and the mysterious lack of thrust had finally, individually, been identified.

With the engine once again given the green light, Watkins and Webb advised a static test at Reno. Right at the start of the 1983 attempt the Air National Guard had allowed the team to test and readjust the Avon for altitude at Reno Airport, and on the Monday the car was returned there and again shackled to the ground. One of Webb's suggestions was to reduce engine temperature by washing out the compressor, and as the engine was spun with the ignition off a water jet was played into the intake. In the course of a long day the inlet guide vanes were put back to 302 specification and their ram was purged, the reheat selector and nozzles were reset, and the unit was tweaked to operate at 104 rather than 102 per cent. By sunset the diamonds were again dancing and the Avon was bellowing in rude health. The load cells revealed 14,400lbs of thrust. Corrected for the desert's 4,000ft altitude that was 16,800lbs. That would rise above 17,000 with ram effect and, at last, it seemed the power really was there. All that was needed now was suitable weather.

We certainly didn't get it that night. With no specific roles to play at the static test, Trish, Birgit and I left the team to it halfway through and went shopping in Reno. The day started fine but as the night closed in and we headed up State Highway Thirty Four it began raining heavily. The windscreen wipers on the Olds were pretty useless and our visibility problems were compounded when the already weak headlights began cutting out intermittently. The first rain spots hit us with forty miles to go but by 27 Mile Rock, which is twenty seven miles from Empire and thirty four from Gerlach, the storm had us fully in its sights. As we ran into Empire a car headed towards us and I sensed shadows in front of its headlights. Fortunately, one of those sixth sense messages made me ease up, which was fortunate as we came across a herd of beef steers standing right in the middle of the road, lapping rain water from the puddles. We made it round them and made Gerlach safely, but Arley Osborn was less lucky as he followed us in an hour later. A Chevrolet Impala is a pretty large chunk of iron, but the front end was wrecked when he ran right into one of the hapless animals. He was lucky to escape injury as it smashed his screen, while the Hearns also had a lucky escape when they had a less damaging brush.

The rain continued well into the night but abated with the dawn and we stood by, ready for a fourteen thirty roll-out. Progress was better than expected and by two the vanguard departed. The storm had missed the desert, but as if to correct its oversight we met the first parties returning as we headed out. The rain had transferred itself to the playa after all and we were placed on forty eight hour standown.

In such a small town, finding ways to keep oneself amused during such periods was part of the trick of staying sane. That Tuesday evening, shortly before dusk, Dick and Leslie introduced us to the pleasures of rattlesnake hunting as we toured the dirt road that lead eventually to Sutcliffe on the shores of Pyramid Lake. Packed into Dick's blue Ford pick-up we went in search of the reptiles. Contrary to what I'd always believed when walking the crown of the road at night, the snakes actually make for that very spot to seek the extra warmth. They'd always been enough to give me a healthy phobia, but with six thousand square miles of Washoe County to patrol Dick couldn't afford to be squeamish and had perfected a neat beheading trick with a five foot hoe. Our headlights didn't pick out any prey that night, to our secret relief, but when we returned home Leslie mentioned there was a headless snake in the garage. It was one Dick had killed earlier, and if either of us felt like skinning it we should feel free. Eventually I decided my fear might best be tackled by doing just that and sauntered casually out to have a go before anyone realised and came to watch. The reptile was softening in a bucket of salt water and I was just about to hoist it out when I noticed to my horror it was still moving, four hours after its death...

The rattler has a hyperactive nervous system and even when beheaded its natural reaction upon being picked up is to wrap itself around your wrist as its headless neck stabs at your forearm. No sooner had I got over that shock to my nervous system than local trapper Tony Diebold told us another skin-creeping snake tale. He is one of those gentle giants, six feet four and no broader than a Peterbilt, and takes photographs of outstanding beauty and feeling for *National Geographic Magazine*. While out with his dog one winter morning, he killed two rattlers, beheaded them, and dumped the bodies in the back of his pick-up. As he drove home the sun broke through the clouds and, sensing his dog cringing in terror beside him as it looked out the cab's rear window, he turned to see two headless reptiles peering in as their necks strained towards the sun's warmth!

Despite the setbacks, and certainly following the positive results of the Reno tests, spirits remained high during the lull, but the next spot of mayhem in Gerlach was caused not by any team member but by the Deputy Sheriff himself. Over dinner at Bruno's on the Wednesday night things got a little out of hand as Trish fired a water pistol at unsuspecting victims while I captured their reaction on film, and eventually everyone transferred to the Miners'. There, Dick produced *his* water pistol and began putting a skill honed to perfection with a Magnum .38 to less deadly effect by taking random potshots. Before long a drenched Noble had grabbed one of the guns and within seconds a full-scale shoot-out was raging. It was childish behaviour that took its toll on Bev's floor, but though it was soaked by the time the last victim stumbled out the door to tell anyone who would listen that the Deputy Sheriff had just shot him, she didn't bat an eyelid.


By Thursday morning the weather forecast was getting better, with only a twenty per cent chance of thunder and showers. In fact, we'd been quite remarkably lucky, for the majority of the rain had fallen away from the desert, and Ken remarked: "We aren't ready for the mops, squeegies and buckets just yet". The forty eight hour standown became twenty four and a thin ray of light began to grow brighter as the forecast beyond the current unsettled weather was for better conditions. As we convoyed out to the desert that day for another run few felt we had had reached Record Day, but there was no denying the sense of gathering climax. Within the week or so, it would surely be make or break.

Again, with a cool day in prospect, things started early, and by seven fifty six Noble was all set for Run 8 when the timekeepers advised a delay as the wind gusted to 7mph. Within ten minutes it had dropped as suddenly as it had sprung up and once again the giant car launched itself down the course, its ever-more muted thunder and the huge roostertail signalling its passage. The instant it departed Ackroyd paused, petrified, listening minutely to the engine's note. The reheat was behaving itself perfectly.

This time the speeds were much more impressive, and as MacGregor informed us Richard had managed 622.837mph through the mile and 622.927 for the kilo we all felt a spurt of elation, and everyone began avoiding one another's eyes in case the hope that lurked there became too obvious. Maybe, after everything, the record was suddenly going to fall into our lap when we least expected it.

Noble had started his run at the softer north end five and a half miles away from the timing traps, and had just recorded Thrust 2's best ever speed. Its average through the mile had improved by a mammoth 14mph. It began to look as if the jetcar and the outright records might just fall in one swoop. As we had experienced so many times before, our feeling of elation rose in direct proportion to the speeds, but the faster Thrust 2 went and the closer Richard came to the record, the more acutely we felt any disappointment. Gradually the sixty minutes dawdled past before he started his return run, but once again there was a cruel anti-climax. Once again the engine failed to stabilise properly and reheat wouldn't select. Noble aborted the run early and any further passes were cancelled for the day. We knew he would have been lucky to have broken the record that day, despite matching Gabelich's two-way figure, for to beat it by one per cent he would have had to average 635mph on his way back. That seemed unlikely in the circumstances, even given the start at the harder southern end, but the human mind is not always rational in such situations. Everyone was again subdued as we returned to base, frustrated at how difficult it all had to be. But nothing worthwhile is ever won without sacrifice and clearly Noble, like all the others, was going to have to fight for his record right down to the wire. On the desert that day I had asked him the one question I never thought he would answer direct.

"What will you do if you fail this year? Will you try again?".

And he had looked down the course, with his hands in the pockets of his black overalls, and had kicked a toe against a polygon until it crumbled into dust. "No, it's this year or never", he had replied quietly. "If we fail at least I can say I had a go. . ."

It was the nearest he ever came to admitting the possibility of defeat.


The meeting that day threw up several interesting points, and as usual good was balanced by bad. As the problem of stabilising the Avon was debated, Ackroyd finally propounded a theory that seemed to provide the elusive answer. Leaning back in his seat, twiddling the end of his ever-present pencil and rolling it around the table top, he outlined his thoughts.

"What we feel is happening is that under the fierce 5G deceleration Richard experiences when he deploys the parachutes, fuel in each tank is slopped violently forward and drains away from the pick-ups. Consequently they gulp air into the system and the resulting aerated fuel prevents the engine running properly.

"The root of the problem lies in our high fuel consumption during a run and the way the fuel flows from each tank. We know definitely that the starboard tank doesn't drain as fast as the port, for example. What we've got to do is come up with a system that stabilises the flow and balances it".

At one stage Noble suggested using the electric pump for a predetermined period on each run, but since that would mean him removing a hand from the steering wheel at a crucial point it was rejected. Instead, Mike Hearn suggested incorporating an automatic timer to balance the flows. It was quickly adopted.

Noble himself seemed delighted with the day's progress. "That last run was absolutely fabulous! Terrific! The most incredible thing was the way I could actually see the shockwaves over the front wings. They were real opaque waves! And because the cockpit seal is much better this year I'm not suffering that dreadful ear-popping problem that was so painful in 1982".

He looked fresh and relaxed, and with the driver performing so well each time out the focus of attention was tending now to turn on John Ackroyd. The driver was doing his stuff, but could the car?

Inevitably, some of the old queries about the air intake design began to crop up again. Should it really have had a centrebody to smooth airflow in the transonic range? If so, what were the chances of modifying the car on site? Several people I'd talked to believed the car would hit a brick wall at 600mph, and as we studied the peak from Run 8 it seemed they might after all have a point. While the average through the mile had been 622.837mph, the peak had only been similar, possibly indicating that Thrust 2 had finally reached the point at which it had stopped accelerating.

With the high rolling drag – Ackroyd once calculated the surface drag at 14,000lbs was twice what it had been at Bonneville in 1981 – anything that reduced Thrust's frontal area was worth considering. Thus while the automatic timer was fitted that afternoon after the meeting, and an access hatch was cut in the bonnet cowling so the fuel system could be bled between runs to enable the car to make its back-up passes, the old four inch wide front wheels from Bonneville were dusted off and bolted on.

"I designed the six inch wide wheels for Bonneville, for our 1982 attempt", said Ackers. "When we were rained off and came here we simply kept them on and have used them ever since. We don't have any data on how they compare to the fours on this surface, so tomorrow we're going to make a relatively low-speed test run to try them out and to see if our new fuel system device works. I feel we might find an advantage in their smaller cross-sectional area".

As a backdrop to all this technical drama, something infinitely more worrying was occupying Noble's mind. Thrust Cars Ltd was officially due to cease operating on September 30th, and all the arrangements with the eleven sponsors ran only to that day. Urgent talks were taking place with them all in the hope that they would inject the extra £20,000 needed for a final week of effort. Earlier in the year, at one of the many meetings held with sponsors, an agreement had tentatively been reached whereby if it seemed likely the record might fall just after the 30th a contingency fund would be made available on a pro rata basis. By the 22nd a best of 608mph looked unlikely to secure that extra budget, but the 623mph clocking from the 29th went some way to manipulating the purse strings.

On the 30th, on the sixth lane of the sixteen lane track, the crucial test run was carried out. The overnight rain had made much of the surface soft and claggy, but despite that Noble reached 485mph in twenty seven seconds. This time it was Craig Breedlove, intending to return with his own rocket contender, who was in town to watch, and he seemed more impressed with the car than had Gabelich. As far as drag reduction was concerned, Noble's expression as he climbed from the cockpit after the run told an immediately negative story.

"All the old Bonneville stability problems came back immediately", he reported in matter of fact tone. "You wouldn't believe the difference the six inch wheels make".

One possible avenue of salvation had been closed, but the run did have a positive benefit as the automatic timer had worked perfectly. If Thrust 2 was to have any chance of the record it was vital it could make its return run within the allotted sixty minutes. Now that the timer had proved itself it seemed Project Thrust had moved at least one step closer to its goal.

When it came to the problem of gaining a significant improvement in its maximum speed, Ackroyd still had some aces up his sleeve. The most important was the ambient temperature and its effect on transonic drag, and he produced some figures to explain why. From the standard charts he knew that at 43 degrees F, the temperature at which Thrust 2 had reached 623mph on the 29th, the speed of sound was 747mph. By dividing the higher speed into the lower he was able to calculate the vehicle's Mach number as 0.834. That represented the percentage of the speed of sound it could obtain. From the standard charts he could then calculate its expected speed for given temperatures. Thus a temperature of 53 degrees F would yield a speed of 629mph, 63 degrees 636, 73 degrees 643 and 83 degrees 649, or a maximum potential speed gain of 26mph purely through changes in temperature. He was quick to point out that the full benefits of temperature would not be realised since the thrust would drop slightly with the increase in the ambient reading while rolling drag remained constant, but his meaning was clear. In its present state, with its 16,800lbs of thrust and the desert surface the way it was, Thrust 2 would need much better weather if it was to stand a chance of success.

He wasn't prepared to rely on the weather, however. He'd lived in Gerlach too long for that. Instead, he launched an investigation into the design of the intake, just as a precaution to determine that its shape *was* correct, and he had Barrett make up small shockwave deflectors which took the form of small triangular wedges mounted on the underside of the chassis just ahead of the front wheels. Brian Ball, meanwhile, was given the unenviable task of lying flat on his back beneath the car, polishing its aluminium floorpan to a mirror finish to reduce drag to a minimum. Watkins was delegated to give the reheat fuel control a thorough checkover, and to make any necessary adjustments.

The final mechanical ace was possible only because of Thrust 2's basic soundness of design. Up to and including the 623mph run it had run at zero angle of incidence, in which condition there was a total downforce on the front wheels of 6,360lbs. 5,760 of that was dead weight, the remaining 600 being aerodynamically induced. Now, after very careful calculation, he decided to reduce the weight on the front, and hence the rolling resistance of the wheels, by running the car at an angle of attack that gave 0.17 degrees of nose-up incidence. When Thrust 2 had first been run at Bonneville the rear end's ride height had been higher than the front's and during subsequent test runs up until October 1983 Ackroyd's efforts had concentrated on reducing the amount of downforce that was generated by altering the suspension ride heights. Eventually the car had been run with them equal; now his proposal meant for the first time that the front would be fractionally higher off the ground than the rear.

Thus a maximum downforce of 1,200lbs at 450mph would become zero at 600 and at a peak of 650 Thrust 2 would have

2,040lbs of positive lift at the front. That meant the static weight on the front wheels would be reduced from 5,760lbs at maximum speed to 3,720. With parts of the Black Rock Desert course still soft and flaky anything that might reduce the car's tendency to plough and encourage it to plane was going to assume vital importance. Though the underside of Thrust 2 is virtually flat until it tapers up towards the diffuser just ahead of the rear wheels, it was still able to creat fantastic downforce through ground effect due to the large area and the speeds involved. As air squeezed beneath the chassis it was restricted by the low ground clearance and a venturi effect was created as the air was forced to accelerate. Through Benoulli's law its pressure thus became lower than that acting on the top surface of the car and that pressure differential was how the downforce was created.

Ackroyd explained that the transition from downforce to positive lift was created by the increasing strength of the shock-waves emanating from the front wheels damming the airflow beneath the car once it exceeded 600mph, and partly breaking down the venturi effect. Despite the deliberate reduction in loading on the front wheels, he was confident there would be no risk of Thrust 2 flipping over backwards.

Not surprisingly, the plan gave Noble some cause for concern, and we all knew from Breedlove's experiences what could happen if the front end of a land speed record contender developed too much lift over 600mph. John, however, always put safety first and pointed to the 3,720lbs of static weight which helped to keep Thrust's wheels in contact with the track. By contrast, Breedlove's Spirit of America – Sonic 1 had had appreciably less than 1,000lbs of either aerodynamic or static weight acting on its front wheels when he set his last record.

By Saturday, October 1st, fifteen days after Thrust's first 1983 run on the desert, it was ready again for action, but the course was still too damp after a rainstorm through Friday had left parts of it in poor shape. Further rain that day ensured that while the Man and the Machine were ready to face their final challenge, the Medium wasn't.

In the afternoon Ken Norris continued his calculation for what he hoped might prove the final ace: a new course. His potential new track was located to the west of Ackroyd's, ran almost parallel, and looked at first as if it might yield up to eleven miles of hard, dry mud. The opportunity of such a surface was too good to pass up so on that warm, dry Sunday several small groups were deployed at various sections, checking out the surface and plotting humps and depressions. Trish and I spent many hours in our allocated region, our hopes raised as it seemed suitably devoid of troughs. In fact, the northern end of Ken's projected 'four lane yellowtop' looked really quite promising, but when we got back to base there was disappointing news. Richard and Eddie had come up with an ingenious means of grinding away any bumps but the overall verdict was unfavourable. The southern end was too bumpy and the work involved to render it fit would have taken too long. There was a feeling we had been wasting our time seeking the proverbial needle in that great polygonned haystack, but any and every avenue that might lead to the record had to be assessed and explored.

Once the proposed new track was abandoned once and for all, we began to reassess the condition of Ackers' sixteen lane course, and for once the prognosis looked favourable. Using his California Load Bearing Ratio machine – a spearlike device which he pressed into the track in order to assess the strength of its resistance and which Trish referred to as Ken's prodometer – Norris was able to determine that the majority of the course was in virtually the same condition as it had been for the 623mph run. On Monday October 3rd the weather forecast suggested ambient temperatures in the mid sixties for the following day, with the possibility of high winds later in the week. The news was met with a sense of growing anticipation which was heightened when the decision was taken later in the day to make a run on the Tuesday. Nobody had to be told it was likely to be the all-out attempt.

It wasn't just the weather that looked like running out. That Monday Thrust seemed to have three chances left: Tuesday, Wednesday and Thursday. With seven of the course's sixteen lanes still intact, that left sufficient track for three and a half attempts, given two tracks per attempt.

By that Monday, Richard also knew exactly where he stood in the Money stakes, for Fabergé had finally confirmed it did not intend to extend its sponsorship beyond September 30th.

However, seven of his sponsors sensed imminent success and when they all agreed to provide enough for one final week Castrol, Champion, GKN, Initial Services, Loctite, Plessey and Trimite were immediately dubbed the Magnificent Seven.

With finances severely limited and the weather running out, everyone knew the coming week represented the final challenge, the last big push to the top of the nine-year mountain. It would be now, or it would be never. And the gut feeling suggested that when – if – that window in the weather finally opened, it would only be for a very brief period. . .

# 12. The one-day window

There was electricity in the air the following morning. Even as I shaved hastily the golden glow of the sun filtered through the crinkled glass of the bathroom window. It was a delicious feeling, as satisfying as being able to sneak an extra few minutes in bed after waking up too early. No one felt like lazing about, though. In Bruno's, where animated conversations were backed by the slip-slop of the waitresses' soft slippers on the linoleum floor, the atmosphere was edged with excitement but not tension. It was a curious contrast to similar mornings earlier in the project, as if everyone knew in their heart that Tuesday, October 4th 1983 was at last going to be The Day.

Most were far too keyed up to eat much, but deep inside there lurked the most incredible feeling of certainty. After all the setbacks that had been strewn in the team's path, I for one had this inner conviction that Fate was finally going to play ball. Months later, while we were indulging in some nostalgia, it transpired Ackroyd felt the same way, and shared the same feelings about Fate.

"I felt Project Thrust was fated to get the record all along", he confided, and I was surprised such a practical man should believe in that sort of philosophy. "Just look back at all the stages we've been through. When we built Thrust 2 I was just thinking I knew nothing about that jet engine when Tony Meston literally walked in. Then when we were worrying about the electrical system Tony suggested his friend Geoff Smee. Fate was apparent in all manner of things.

"Look at the way Rolls-Royce refused to tweak the engine for 1981 and 1982. What a good job they didn't, because there's no way we were ready for that until the final year. Fate really was very kind to us, although it often didn't seem so at first glance. It even gave us good excuses for packing up in 1981 and 1982, and we really did need three years to lick ourselves into shape. I always looked on the previous two attempts as test runs, and we'd never have been able to persuade any sponsors to back a three-year programme if we'd known at the outset just how long it would take".

At eight o'clock Norris convened a post-breakfast meeting in Bruno's back room. He looked fresh and confident, his open white shirt collar exposing a sun-browned throat and making him look very young and boyish. He was at pains to portray the exact situation as he addressed team members, to make sure nobody dressed things up in any way.

"I reckon today could be what we're looking for", he began. "The weather is excellent – with no wind – but the track is only reasonable. It's certainly not as good as we'd like. I'd say it's up to the 623mph condition, but it doesn't seem likely it will get any better. . ."

The previous day Ackroyd had echoed Ken's original sentiments about the Black Rock Desert, with one important qualification that had become apparent the more the 1983 campaign progressed.

"It's the best site in every way bar its softness. That really is going to be the key. Our biggest problem here is that the rolling drag is just so high compared to Bonneville – probably double – and that's not just because the desert is damp in places or too flaky. Unfortunately it depends to some extent on the very make-up of the basic alkali, and that's something we'll just have to live with".

What delighted both, however, was the ambient temperature, and for once the forecast had been pessimistic. It seemed likely even at that time of the day that temperatures in the seventies might be possible later on, and Ackroyd lost no time in stressing the importance of that to the meeting.

"If we get, say, 73 degrees, that would add 20mph to our Mach number – not necessarily to Thrust 2's top speed – and that could make all the difference. As you know we are also now running positive incidence on the car and, frankly, I think we're erring on the side of caution. But we are doing it safely, and that's what counts. Our front wheel spats are in position and Brian has polished the bottom of the car so much I don't think we need any thrust!"

He also outlined the contingency plan whereby Watkins would bleed the fuel system on the electric pump during the turnround, as a belt and braces operation to back the automatic timer. Project Thrust was taking no chances, bearing in mind the speeds Noble sought. If he was going to exceed the record in one direction, everything would be geared to making certain he could complete his all-important second run within the time allotted.

Noble himself had missed the early part of the meeting. At Chisnell's suggestion he had been given the luxury of breakfast in bed, although everyone tried hard to ignore the parallel of the condemned man eating a hearty meal. Predictably, he didn't stay there long, and when he sauntered into the meeting he looked bouncy and relaxed and more than ready to realise his long-held ambition.

By two forty five everyone was in position on the desert, and no-one could believe the conditions. There was zero wind, and the ambient temperature was sidling gently up by the minute and sitting happily in the low seventies. It was more than we had dared hope, and the omen simply added strength to the conviction that the record would fall. After so long the final pieces of the jigsaw were falling into their designated places.

Thrust 2 would start Run 9 at the flakier north end, saving its better chance for the second pass. I'd taken a party of Fleet Street's Los Angeles-based reporters up to the start position and patiently we basted ourselves under scorching sun as Sally, Ninetta Hearn and Trish played with Miranda and Genevieve, neither child in the slightest bit aware of the enormity of the task facing their father, nor of the strain their mother must have felt. Occasionally Mimi would wave her Union Jack, and Genny would quickly, if uncertainly, follow suit.

A quarter mile away Noble sat, fully kitted in his black Panotex flameproof driving suit and Cromwell jet pilot's helmet, broiling in the sweltering heat of the jetcar. Quietly, methodically, he worked through his routine checklist. Already he had checked some thirty four separate external points on a list prepared by Ackroyd. Now he checked first that the 'chute switch caps were in position, all switches were off, the high pressure fuel cocks were closed, that his radio to helmet connection was secure, and that his seat harness was properly buckled and tightened. Then he checked the instruments and flicked on the master switch before taking the reading on the voltmeter and registering the contents of each fuel tank. Next he checked the speedometer and the test lamps in the power packs, tested the lamps in the brake pressure monitoring system and ensured that the reheat nozzle position indicated closed. He followed that with a radio check, armed the fire extinguishers, tested the system's electrical circuit and connected his air hose to his helmet and switched on the breathing apparatus. When he received confirmation that the primary and secondary 'chute mortars had been armed he removed the 'chute switch caps and stored them in a special cockpit pouch to prevent them rattling round during a run. He then awaited clearance to signal to start the Palouste and, in turn, the Avon.

So far he had performed another twenty tasks, with a similar number to follow before he began his run. Next he started the stopwatch mounted on the dashboard directly ahead of his wheel-mounted main parachute switch. As soon as the Start Team indicated the Palouste's rpm and jetpipe temperature were satisfactory he pushed the start button to set the Avon rotating and at ten per cent of its revs opened the HP fuel cock before carefully monitoring the jetpipe temperature to make sure it stayed below 850 degrees. When the Avon reached twenty per cent he released the start button, watched that the oil light went out at thirty four and let the engine run up to its forty per cent idle. Once it had stabilised at that figure he checked the jetpipe temperature had fallen to 550 degrees and switched off the electric fuel pump. He then reached across to open the low pressure reheat fuel cock, ensured the brake pressure maximum light was on as he held Thrust 2 stationary on its wheel brakes, and then signalled to the Start Team to disconnect the Palouste before awaiting confirmation that the panel had been replaced over its connection socket. That was when the cockpit hatch was finally shut.

As we watched what we could of the procedure for Run 9, the closing of that gullwing canopy brought to mind the paradox of land speed record breaking. As an undertaking it requires enormous support from skilled personnel, yet it is ultimately one of the loneliest challenges a man can face. Breedlove told me: "If you're not a little bit scared of this thing, you're not dealing with it from a full deck", and made no bones of the fact that unless a man *really* wants the record, no amount of money will ever persuade him to keep his foot right on the floor once that canopy closes. As Noble received the final double thumbs-up from Gordon Flux, he was already far away, out beyond the pale. Whatever our individual roles, we had all done our bits and now it was up to him alone to face the real challenge, to take the risk, to determine whether or not the great dream would be realised. Or, if that was what Fate decreed, to die. The latter was a sobering thought.

This day, however, this vital day when conditions were so perfect, there was a problem. Once, twice, the jetcar refused to fire. A blown banger fuse in the ignition system was diagnosed and for the second time that year a desperate call was put out for Gordon Biles to dash from the southern end to the north to administer electrical first aid. We could only watch and wait, and it was not until three nineteen that Flux's voice came over the radio to explain that the fuse had been replaced. Even then there was a further delay as Gordon sped back to his position with Start Team 2, and by now the tension was right out in the open, taking over from the calm air of confidence that had pervaded breakfast.

In the cockpit Noble maintained his calm, worked through the starting procedure again, received the all-clear from Start Team 1, and saw the canopy close again. Flicking on his recorder he then took the Avon up to ninety per cent, took his foot off the brakes and pushed the power to a full one hundred and four per cent with reheat as Elsom made his now classic announcement into the radio: "Speedy One is rolling".

As Thrust 2 rolled forward to blast into its high-speed run, observers were left to protect their eardrums as best they could, and to choke in the orange-brown roostertail of dust. With almost 34,000bhp pushing it forward and acceleration of 2G, the four-ton projectile was up to 180mph within four seconds. Inside it, Noble made gentle corrections to curb its initial tendency to wander below the 300 to 400mph speeds at which the aerodynamics began to control its straightline running. As he moved towards 590, and Thrust's critical Mach number, airflow over the top of the screens went supersonic, the tops of the wheelarches following suit 20mph up the speed scale. As this happened his mental processes had long been working four to five times faster than normal. He reported that everything occurred in slow motion, to the point where he could actually detect the minutest course detail as the track slammed towards him before disappearing beneath the car, where the airflow was also way over the speed of sound. Over 600mph he found he could steer with uncanny accuracy, although he was surprised that he needed twenty degree movements of the wheel at times as he drove delicately with fingertips rather than clenched knuckles.

As usual it was totally impossible to gauge the speed with any kind of accuracy, especially as we'd watched from the start of the run, but we were gripped with excitement as we ran pell-mell for our cars and convoyed back to the pits. There virtually everyone in Gerlach and Empire – and several friends from Reno as well – had congregated to hear the news. For agonising minutes we had to endure the wait before the speeds finally came through. 624.241mph in the mile, 626.240 in the kilo.

It was a sickening feeling, like being punched in the stomach, even when it transpired the peak had been 632. All that effort. All that hope. For a miserable two extra miles an hour! In the pits the news raised a cheer, but the speed was so far beneath a one per cent improvement it seemed unlikely the back-up run could possibly be fast enough to bridge the deficit. The sense of anti-climax was incredible.

What nobody knew then was just how bad the rolling drag had been at the friable northern end, though, and as Noble embarked on Run 10 well within his allotted sixty minutes, another bonus developed as the ambient temperature eased up another three degrees to seventy five. Thanks to the harder southern end a longer run-up was available. Where Noble had started Run 9 five and a half miles from the timing traps, Ackroyd had really stretched the elastic to breaking point for

10, giving Thrust 2 six and one eighth miles. The differences were to prove crucial.

As the dust cloud and the distant rumble signalled Noble's return, necks craned and binoculars were screwed into eye sockets. As usual the optic warp played some strange tricks. Way across the playa it seemed as if the car was riding on water and heading up towards the mountains on the east side, but the closer it got to the measured distance the less twisted the image became until it could be seen clearly, thrusting over the polygons, running straight as a die.

"Pedal to the metal, Richard!"

"Go for it!"

"C,mon, babe!"

The exhortations rang out across the desert, willing Noble and Thrust 2 on to higher speeds, and such was the level of excitement it didn't even register that the car had safely reached the northern end. Through every run, in fact, one never consciously worried about the possibility of an accident, only how fast the car had gone. Like most of the other team members, I somehow always felt the tightrope walker would make it to the other side.

What Don MacGregor actually said when his voice drawled on to the airwaves was: "The speed is, for the mile, 642.971mph – it's a new record. Congratulations!" But all anyone in the pits heard was "Six-four-two" before the remainder of his words were ripped away in screams of relief and elation. 642mph was so *strong*, so far above Run 9's speeds, that the fine details didn't matter for that split second. Whatever, the 622.407mph two-way average for the mile was surely history. As it transpired, Thrust 2 had hit 642.971mph in the mile and 642.051 in the kilometre, peaking at 650.88mph, a hair over its design figure. The average for the mile, the new land speed record, was 633.468mph.

The kilometre average was also better than Gabelich's 630.388mph mark, at 634.051, but that wasn't quite enough to improve it by one per cent. It was something which began to worry me a lot, but at that moment we were all concerned more with getting up to the northern end to join in the celebrations. We were prevented by the decision to try for a 'best of three', and despite the elation Start Team 1 performed a superb turnround to send Noble back on a third run, north to south, in the hope that the higher temperature might yield a fractional increase on Run 9's figures to boost the new record even higher and capture the kilo. Thrust 2 had to be towed out of the ruts it made slowing down on the flaky northern end, however, and three times during the run into a headwind that had just sprung up, he tramlined into Norris' guiding wheeltracks. He was tired and had always shunned the idea of more than two runs in a day, and in any case he knew psychologically that he'd already done enough on the previous runs. Run 11's speeds were much slower, with 620.555mph through the mile even with six and a half miles of run-up. It wasn't important. After Run 10 Richard Noble had uttered a two-word Anglo-Saxon expletive of sheer relief and now the team he had built up unceremoniously grabbed him and hoisted him shoulder-high. Somebody initiated a chorus of 'For he's a jolly good fellow', as only the British can, and as Noble whooped and hurrahed Ackroyd shook the champagne bottle that had been brought along in readiness, before squirting its contents over him. He got one jot square in the eye, but nothing could faze him as he waved the Union Jack aloft. The new speedking had been crowned.

"Thank you everybody! *Thank* you!", was all he could exclaim initially as the photographers moved in to pose everybody for team pictures.

"Was it worth it, Richard?" asked Rob Widdows.

"Good God, yes. But it's only just beginning to sink in what we've done!"

As the sun began to set on the yellow-brown mud, throwing long shadows across the crumbly polygons, Thrust 2 sat impassively, like a giant animal awaiting affection after exemplary behaviour. I was reminded of the time I'd walked the salt at Bonneville. For once the car, so often the focus of attention, was now left alone. Only its driver, it seemed, was important now. I patted its gold flank and as I took a last delicious whiff of the burnt kerosene fumes still lingering in the jetpipe I caught Noble's response to Rob's inevitable question "Why did you do it?"

"I suppose for Britain, and for the hell of it", came his reply. It couldn't have summarised things better.

As the rest of the team completed their work, mine was really just beginning and as I dashed back to the Gerlach press office I began to worry more about the significance of the failure to break the kilometre record. Nobody seemed able to provide a real answer to the one thing that was so worrying. Did Noble's best speed have to better Gabelich's best by one per cent, regardless of the distance? For if that was the case the Thrust mile figure did not break the Blue Flame's kilometre figure by sufficient margin, even though it was faster. And if that was the case it meant that Noble had to find another four or five miles an hour on a crumbly track. After all the deliberate fuss we'd made pointing out how unofficial the Budweiser Rocket's publicised speed had been, I was secretly terrified the team might decide to accept what it had won, only subsequently to find when it was too late that the rest of the world wasn't so convinced. That would have been a tragedy.

By the time I reached Gerlach there was too much to do to dwell on the matter further, and by far the greatest problem proved to be dragging Noble to the telephone to talk to the press. I'd always felt Ken's parameters should have a fifth M added, to read Man, Machine, Medium, Money and the Media – for Campbell's final effort at Coniston had shown just how fatal an effect excessive media pressure could exert. All the same, Richard and I never quite saw eye to eye on how the pressmen on site should be treated. He'd always wanted the shoestring operation run on as low-profile a basis as possible, yet clearly that wasn't workable as more journalists and photographers took the trouble to drive up to Gerlach.

If we'd had ten dollars for every call the press office received that night we could probably have reimbursed the Magnificent Seven, but getting Noble to talk for very long at times proved pretty damn impossible.

The luckiest man in that respect was an American journalist called Dene Strunk, who reached Gerlach in the early hours of Wednesday morning as we were pausing with a beer between calls.

"Is Richard Noble available?", he asked as he dropped his bag on the carpet. An hour later they were still talking and Richard showed no sign of wanting to rush off. Dene got one of the best stories off all the American reporters, even though he'd arrived too late to see any of the record runs.

That night the partying began in earnest, and eventually any thought of further runs the following day was abandoned. Project Thrust was happy enough with what it had won.

The final team meeting was held at ten o'clock the following morning, when one or two faces showed every sign of a heavy night. Norris' first step was the most sensible as he called on Dave Petrali to clear up the kilometre business, and in his easy-going, laconic manner Dave did just that. The heavy-set, bearded figure, who seems to have a perpetually wry expression on his face, exorcised any doubts that lingered.

"First of all, let me tell you exactly what you *have* achieved. You've set six new records. The world unlimited record for the mile, at 633.468mph; the American unlimited record for the mile with the same speed; the International Category C jet record for the mile with that speed and for the kilometre at 634.051mph; and the national Category C jet record for the mile and the kilometre with the same speeds.

"No rule says the mile or the kilometre takes precedence over each other. So don't worry. Richard's 633.468mph for the mile makes him the fastest".

As waves of relief flooded the meeting and it was confirmed that no further attempts would be made, Petrali made one last point.

"When I first saw you guys at Bonneville in 1981 you were the *greenest* land speed record team I'd ever met. I'm here to tell you now you are the most *professional* team I've ever met".

It was a point which brought home just what Richard Noble and his dedicated band had achieved. They hadn't just created their mammoth car; they'd finally taken it to the very top. Not one man or woman in the team worked regularly around race cars on a technical or even managerial basis before they joined, and what they learned had been learned the hard way, from bitter experience. What Project Thrust achieved out on the Black Rock Desert was not so very different from a team of greenhorns producing its own Grand Prix car after · sourcing the finance, going racing one season, and winning the World Championship only two years further on.

It was then Noble's turn to address the team, and he too came straight to the point. "We came here for the land speed record, which we have always defined as 622.407mph, Gary Gabelich's figure for the mile. Our second aim was to get Thrust 2 up to its design speed of 650mph. We have achieved both objectives".

After everything – the weather-related cancellations at Bonneville and Black Rock, the Greenham Common disaster and the panic rebuild, all the 1983 cliffhangers – Project Thrust had finally delivered the goods. Even a pin which had worked loose in Noble's fireproof balaclava on the fastest run, as the hood itself began to slip down over his eyes at 600mph, or a helmet visor which had worked loose, had failed to frustrate that final breakthrough. And all the doubts about Thrust 2's air intake design had been proved invalid. Ackroyd had always hoped Thrust 2 would achieve 650mph; Noble had always said he would break the record. Both men had finally realised their ambitions.

As the meeting drew to a close Noble yet again thanked his team and added a rider to his speech. "For the past nine years I've put myself first. Now it's time to put my family first".

With that he sat down next to Sally on a black plastic-upholstered chair in the back room of Bruno's Country Club, in the tiny town called Gerlach out in the desert all those miles from the electroluminescence of Reno. And as he sat the rest of the room stood to offer loud and enduring applause. Many eyes wore the sheen of tears.

# 13. Reluctant hero

On record day Sally Noble had got off to a bad start when she broke a mirror.

"I was so worried when I did it", she recalled. "But after today I've decided it means we're going to have seven years of *good* luck!"

If October 5th was the first full day of that seven years, it got off to a flying start. After the final meeting the entire team was taken out to the desert for the last time for the final batch of photographs, and it became apparent just how kind the weather and Fate had eventually been to the project. It was a blistering hot day, with ambient temperatures even higher than the 4th's, but the wind was so high there could never have been any question of running Thrust 2 that day, had such a decision been taken the previous night. In fact, it stayed windy right through to the end of the week, despite the brilliant sunshine. The team had been ready and waiting for the window in the weather, and it was just as well. It had literally stayed open for just one day.

The following day brought more good news when a message from the Queen arrived in the Gerlach press office. 'I was very pleased to hear of your success in recapturing the World Land Speed Record', it read. 'I send you and all your team my hearty congratulations'. More was to come. A civic reception was planned for Richard and the team at Reno's Peppermill on the 7th, and there it was announced by the mayor that October 4th would be Richard Noble Day in Reno, while the 7th would be his Day in Nevada. The same day would also be Project Thrust Team Day in the City of Sparks. That evening, courtesy of Tom Reviglio, the Reno businessman who had supplied much equipment to the project over the past two years, everyone was entertained at the MGM Grand Hotel. On the flight to Los Angeles from Reno the day after, on the first leg of the homeward journey, Noble's newfound fame had spread to the pilot of the aircraft. As drinks were served and he introduced himself over the radio, he provided the usual details of altitude and air speed.

"Right now we're doing 550mph. We have Mr Richard Noble, the Fastest Man on Earth, aboard with us this flight but if he was on the ground right now, I guess he'd be overtaking us any minute!"

Back in Britain he finally got some decent publicity from the dailies, and another press conference was held at the SMMT as soon as the team touched base. Later that month there was just time to squeeze Thrust 2 into Motorfair at Earls Court, alongside Sir Henry Segrave's 1929 Golden Arrow. It was fitting Motorfair should be the car's first port of call, for it was almost exactly six years to the day since the bare concept of Thrust 2 had been announced publicly at the same event.

In the aftermath of the record and his return home, Noble spoke of his feelings once it was all finally over.

"It's always the most enormous letdown whenever you come to the end of a project. Everyone on the team is bound to suffer the most awful withdrawal symptoms".

Gordon Flux summarised another of record breaking's paradoxes. "It's a stupid situation, really. The moment we establish ourselves as the best team in land speed record breaking, we find we can no longer practise our skills".

As 1983 drew to its close there were some palliatives. In early November Richard and John were invited to attend the annual British Racing Drivers' Club dinner and dance at the London Hilton, for among the many accolades heaped upon the former was the John Cobb Trophy. It is awarded annually to 'the British racing driver, driving a British car, who has achieved success or successes of an outstanding character'. Bearing in mind the influence Cobb exerted on him, it was a particularly apposite award. At the same time, in one of those rare moments when the motor racing and record breaking fraternities come together nowadays, he was also made a member of the exclusive club and

*199*

awarded a special Gold Star as British Formula Two Champion racing driver Jonathan Palmer received his. Only a few weeks later, as he was awarded the RAC's Sir Malcolm Campbell and Diamond Jubilee Trophies, he received a five minute standing ovation from members of the racing and rallying worlds, neither particularly noted for their interest in record breaking. Later he also received Castrol's Segrave Trophy.

At the Lord Mayor's Show on November 12th Thrust 2 and the entire Thrust team comprised the penultimate float. The public response to Noble and the car was rapturous applause, which was repeated when the duo appeared in 1984 at the Birmingham On The Streets cavalcade and again in 1985 at the World Motoring Centenary celebrations in Coventry.

The last display at the Lord Mayor's Show was an Enfield 8000 electric car, the vehicle for which John Ackroyd had been responsible for six years from 1970. He had started with Enfield Automotive as a designer and moved as chief designer and then works manager to a special factory in Syros, Greece, before finishing as managing director. Now, apparently by pure coincidence, his fastest and slowest designs were on unique display together.

Throughout such public functions Noble remained what he had always been, a reluctant hero. If at all possible he would always try to avoid the limelight, and at the Lord Mayor's Show pointedly refused to wear his distinctive black Panotex driving overalls, preferring the anonymity of a set of blue Thrust overalls like the rest of the team. Many bystanders actually appeared to believe Benton or Brinn were the driver of the world's fastest car, and a grateful Noble did nothing to disabuse them.

On occasions when the equally retiring Ackroyd was with him, he would always go out of his way to ensure the designer received his fair share of the credit and publicity.

By November 30th it was intended to disband the team, much to Noble's regret. Very early on in the Thrust programme he had explained how he hoped any record he might set would be beaten quickly by the Americans, so he could go back for another attempt.

"The thing is, we don't really want our record to last for long because the basic idea is that this thing is an industry, and we all want to come back and have another go at it.

"Look at the problem the Americans had. They haven't been able to finance a proper attempt because an American holds it. If you try to break a record that is nationally held, there is always the danger sponsors will be frightened off because they think you're simply on an ego trip.

"What we would like to see happen is that we should break the record and the Americans should get it back within a year. That way with luck we should be able to hold the team together and then have the incentive to go back and build Thrust 3".

Sadly, without any serious American contenders within a year of making their attempts, it became obvious in late 1983 that the team couldn't be held together, and faced with the need to make such faithful allies redundant, Noble took the extraordinary step of arranging an auction of all the project's equipment. All proceeds would then be distributed according to service, to the fulltime team members.

It was scheduled for December 18th at the Sheraton Skyline Hotel near Heathrow Airport. On the 17th Christies, which had agreed to sponsor the sale, packaged lots in its Victoria warehouse prior to transporting them to the venue. As we helped package and label parts it was rather like butchering an old and trusted pet. The following day, with business briskly conducted by Christies' Robert Brookes, a surprising amount of stock was sold, including both Palouste starter turbines and all the curious parts which had no obvious practical value, such as the wooden formers around which Benton and Ball had shaped the curved front panels. Sufficient money was raised to give the fulltimers some leeway in their search for fresh employment.

If Noble looked after his team in that respect, he also did so in others. Shortly before the auction the sponsors had laid on a celebration dinner for everyone at Kensington's Royal Garden Hotel on November 29th. After a speech honouring the team and its achievements had been given by former GKN Group Chairman Sir Barrie Heath DFC, Noble was called upon to respond. He did so, at length, before neatly turning the tables. He then insisted on naming every member of his team and outlining to the gathered guests exactly what role they had played in Project Thrust's success. As he did so, he further insisted that each of them rose to make a speech of their own. It was a quite extraordinary and unselfish gesture and in some ways helped to answer the enigma of his attitude to the press, curiously enough.

It had become clear that he certainly doesn't trust the media, nor liked his progress monitored publicly, but his true underlying motivation was a reluctance for any kind of personal publicity, good bad or indifferent. He hated anyone who ballyhooed themselves for pure self-aggrandisement. That was why he was so insistent he wasn't going to be the only one singled out, and that everyone who had played a role in the realisation of his dream should have their part acknowledged and have the chance to speak. There had been round-the-table speeches in Gerlach immediately after the record, but that had been at a private meeting. This was altogether more public and was his way of expressing his gratitude.

What he didn't publicise, to the relief of many gathered there that night, were the Silly Boy Awards. These record breaking Oscars were the invention of Barrett and were awarded to team members guilty on occasion of foolish blunders. John Griffiths, for example, qualified the day he was found on hand and foot grovelling in a puddle outside Bruno's Motel looking for the keys to the Jaguar, only later to discover they were in his pocket. There must have been something about that car, for later that very day Elsom won the award after a high-speed dash across the playa. It was only as he braked sharply to a halt that he realised one of the Paloustes was still roped to the rear bumper. On one occasion in 1983 I felt close to winning. I'd finally got my hands on the Jaguar and whisked up State Highway Thirty Four to celebrate my first drive in America in a decent set of wheels, when the oil pressure zeroed. As the engine had just undergone a $4,000 rebuild after being run without an octane booster I felt very silly coasting back to Gerlach with a dead engine, knowing nobody would believe it wasn't my fault. It transpired, to my relief, that it was only a fault in the gauge's electrics.

One individual who shall remain nameless probably won the Silly Boy Award in perpetuity for the occasion on which he inadvertently drove across, and damaged, Petrali's timing wires, earning the rebuke from the normally placid photographer: "Don't you ever, ever, *ever* do that to me again!"

There were more round-the-table speeches early in 1984, but that was at another private function to mark the official end of Project Thrust. It took place at Shambles in Teddington, and it was as well there were only Thrust people present, for to a man and woman everyone behaved in a disgusting manner. Franco, the proprietor, was a longtime Thrust supporter and had insisted on laying on the feast himself as his gesture. His credentials were immediately established by the huge photograph of the late Gilles Villeneuve which hangs on one wall. There were food fights and FISA's engraved silver cup – presented to the land speed record holder – was frequently filled with champagne before being tipped over an unsuspecting victim's head, but Franco merely smiled tolerantly and turned a blind eye to the childish antics. Noble, as usual, was at the centre of most of the trouble, and didn't bat an eyelid when Sally poured a complete bottle of red wine over his head. . .

The New Year also brought the Order of the British Empire in the Honour's List for the Queen's Birthday, although prior to that Richard's life expectancy might have been affected significantly when the team was called upon to help Eamonn Andrews for *This Is Your Life*. In time-honoured style a plot was hatched to surprise the programme's victim. He was duped into meeting John Viner of the television programme *Drive-In* at Thames TV's Twickenham premises, where Thrust 2 was present on a flat-bed trailer awaiting delivery to another venue. *Drive-In* had closely followed the Thrust project from the beginning, so Noble suspected nothing as he and John chatted. He was then asked to talk him through a video film of the BBC/Filmscreen documentary of the record run, which was shown on a special fullsize screen which stretched down to the floor. On cue, the entire team would then literally leap through the paper screen.

The plan worked to perfection, but Noble jumped at least a foot in pure shock as twenty or so blue-clad figures suddenly burst from the Black Rock Desert. By the time we reached him and he began automatically pumping hands as a reflex action, he was virtual dead weight. As he admitted later, it was "one *hell* of a shock!"...

As everyone concerned with the project struggled to get back to normal life, and to existence without a continuing series of cliffhangers, Noble had a head start. Ever since he had learned to fly as part of his driver training, he had discovered another subject he found nearly as exacting, exciting and exhilarating as chasing the land speed record. Aviation.

Already, after those initial lessons, he had been bitten by the flying bug and had also been toying with an idea at the back of his mind. The sheer cost of lessons had horrified him, and he began forming a concept that was to guide him to the next stage of his life after Project Thrust.

He had already started keeping tabs on the light class of aeroplane rife in America, the Air Recreation Vehicle or ARV, and from these initials his new company venture subsequently took its name. He visited ARV meets in America, especially those at Oshkosh, the Bonneville of light plane pilots. He employed exactly the same tactics as he did when starting Project Thrust or seeking sponsorship, going to great lengths to learn as much as he could about the background to his new subject and making sure he did his homework. The more he discovered the more determined it made him to produce his own light aeroplane in Britain, and to attack the high costs facing private pilots the world over.

Even now the market in Britain is dominated by the Americans, with Piper and Cessna ruling the roost. Both are well established companies, but it is not difficult to draw comparisons between ARV Aviation and the challenge that faced Project Thrust when Noble set out to break the land speed record. The fact that light aviation is as strewn with debris from previous projects as Bonneville was with unsuccessful land speed record contenders did nothing to deter him. If anything, it further stimulated him, for here again was a real challenge. Here again was a situation in which people had to be turned round, and attitudes modified. The fact that most of the previous failures had foundered for financial reasons was an added incentive, for he loved the business side of his projects every bit as much as the action side.

When he first disclosed his ideas to a few of us, we listened politely and probably masked our true thoughts. But the more one learned of what he intended to do, the more feasible it all sounded. The fresh challenges suited him ideally.

Throughout 1984 he would excitedly reveal fresh progress whenever we met. On one occasion after lunch he dragged out a sheet of Alcan's new Supral alloy, explaining how the material would be used in the new plane – the ARV Super 2 – that was under design. Ackroyd did the tailplane, but the main fuselage and running gear of the Super 2 is the work of three talented engineers, Bruce Giddings, Nick Sibley and James Morton. It came as no surprise to hear subsequently that Alcan Aluminium Company had agreed to sponsor production of the second prototype, such was its satisfaction with the way things were going.

From the outset Noble was aware the new plane would stand or fall on its power to weight ratio. A heavy powerplant with a low output would mean a heavier airframe with less economy, less manouevrability and, the great enemy, higher running costs. What he needed was a modern, lightweight British engine. Via Champion he was led to Mike Hewland of Hewland Engineering, the company best known for its domination of the motor racing gearbox market. Hewland had produced a high-performance twin cylinder two-stroke engine for use in microlight aircraft, but it had never gone into production. Noble put his charm to optimum use, and as Hewland listened to his incredible enthusiasm and his logical line of argument he agreed to add a third cylinder and to switch over to water cooling. The revised engine immediately proved impressive on the test bed, and now endows the Super 2 with superior take-off characteristics to its major rivals, and a better power to weight ratio.

If Project Thrust's early days had been a struggle, Noble was at least prepared for the fight for backing for ARV. The struggle with bureaucracy at its worst, with tight-fisted government aid departments which always seemed to have millions to give away, yet never heard sound commercial arguments, and with financial bastions in the City, ran well into 1986. But on July 21st at Heathrow Airport, he was finally presented with Public Transport

Cover for both engine and airframe. That was the final key that allowed him to market the 'plane and the very speed with which such cover was granted took industry observers by surprise. Following a highly successful appearance at the Farnborough Air Show in September, ARV had begun to run in full reheat.

When he set the land speed record Richard Noble made Sally a promise. In our first interview he had concluded by saying: "I'd like to break the record twice, then retire. After that? We'll spend the next fifteen years doing what Sally wants to do!"

After the Black Rock Desert triumph he promised that, while he would involve himself as closely as possible with any subsequent British attempt, he would not drive again. But though he still works flat-out on ARV, a far more long-term undertaking than Project Thrust which by its very nature had to have a finite life, he still thinks of record breaking. For some time he gave a series of lectures on his achievements, after a hectic round of similar engagements in 1984 and '85, and his thoughts still turn to Thrust 3.

"I envisage a forty foot long, incredibly slim car – something really exotic", he once outlined, rubbing his hands at the prospect. "These things always depend on the sort of powerplant you can lay your hands on, but a Rolls-Royce Olympus 593 similar to Concorde's engines, with a basic 32,000lbs of thrust plus at least another 3,000 with reheat, should provide us with the means to produce the ultimate car and kick the record up to a point where it will stay with Britain for a long time.

"Perhaps Thrust 3 might take the land speed record right up towards the 1,000mph mark, which is going to be the next big goal after the sound barrier".

One thing is sure. If the Americans do break Richard Noble's land speed record in the near future, he has earned the highest credibility in such undertakings, so a future project should be less difficult, if much more expensive, to mount. Few could envisage him having any trouble getting hold of the right engine for the job, although Ackroyd is known to have reservations about anything as heavy as the Olympus and talks more in terms of another type of jet with rocket assistance.

Certainly the ability to produce the ultimate land vehicle exists in Britain, within the nucleus of the old Thrust team. Thrust 2 was only ever intended as a transonic car, yet had it been able to run at Bonneville, in suitable conditions on a harder surface than the desert's and with less rolling resistance, its eventual record might have been significantly closer to its 650 theoretical maximum.

Whatever, it was a far better engineered car than anything the Americans produced, with the possible exception of the Blue Flame. It met with many problems, yet when it was running its stability was so impressive it made things look easy. There was never any suggestion of dangerous lift at speed, and even on the final runs, with the greatly reduced downforce, Noble admitted the feel of it was exactly the same. In other words he was nowhere near close to flying, as Breedlove had been. The bodywork withstood supersonic airflow without any distortion or buckling and the same Lucas-Girling disc brakes were used on all the 1983 runs, seven of them over 600mph. Wheels and discs rotated near 8,000rpm, the discs themselves surviving a peripheral velocity of 525ft/sec, or twice the speed at which a traditional cast-iron flywheel will shatter.

Before the turn of the century man will probably exceed the speed of sound on land, in officially ratified runs, one in either direction over a measured mile or kilometre, within sixty allotted minutes. Noble is under no illusion that his mark will last forever, and already Ackroyd has made some tentative design studies for a jet-powered supersonic vehicle. Whenever he talks of contenders such as Craig Breedlove or Sammy Miller, Noble is open yet impatient.

"I really hope someone will come forward and gave a go. What's the point of holding the record if there isn't any competition? The sooner our record falls the sooner we can start to raise the budget for another go".

In the meantime, Thrust 2 rests at the Museum of Transport in Coventry between exhibition engagements that have taken it as far afield as Detroit, Essen and Vancouver, while the Thrust teamsters stay in touch via the 633 Club, which meets every year on October 4th and of which Sally is Secretary. Past Chairmen include Benton and Ball, and in typical Thrust style they had apposite mottos formulated by Andrew Noble. For Brian there was 'May we be led by the Balls', while for Ron there was the immortal summary 'Give me more time and I'll get the job done quicker'.

Winning the land speed record in no way changed Richard Noble, the man who still shuns the limelight yet thrives on a challenge, be it driving a car faster through a measured mile than anyone else in history, slashing the cost of learning to fly, or the planning of another secret, non-automotive project on which he has been engaged. Some people aim for a quiet life, others need continuous stimulation and action. The former rarely break records.

If there is a Thrust 3 it is highly unlikely he will be tempted back into the cockpit, but if another country does recapture the glory, expect him to spearhead the British response, even if only in an advisory capacity. He may have won the gold and moved on, but the way in which his eyes twinkle when the subject is mentioned underscores how strong a hold it still exerts.

"The land speed record is one of the most fascinating challenges in the world", he asserts while making the mental switch from air to land. "If things happened properly it could become one of the greatest sporting events. I could even see the day when it is run along the lines of the old Schneider Trophy seaplane races. The high-technology image is still attractive to many and the costs, even for a supersonic vehicle, are still within reach of corporate budgets, especially when you look at Formula One".

He again rubs his hands as inevitably he warms to his theme. "All we need is the challenge. . ."

# *Appendix One – The Team*

## 1981

| | |
|---|---|
| Richard Noble | Driver/Team Manager |
| John Ackroyd | Designer |
| Eddie Elsom | Operations Director |
| Gordon Flux | Chief Engineer/Start Team 2 |
| Ron Benton | Development Engineer/Start Team 1 |
| Geoff Smee | Start Team 1 Leader |
| John Watkins | Start Team 2 Leader/Engine |
| Tony Meston | Engine |
| Mike Barrett | Parachutes/Tow Car |
| Brian Ball | Start Team 1 |
| Andrew Noble | Start Team 1 |
| Terry Hopkins | Transporter driver |
| David Brinn | Financial Director |
| Glynne Bowsher | Brakes (Lucas Girling) |
| Jess Sharpe | Bearings (British Timken) |
| John Griffiths | Fire Chase |
| Mike Hearn | Fire Chase |
| Bruce White | Parachutes |
| Richard Chisnell | Sponsor representative |
| Tony Jeeves | Public Relations |
| Sally Noble | Club Secretary |
| Birgit Ackroyd | Team Secretary |

*Also present as team members:* Ninetta Hearn; Lorraine Culkin; Clive Benton; Tom Palm; Charles Noble; George Myers; Richard T. Briggs; Richard Aston (Loctite); Jack Nichol (Loctite); Earl Sperry (GKN); David Hannay (GKN); Peg Griffiths.

## 1982

| | |
|---|---|
| Richard Noble | Driver |
| John Ackroyd | Designer |
| Ken Norris | Team Manager |
| Eddie Elsom | Operations Director |
| Gordon Flux | Chief Engineer/Start Team 2 |
| Ron Benton | Development Engineer/Start Team 1 |
| Geoff Smee | Start Team 1 Leader |
| John Watkins | Start Team 2 Leader/Engine |
| Mike Barrett | Parachutes/Tow Car |
| Brian Ball | Start Team 1 |
| Andrew Noble | Transporter driver/Start Team 1 |
| David Brinn | Financial Director |
| Glynne Bowsher | Brakes (Lucas Girling) |
| Jess Sharpe/Mick Chambers | Bearings (British Timken) |
| John Griffiths | Fire Chase |
| Mike Hearn | Fire Chase |
| Richard Chisnell | PR/Sponsor representative |
| Sally Noble | Club Secretary |
| Birgit Ackroyd | Team Secretary |
| Peter Hand | Electronics |
| Charles Noble | Photographer |
| Phil Goss | Engineering |
| Bill Ryan | Engineering |
| John Norris | Operations Assistant |

*Also present as team members:* Ninetta Hearn; Lorraine Culkin; Tom Palm; Earl Sperry (GKN); Peg Griffiths.

# 1983

| | |
|---|---|
| Richard Noble | Driver |
| John Ackroyd | Designer |
| Ken Norris | Team Manager |
| Eddie Elsom | Operations Director |
| Gordon Flux | Chief Engineer/Start Team 1 Leader |
| Mike Barrett | Parachutes |
| Gordon Biles | Electrics/Start Team 2 |
| John Watkins | Start Team 2 Leader/Engine |
| Brian Ball | Start Team 1 |
| Glynne Bowsher | Brakes (Lucas Girling)/Start Team 2 |
| Mick Chambers | Bearings (British Timken)/Start Team 2 |
| Andrew Noble | Transporter Driver/Start Team 2 |
| Ron Benton | Development Engineer/Public Relations |
| David Brinn | Financial Director/Pits Boss |
| Peter Hand | Electronics/Start Team 2 |
| John Griffiths | Fire Chase |
| Mike Hearn | Fire Chase |
| David Tremayne | Press and Public Relations Manager |
| Ian Robinson | Track Team/Start Team 1 |
| John Norris | Track Team/Start Team 1 |
| Charles Noble | Photographer |
| Sally Noble | Club Secretary |
| Birgit Ackroyd | Team Secretary |
| Tom Palm | Start Team 1 |
| Richard Chisnell | Sponsor representative |
| Simon Walmesley | Electronics (Plessey) |
| George Webb | Engine (Rolls-Royce) |

*Also present as team members:* Ninetta Hearn; Lorraine Culkin; Trish Tremayne; Peg Griffiths.

*USAC Timekeepers on all three attempts:* Dave Petrali (Chief Steward); John 'Buck' Wetton (Chief Timer); John Banks (Chief Scorer); Jess Tobey (Chief Observer); Don 'Mac' MacGregor (Technical Representative).

# Appendix Two – The Records

*British National*

24&25/9/80 RAF Greenham Common

| | |
|---|---|
| 1 Mile (standing start) | 166.47mph |
| 1 Kilometre (standing start) | 149.57mph |
| Flying Quarter Mile | 259.74mph |
| Flying 500 Metres | 255.06mph |
| Flying Kilometre | 251.19mph |
| Flying Mile | 248.87mph* |

\* *British Land Speed Record*

| *British Car and Driver* | *Mile* | *Kilometre* |
|---|---|---|
| 10/10/81 Bonneville Salt Flats | – | 418.118mph |
| 21/10/82 Black Rock Desert | 463.683mph | 468.972mph |
| 3/11/82 Black Rock Desert | 575.489mph | 575.652mph |
| 4/11/82 Black Rock Desert | 590.551mph | 590.843mph |
| 21/ 9/83 Black Rock Desert | 606.469mph | – |

| *World Unlimited* | | |
|---|---|---|
| 4/10/83 Black Rock Desert | 633.468mph | – |
| *American Unlimited* | | |
| 4/10/83 Black Rock Desert | 633.468mph | – |
| *International Cat C Group Jet* | | |
| 4/10/83 Black Rock Desert | 633.468mph | 634.051mph* |
| *National Cat C Group Jet* | | |
| 4/10/83 Black Rock Desert | 633.468mph | 634.051mph* |

\* *Exceeds kilometre record but not by mandatory one per cent.*

## Previous records

| *Unlimited* | *Mile* | *Kilometre* |
|---|---|---|
| Gary Gabelich/Blue Flame | 622.407mph | 630.388mph |
| *Cat C Group Jet* | | |
| Craig Breedlove/Spirit of America – Sonic 1 | 600.60lmph | 600.841mph |